The Apocalypse—
Letter by Letter

The Apocalypse—Letter by Letter

A Literary Analysis of the Book of Revelation

Steven Paul
http://www.stevenpaul.org

iUniverse, Inc.
New York Lincoln Shanghai

The Apocalypse—Letter by Letter
A Literary Analysis of the Book of Revelation

iUniverse books may be ordered through booksellers or by contacting:

iUniverse
2021 Pine Lake Road, Suite 100
Lincoln, NE 68512
www.iuniverse.com
1-800-Authors (1-800-288-4677)

Scripture quoted in this book is from the Holy Bible:

New American Bible
Revised Standard Version
Douay-Rheims Version
Westminster Version
St. James Version

ISBN-13: 978-0-595-38028-2 (pbk)
ISBN-13: 978-0-595-67591-3 (cloth)
ISBN-13: 978-0-595-82398-7 (ebk)
ISBN-10: 0-595-38028-X (pbk)
ISBN-10: 0-595-67591-3 (cloth)
ISBN-10: 0-595-82398-X (ebk)

Printed in the United States of America

In loving memory of Steven Paul

Semper Fi, brother!

CONTENTS

FOREWORD

Dear Reader,

The last words of the author of this book were, "I understand now." Steven Paul was much older than his sister, my wife. I met him at their parents' home for one of many family gatherings that they held through the years. Steve would always start into a discourse, a debate, or a discussion depending on your point of view. Nearly every time it would turn to the Apocalypse and Steve would try his case with anyone who dared to challenge him. Steve would passionately quote from the Bible, from classical literature, history books, and books by the Church Fathers such as, St. Augustine, St. Thomas Aquinas, Tertullian, and others. As a casual Catholic by upbringing, I was astonished at the depth and breadth of the argument. One book that really struck Steve was The Book of Destiny, by Rev. Herman Bernard Kramer, [Tan Books, 1954], and this book owes much to it. Steve once said that Rev. Kramer was on the right track but missed some important clues.

As time went by, I began to look forward to these oratories. I'd never heard anything like it. How did he gain such knowledge and insight?

My wife related that Steve had attended Our Lady Queen of Angels Seminary in the Los Angeles area but then enlisted in the Marines and served in the Vietnam War. He picked the toughest unit he could. While serving his country, he was diagnosed with cancer. Surgery and chemotherapy saved his life but required a long convalescence. Though given a short life expectancy, Steve beat the odds. During this period, Steve read many books. Literary analysis and the use of language became his passion. This influence will be evident in the book.

He studied religion, history, and classical literature and graduated Magna Cum Laude in 1974 with a Bachelor of Arts in English Language and Literature from Boston University. In the evenings, he volunteered to teach English to refugees from South Vietnam. He also shoveled snow at the local parish and served as lector. We didn't see him much over the first dozen years we were married. An occasional barbecue or holiday gathering was about it.

Then we got word that his cancer had recurred and he was undergoing chemotherapy. He seemed to be improving but then disaster hit. While I was working as a consultant about three hour's drive from home in 1996, I received a message from my wife. She was shaken and had trouble explaining to me that her brother, Steve, had been brought to the hospital with a ruptured colon and was not expected to survive the day. "He's not going to get out of this one," she said. Apparently, a thinning of the intestinal walls is one complication from the cancer treatment. I jumped in the car for the long three-hour drive home with a deep sense of sadness and remorse. The nagging feeling in the back of my mind was what a waste it would be if the knowledge Steve had of the Apocalypse and his faith would not be passed on, especially to my children.

And so I began to pray as my wife and children had been doing ever since Steve had become sick. I asked that if it were possible, for "with Him all things are possible," [cf. Lk. 1:37], to spare Steven so he could pass along what he knew to my children and they in turn could preserve it. Due to my weak faith, I assumed this was folly but there was nothing else to do. I continued my drive and my conversation with the Lord.

When I got home, I expected to be greeted with the news of Steve's passing but instead was informed by my wife that he was hanging on by a thread. The doctors were in a dilemma. He was too weak to operate on and too sick not to. His vital signs were unstable. They decided to operate and by some small miracle, he survived the night. The next few days, I watched the children while my wife and her family went to the hospital. They arranged for the sacrament of healing from a priest at the hospital. Steve was in a death grip. His face was contorted and pale. During the prayers for the sick, he changed. He took on a pinkish color and his whole body seemed to relax. He lived. By one count, he had 14 IV bottles hooked up at once. Although he survived, he was mostly in a coma and so after a week or so I went back to work. For four weeks, he lay in a coma, heavily sedated and with a tracheotomy tube.

When I arrived home for the weekend, I decided to go see Steve with my wife. I felt really strange because it had been awhile since I'd seen him and was afraid he wouldn't recognize me. I was told he was so out of it that he wouldn't know much of anything. When I walked into the room, Steve motioned to me and kept trying to communicate. I asked if he knew who I was and he smiled and nodded. He would get very frustrated because you can't talk with a tracheotomy tube. Then this 300 pound former Marine began to cry. I grabbed his hand and repeated over and over, "we're going to get through this, God has work for you." Four days later, he was sitting up; taking short walks and was talking. Two days after that, he walked out of the hospital and went home.

As he recovered, I told him how I had prayed that he would live so that he could write down what he knew about the Apocalypse. At first, I think he thought I was crazy. Then the letters started coming, typewritten on an old manual typewriter. [Steve had no use for technology. He still had a rotary phone in 1999. No computer, no cell phone. He was still driving a 1974 Ford Escort in 2000]. First, a short letter arrived that explained the symbols in the Book of Daniel and how they will be important in interpreting the Apocalypse. Then a beautiful letter, a commentary, an Introduction to the Apocalypse followed.

As the letters kept coming, they kept getting more detailed, and more beautiful. Because of Steve's medical history, he knew that time was short to complete the task. He would stop by from time to time, always armed with a box of Boston Crème donuts, to explain some aspect of his letters. I kidded with him that he should never complete his commentary because then his mission would be over. His letters also changed during this time. He began to feel the strong hand of God in his work and began to see it as more than just letters for the family. He wrote, "When I look at what I have written, I am greeted by evidence of the grace of God, for some of the things explained have not been explained in nineteen centuries. When I was young, I never thought I would write something like this. When it is all typed up, I will not even speculate on what God will do with it. I have not the foggiest idea. I only know I must finish it. And, that is my cue to get back to the typing." And he started to give instructions on how it should be shared.

In each letter, Steve showed how previous commentaries failed to let the grammar and structure of the Apocalypse lead the reader to clues as to the symbols and sequence of events. This book is not a wildly speculative work of fancy, or a fictional novel.

Steve also demonstrated how translators often inserted their own opinions into the text and distorted it from its original meaning in Greek. By meticulously giving examples from the original Greek text and the available English translations, Steve showed how subtleties in the work answered the most vexing questions that had gone misunderstood or unexplained for 1800 years. At first, his method may seem tedious, especially to this sound-bite generation used to the paradigm of "browsing" as on the Internet. This book appeals to the reader who is ready to apply their own reason and effort into evaluating the rational proofs presented. In some cases, the author challenges the reader to prove him wrong with their own explanations. He often advised us to use only the Bible as our main reference, though history books and writings by Church Fathers also prove helpful.

I think it must have frustrated Steve that we would often tell him that what he wrote was very confusing for us. He often stated that the Apocalypse was written in fourth grade grammar and anyone should be able to see what he saw. We told him we would try harder. Alas, he had only sent his analysis up to Chapter 12 when he got sick again and went to the hospital. While there, he implored me to complete it from his notes.

As the reports from the hospital became more negative, I began to suspect this project would never be completed. I just didn't have the combination of intelligence, faith and reason that Steve possessed. Usually we would all go visit Steve together on the weekend. On a Thursday in October, I told my wife to go see him THAT DAY. I had a feeling that the end was near. He was mostly unconscious but for a few moments, he opened his eyes. My wife told him that we were reading his work and were beginning to understand it. It was at this point that he mustered the strength to utter, "I understand, now." It reminded me of the last words of St. Thomas Aquinas, "All I've written is straw." The next morning he was in God's arms. He was 54 when he died. I was deeply saddened not only at the loss of someone who had become my brother but also by the fact that our mutual project had not been completed.

On the drive to the funeral, I said to the family that we could be comforted that Steve's "<u>works will accompany him</u>" as it says in the Apocalypse. My children herein referred to as "Friends" and the principal recipients of the letters, served on the altar and performed the scripture readings at the funeral. One of the readings selected by the presiding priest (who was unaware of Steve's work in this regard) was from the Apocalypse Chapter 14 verses 12 and 13: "Here is what sustains the holy ones who keep God's commandments and their faith in Jesus. I heard a voice from heaven say, 'write this: Blessed are the dead who die in the Lord from now on.' 'Yes,' said the Spirit, 'let them find rest from their labors, for their works accompany them.'"

After the funeral, we went to his house, and there, in the typewriter, a manual typewriter, was another page. I had no idea how many pages he may have finished that he hadn't sent. When his wife sent me six more pages that got me most of the way through Chapter 13, I again thought that the project was over. Then, a month later, my wife sent me a message at work. "Guess what showed up in the mail today?" I had no idea. She answered, "a package from Steve's wife…68 pages of his notes." They weren't just notes. He had written out the entire commentary prior to sitting at that manual typewriter day after day. His wife had copied it and was fixing the places where the copier had cut off parts of words. I was filled with such joy that all I could think of was typing the whole thing into the computer so that it could be shared.

The book will cover the time from the late first century when St. John wrote the Apocalypse to a time as yet unknown in the future, and show how some predicted events affecting God's people have come to pass, such as the Arian Heresy, the Barbarian Invasions, the rise of Islam, the Greek Schism, Martin Luther and Protestantism. Each of these events then sets the table so to speak for the climactic events of the second and third woes. The book was written beginning in 1997 and Steve finished the letters in 2000. He did not live to see the attack on the World Trade Center, the invasions of Iraq and Afghanistan, the sex abuse scandal in the Church, the death of Pope John Paul II and election of Pope Benedict XVI. Other events that would have piqued his interest include the accelerated de-Christianization of Europe and unregulated Islamic immigration, the recent riots in France, and the pronouncements concerning entry to the priesthood from the Vatican. As you read the book, it should become clear how they all fit with what he wrote.

Steve once related to my wife that when he was sick as a young soldier, he was walking along a beach in Viet Nam and spotted a lone seagull circling overhead. At that moment he says he was infused with the certainty that "everything is exactly the way it is supposed to be."

What follows is the result of a life's work. It is Steve's Apocalypse, Letter by Letter.

Yours in Christ,

A Friend of the Lord

Introduction

—

Analysis Book of Daniel Chapters 2, 7, 8

June, 1997

Dear Friends of the Lord,

I cannot remember, Friends, whether you suggested or requested that I put my thoughts about the prophetic books to paper. In either case, I send this letter in which I will deposit some notes on Daniel, as principal to those on Revelation. May they yield interest.

I hope you have had time to read Daniel, especially, Chapters 2, 7, & 8, because I must keep brief what only two fingers must type. Besides, I intend not to comment on minor matters or to raise speculative questions, since such do not profit much.

One thing more: concrete persons and things make that unique evolvement called history; therefore, prophecy about the future can have only one correct interpretation or explanation. Such prophecy is not a prediction in the human manner, but a DIVINE REVELATION—and God never guesses.

The second Chapter unequivocally informs the reader, that the king's dream and Daniel's are divine revelations of the same unique evolvement, one which spans from the present into the future; and that, therefore, the interpretation or explanation Daniel gives is the only correct one.

The "statue" in the dream represents the time frame [a delectably ineluctable pun] within which, by the time frame's ending, there will have existed four specific kingdoms in succession, the first already existing at the time of the revelation. By correlating the information in Daniel 2, 7, & 8 with Isaiah 13:17, Jeremiah 51:11, and modern history books, the reader can ascertain the identities of the four kingdoms: the Babylonian Empire, the Medo-Persian, the Greek, and last, the Roman Empire.

> 17 Behold I will stir up the Medes against them, who shall not seek silver, nor desire gold: 18 But with their arrows they shall kill the children, and shall have no pity upon the sucklings of the womb, and their eye shall not spare their sons. 19 And that Babylon, glorious among kingdoms, the famous pride of the Chaldeans, shall be even as the Lord destroyed Sodom and Gomorrha. [Is. 13:17-19]

> 11 Sharpen the arrows, fill the quivers, the Lord hath raised up the spirit of the kings of the Medes: and his mind is against Babylon to destroy it, because it is the vengeance of the Lord, the vengeance of his temple. 12 Upon the walls of Babylon set up the standard, strengthen the watch: set up the watchmen, prepare the ambushes: for the Lord hath both purposed, and done all that he spoke against the inhabitants of Babylon. [Jer. 51:11-12]

The seventh Chapter of Daniel shows the same four as beasts that emerge from the sea: the "two-winged lion" was the national symbol of Babylon; and the "four-winged, four-headed leopard" appears, in Chapter 8, as the "he-goat" that eventually grows four horns [Greek Empire of Alexander the Great that became split in four Seleucid Empires].

Since the "statue" in the dream, depicted in Chapter 2, symbolizes the four empires and their evolvement, and since the "stone" symbolizes the "kingdom of God" initially small, the reader can deduce that God would and did establish or begin his kingdom DURING THE LATTER HALF OF THE FOURTH KINGDOM, which became known as the Roman Empire. Bear in mind that the "stone" struck the FEET and not higher, i.e., earlier.

Since Daniel makes it perfectly clear that God would establish an everlasting kingdom, it follows that he would not set up a second one and that, therefore, the kingdom to be established would also be the one established BY THE MESSIAH. Since the "stone" was hewn from a "mountain not on the earth," but became a "mountain on the earth," it follows that the "mountain not on the earth" symbolizes the "kingdom of God" in heaven, and that the "stone" that becomes a "mountain covering the entire earth" is the "kingdom of God" on earth. Divine from Divine is the fact. One can, therefore, deduce that the "stone" also symbolizes the Messiah. Indeed, Jesus made this image personal to himself

> 17 But he looking on them, said: What is this then that is written, The stone, which the builders rejected, the same is become the head of the corner? 18 Whosoever shall fall upon that stone, shall be bruised: and upon whomsoever it shall fall, it will grind him to powder. 19
> And the chief priests and the scribes sought to lay hands on him the same hour: but they feared the people, for they knew that he spoke this parable to them. [Lk. 20:17-19].

Those who pondered the writings of the prophets, correlating them, meticulously, came to the same conclusions and disseminated their findings, until the nation of Israel, by the time Jesus was born, was rife with expectation of the Messiah. But, as Moses said, the Jews were a "stiff-necked people." [Ex. 33:3]

To resume: Daniel relates:

(1) The "statue" had a terrifying appearance. [Dn. 2:31]
(2) The second kingdom would be inferior to the first. [Dn. 2:39]
(3) The "stone", or "kingdom of God" on earth, would destroy the "statue", i.e., all four kingdoms. [Dn. 2:45]

Now, the statue looked terrifying because it looked monstrous; and it looked monstrous because God, who caused the dream, saw the four kingdoms were monstrous. Thus, the statue's "physical appearance" signified the spiritual reality of the four kingdoms. As to what that monstrous reality was, the statue itself signals: idolatry, which was paganism's preposterous falsehood and evil practice. For God, who is spirit, made man in his own image; and so, whenever man worships "graven images" made of "gold," "silver," "bronze," or "iron," then has man become a blasphemous monstrosity.

Note that <u>every</u> succeeding metal was [still is] worth less than the one before it; hence, the term <u>inferior</u> may be applied to every succeeding kingdom, so that the depreciating succession of metals signifies that each succeeding kingdom will be, in some sense, more monstrous than the one before it. Since the four kingdoms were equal, in that they each practiced idolatry, the "succession of metals" must, therefore, symbolize an evil greater than idolatry, but involving it nonetheless. As the Bible and history books have recorded, the greater evil was this: that each succeeding empire was more brutal than the one before it, in attempting to impose idolatry upon God's people.

The Roman Empire eventuated in the most blasphemous monstrosity of emperor worship; its persecutions against the Christians were greater in number, duration, cruelty, and, as the divine "mountain" grew, in extent. But, in 392 AD, Theodosius proscribed paganism as high treason and proclaimed Christianity the one religion throughout the Iron Empire, the empire that had conquered even those lands of the previous three; and this explains why, in the dream, the <u>whole</u> statue crumbled.

Chapter 8 presents more details about the second and third kingdoms; it elucidates their identities. The Chapter unequivocally asserts its contents are a vision of the future [divine revelation]; therefore, the explanation by the angel Gabriel is the only correct one.

That the "ram" represents the Medo-Persian Empire and the "he-goat" the Greek Empire indicates God's perspective: rational beings who worship idols are no better than animals.

> 20 The ram, which thou sawest with horns, is the king of the <u>Medes and Persians</u>. 21 And the he goat, is the king of the <u>Greeks</u>, and the great horn that was between his eyes, the same is the first king. 22 But whereas when that was broken, there arose up four for it: <u>four kings</u> shall rise up of his nation, but not with his strength. [Dn. 8:20-22]

Note, also, that God views the Medes and Persians as combined into one kingdom. Thus, it is clear that the second of the four kingdoms is the Medo-

Persian Empire: simple mathematics. The reason God saw them so is that the Medes did not come into contact with all, or almost all, of God's people until after they were conquered by the Persians and became part of the military force that conquered Babylon. It was then that the Medes participated in the attempts to impose idolatry on the Jews.

The reader can deduce a minor but important point from Gabriel's explanation, then correlate it with Chapter 2: just as the "animals" represented kings—let me be more precise—just as each "animal" represented a king or series of kings, so does a "horn." Moreover, each represents a kingdom. But, note that the "horn" is used to indicate a lesser king or kingdom, or one within the duration and extent of the animal/empire.

For example, the "he-goat" is the Greek Empire and the "great horn" is Alexander the Great, the first of the kings that will come into contact with all, or almost all, of God's people. The four smaller "horns" that replace it are the four Seleucid kings, but the "animal," which represents a pagan empire and culture, remains: God still sees that the same "animal" or "beast" exists. In other words, "king" and "kingdom" are interchangeable terms because there cannot be really a king unless he also has a kingdom, and vice versa.

Correlating this with Chapter 2, the reader finds double usage for the same symbol: Daniel explained that the "gold head" represented King Nebuchadnezzar, but that the "silver arms and chest" represented a kingdom, i.e., the series of kings from Cyrus the Persian to Xerxes III. After all, Alexander defeated Xerxes III at Granicus and Issus, not Cyrus!!! Remember this double usage: you will meet it again in Revelation. Lastly, I will point out important details and aspects in Chapter 8, which I left for last because it concerns a fifth empire that will come long after the Roman Empire has fallen. It will also be the last evil empire to persecute God's people, and it will be the worst, bringing the human race to the brink of extinction.

Excuse me: put Darius III in place of Xerxes III, in the second paragraph above. I am a genius in figuring out prophetic symbolism, but a dunce in memorizing historical names and dates.

The reader, you, meets the four kingdoms again, but, in this Chapter, they appear as "beasts." I think you understand the meaning of that symbolism by now, so I won't comment on it. The important new information comes from the explanation of someone in the vision, about the "ten horns" and the "little horn with two eyes and a mouth."

The person in the vision tells Daniel that the "ten horns" represent ten kings [kingdoms] that come into existence after the fourth beast [Roman Empire] has fallen apart. Sometime after the ten have been in existence, another king springs up in their midst, and three of the ten are torn away to make room for "the little horn." This "little horn" wages persecution against God's people and is victorious for 3½ years; then, God destroys him [and his kingdom, obviously]. Finally, the dominion of all the kingdoms under the heavens is given to God's people [Christ did say that the meek shall inherit the earth].

The first point I'll make is that the "ten horns" in this Chapter are not the "ten horns" in Revelation 12, 13 & 17. Please remember that. The second point is that the "little horn" in Chapter 7 rules for 3½ years, whereas the "little horn" in Chapter 8 rules 6 years and 3 months; the former comes long after the Roman Empire is history, the latter comes in the Greek Empire after the first four Seleucid kings.

Only God knows the name of the "little horn" who still has not appeared to date; the little Greek "horn" was Antiochus III Epipanes, who put an idol in the temple at Jerusalem. Note: the correct spelling is Epiphanes. I told you I type with two fingers.

The "little horn" yet to come is the Antichrist. He and his empire will be the last and worst to persecute God's people. The context implies that the struggle will rage over all the nations under the heavens. There is some kind of cause-effect relationship between the cruelty and extent of the persecution, and the greatness of the victory that God wins through his people, a victory that includes even those not yet belonging to God's kingdom.

One of the Fathers of the Church [Tertullian, The Fathers of the Church, p. 89] wrote that the blood of the martyrs is the seed of the Church. For example, to triumph over paganism in the Roman Empire required a great price. What will it cost for universal victory? His reign of terror [the little horn's] shall throw the human race into the worst crisis that man will ever experience: of that 3½-year period, and the decade or two or three before it, Christ said,

> "Never before, and never again, will there be such tribulation on the earth." [Mt. 24:21]

The last point is that Christ made the expression "Son of Man" also personal to himself; he even quoted a passage to the Sanhedrin on the night before his death, telling them they would see the "Son of Man coming on the clouds of heaven", which is right out of Chapter 8 of Daniel.

> 64 Jesus saith to him: Thou hast said it. Nevertheless I say to you, hereafter you shall see the Son of man sitting on the right hand of the power of God, and coming in the clouds of heaven. [Mt. 26:64]

> 13 I beheld therefore in the vision of the night, and lo, one like the son of man came with the clouds of heaven, and he came even to the Ancient of days: and they presented him before him. [Dn. 7:13]

Some of the symbolism is so obvious that I haven't bothered to mention it: I mean, please don't tell me you can't figure out whence came the "beasts"! If you say, "the glorious country," I shall have a sudden compulsion to baste your pates into paste! Isaiah 17:12 should be enough.

> 12 Woe to the multitude of many people, like the multitude of the roaring sea: and the tumult of crowds, like the noise of many waters. [Is. 17:12]

The symbols you will meet in Revelation are: "sea," "stars," "horns," "heads," "beasts," "mountains," "heaven" = kingdom of heaven [usually, on earth]; but, don't forget the "lion," "bear," and "leopard" in Chapter 7!!!

One thing more: I have to get dinner ready, do you?

Well, I have shown you how you must ponder every aspect, especially, composite symbols like the one in Chapter 2. If you have any questions, just ask.

I must go.

Your local sage,

Steve

Chapter 1

—

Apocalypse Chapters 1–3

Dear Friends of the Lord,

Because those who work daily have little time for Biblical exegesis, and because those who type with two fingers eventually spring a fit of wanting to bite them off, I will keep my commentary brief, but, mostly, because God wants people to do some discursive reasoning of their own, as He has heavily hinted by making some of prophecy, subtle and symbolic.

In this letter, I will outline the Book of Revelation, comment on its first three Chapters, and then begin clarification of its chronology or sequence of major events; for the fact that the sequence of events and that the sequence of visions and their contents are not always the same thing has occasioned many misconstructions. You will see that you already know much, including the symbols. With all Heaven on our side, let's go!

The name of the Christian Bible's last book [it is really an epistle or personal letter] comes from the opening phrase of the same,

> Ἀποκάλυψις Ἰησοῦ Χριστοῦ
> Apokalypsis Iësou Khristou
> [the] Revelation of Jesus Christ

I will, henceforth, refer to it as the Apocalypse. My outline is:

(1) PRESENT THINGS
- A. Chapter 1: Introduction
- B. Chapters 2-3: The Seven Letters

(2) FUTURE THINGS
- A. Chapters 4-9: The Sealed Scroll
- B. Chapters 10-21: The Open Scroll

(3) FINAL THINGS
- A. Chapter 22: Last Warning and Attestation

Perhaps, you noticed that half of the Apocalypse is the OPEN SCROLL, and, perhaps, you surmise the Open Scroll deals with something very important, because so much space was given to it. If you think so, you are right; for that very small scroll, which takes up half of the whole Apocalypse, deals with the climactic battle between the Kingdom of Heaven and the Kingdom of This World. You know who wins. But, let's get going on Chapter 1, eh?

In the New Testament, the term apokalypsis almost always means a revelation directly from God the Father, the Son Jesus Christ, or the Holy Spirit. Even though God unveils certain truths or facts heretofore hidden, he does not unveil them, completely; and so God gives us revelations that often are, as St. Paul says, "difficult of interpretation" [1 Cor. 14:26].

John's opening phrase, then, does two things, immediately:

(1) It informs the reader or listener, that the contents to follow are a DIVINE REVELATION.
(2) Those contents will be expressed in such a manner as to leave the truths or facts still partly hidden.

Now, if one reflects for a moment, one will see that the Apocalypse's first sentence is not a sentence at all: there is no subject and no verb, grammatically speaking—most conspicuous to this literature major! The name Iesou Khristou has the endings of the genitive case; it is the genitive complement to the word Apokalypsis, and so gives precision to its meaning. For, if Jesus Christ is the source of the revelation, then He is the Cause and Subject of it, not merely the Object to whom God the Father gave it. John is emphasizing the human nature of Jesus, the Jesus who acquired for his human nature all divine prerogatives, and said of this,

> "All power and authority has been given to me." [cf. Mt. 28.18]

The Apocalypse, then, will be the revelation of Jesus Christ by Jesus Christ. But, John implies more in the words,

> "...that he might disclose to his servants what must speedily befall."

This means the Apocalypse is not about the happenings of blind fate, but the bringing to completion of the Father's decrees. Because Jesus Christ is who he is, he must, can, and shall do the will of the Father. All the powers of hell and earth will not be able to prevent it.

Since the servants are the Mystical Body of Christ, the Apocalypse will, therefore, be a description of the way in which Christ and his Church evolve the Father's design and achieve total triumph. The words en takhei [speedily befall] do not promise that all will be accomplished speedily or soon, but that the beginning of the process will come soon. This is made clear in Chapters 13 and 14 where John admonishes Christians to await the designs of God.

At this point, I think you realize that John's words are simple but subtle; I will not often discuss a single passage, at such length, because I would have to type 500 pages or so. Don't expect to catch every subtlety in one reading.

John tells the reader that...

> "...he signified it by a message of his angel to his servant John..."

This puts the seal of truth and reliability on the revelations to follow. The angel was sent to help John in receiving them, completely, to explain anything unclear to him, and to guide him in recording everything, correctly. John will later mention that he took notes during the visions, but sending an angel to John makes it evident, also, that John did not begin final composition until after he had received all the visions. Neither the angel's identity nor whether it was visible can be determined from the text.

I think you were, at first, puzzled by something in verse 4,

"...and from the seven spirits who are before his throne..."

If you reflect a moment, you will see that John expresses the doctrine of the Holy Trinity. Throughout the Apocalypse, God is called,

"He that is, and was, and is to come;"

But, here in verse 4, John gives that title to the Father only, because he wanted to emphasize the Father's role as the Creator in the past, Ruler in the present, and Director in the evolvement of the future history of the Church and the world. The same grace [light, life, love] flows from the "seven spirits" and Jesus Christ; this means they are co-equal with the Father.

But, Jesus is again emphasized as to his human nature, the "faithful witness" and "first-born of the dead" and "ruler of the kings of the earth." In short, Jesus will carry out the Father's will and rule as the Father rules: this accentuates, again, the human nature of Jesus, as to his mission in the temporal reality, but the context makes it perfectly clear that Jesus Christ is also divine. Those who deny that Jesus is both God and man in the Hypostatic Union and who deny the Holy Trinity, yet call themselves Christians, are liars.

But, I have not forgotten the "seven spirits!" I think you understand that John is talking about the Holy Spirit. Why, then, the plural? The "seven spirits" here, as in 3:1, is the same Holy Spirit who, in 4:5, appears as the "seven lamps" and, in verse 5:6, as the "seven eyes" of the Lamb [which, may I add, unequivocally declares that the Holy Spirit proceeds from Jesus Christ also, not just the Father!].

These forms denote the Holy Spirit's various external activities in the Church and its mission in the world; therefore, John expresses this idea in the words,

"...the seven spirits WHO are BEFORE HIS THRONE,"

just as, later on, he describes the Four Living Beings and twenty-four Elders and angels and Crystal Sea BEFORE THE THRONE [Chapter 5]. How subtly

John hints at the Holy Spirit's role of humble servant-guide in the Mystical Body of Christ, the Church! He revealed Himself in Isaiah [11:2], as the "seven gifts" of the Messiah, and in Zachariah [4:10], as the "seven eyes." The symbolism is not new.

Let me here interpolate an explanation of the symbolic number "seven." Seven is the sum of three plus four, the number of the Holy Trinity plus the visible creation. This sacred number expresses the perfection and universality in the dealings of God with men. It also expresses the idea of "indefiniteness in such things as time, quantity, etc." Hence, the length of time to actualize the purpose of the visible creation, namely, man, is expressed as SEVEN days. God's purpose for man shall continue until He brings it to fulfillment. The number SEVEN, thus, sums up all God's revelations.

The Apocalypse tells about the evolvement and consummation of God's purpose, and that is why it is addressed to SEVEN bishops and their SEVEN congregations. Indeed, the contents of the whole book [epistle] can be put into a series of SEVENS. It doesn't take much intellectual talent to get the hint: the Apocalypse is Jesus Christ's final message to the whole Church throughout all the ages, even to the end of human history. For Jesus Christ is Immanuel, God with us, for every step and second of the journey.

Interesting, so far? Not so hard to understand! At least, you know why the Church has SEVEN sacraments, neh? A little more to help you with Chapter 1, but please do not infer from that statement I imply any angelic status.

In verse 3, John asserts his book is "prophecy," i.e., divine revelation; and, in verse 10, he writes that he was "in the spirit," i.e., divinely inspired.

In verse 8, he quotes the Lord God [the Father] as saying,

"I am the Alpha and the Omega."

Jesus Christ will say the same thing in Chapter 22. Thus, John, many times, makes it perfectly clear that God is Three Persons in one divine nature, that Jesus Christ is one of those three persons, and that Jesus Christ is both divine and human.

Even before the first Chapter ends, John will allude to Daniel 7:9 when he describes "one like a son of man," for his description matches that of "the Ancient of Days." Jesus is both Son of God and Son of Man: the New

Testament is clear on that point. But, many denominations teach otherwise. The final warning in Chapter 22 applies to them.

From verse 10 onward, the narration of the visions begins. John hears a voice "like a trumpet." This alludes to such as Joel [2:1], wherein the priests are commanded to blow the trumpet to announce the coming of God's judgments or to Paul's first epistle to the Thessalonians [4:15].

> 1 Blow ye the trumpet in Sion, sound an alarm in my holy mountain, let all the inhabitants of the land tremble: because the day of the Lord cometh, because it is nigh at hand, [Jl. 2:1]

> 15 For the Lord himself shall come down from heaven with commandment, and with the voice of an archangel, and with the trumpet of God: and the dead who are in Christ, shall rise first.
> [1 Thes. 4:15]

It is not clear whether the voice was that of the angel mentioned in verse 1.

John turns and sees "one like a son of man" standing in the midst of "seven lampstands," and holding "seven stars" in his right hand. From John's description of the figure and from the dictation to follow, it is clear that the person is Jesus Christ. His "white [fore]head and hair" [hairs, actually] symbolize his eternity and divine wisdom.

John means "forehead" because, if you read a few verses down, he says Christ's face was "like the sun shining with full force"; and the "hair" is actually "hairs" because John uses the plural. "Every hair on your head is counted," Jesus once said; and, thus, the plurality of "hairs" connotes that God is omniscient and pays attention to every little detail.

The "sun" symbolizes divinity in knowledge and power to be "the light of the world." John's description of the face recalls the Transfiguration on Mt. Tabor [Mt. 17, Lk. & Mk. 9].

The robe Christ is wearing was the kind made of white linen; it is "long," i.e., it reaches to his ankles: that is why only the feet are described as "burnished bronze, refined as in a furnace." The "long robe" is the emblem of his priesthood, and the color "white" is the symbol of victory.

The "sash" around his breast symbolizes the purity of his desires and thoughts; the "gold" symbolizes his royalty, for, in John's time, gold was given only to kings.

Thus, Jesus presents himself as prophet, priest, and king in his very first appearance, one who is victorious and has already overcome the world, the flesh, and Satan.

As to the meaning of the Thracian two-edged battle sword coming out of Christ's mouth, I will not tell you!!! I have explained too much already. I do suggest you remember it, because you will meet it later. I am permitted to hint part of the answer: think of Perry Mason or the statue outside of a courthouse.

Yet one thing more: Christ explains the meanings of the symbols of "seven stars" and "seven lampstands." He thereby informs us, as the term apokalypsis has already suggested, that the revelations will be expressed partly in symbolism. Obviously, Jesus dictates the "seven" letters to "seven" bishops and their congregations, as both the symbolism and the next two chapters and common sense make clear enough.

Hence, unless the context indicates otherwise, "angels" are members of the clergy, ones with high authority, such as bishops or cardinals. Need I point out that the angel, mentioned in verse 1, is a real celestial spirit?

Now, I must pause to get my head straight again. Typing has always been tedious for me. No, no, no! I will not tell you the meaning of the "sword!" **YOU FIGURE IT OUT!**

Chapters 2-3 comprise the seven letters Christ dictates to John; they deal with "things that are," as Jesus said toward the end of Chapter 1. As you peruse the letters, notice their format: Jesus, after repeating one or more of the characteristics/titles from Chapter 1, first states the good news, then the bad news.

Nota Bene: each characteristic/title is what will manifest itself in inflicting punishment on that bishop or congregation [if they don't repent], because it is the one most proper to apply to them. THEREFORE, if you discern the relationship between the characteristic/title and the offense to be removed, you will also discern the meaning of the symbolism in John's initial description of Jesus Christ.

For example, in the letter to the angel of the church in Pergamum [2:12-17], Jesus implies the relationship between "the sharp, two-edged sword" and the fact that…

> "thou hast some there holding fast the doctrine of Balaam who taught Balak to cast a stumbling-block before the children of Israel, the eating of idol-offerings and the committing of impurity."

The Nicolaites did not keep the decrees of the Council of Jerusalem, rejected the apostolic traditions and restrictions, and compromised with pagans [Acts 15:29].

Jesus refers to Numbers 25, when he mentions Balaam. However, I could not find any passage therein that unequivocally stated that Balaam [a soothsayer or fortuneteller] did deliberately inform Balak, King of the Moabites, as to how he could get God to curse the Israelites.

Perhaps, Balaam's seven holocausts on seven altars suggested to Balak the idea or sly scheme of having the princes of Israel lured into sinful acts by Moabite princesses; to wit, the princesses invited the princes to commit fornication with them, and then to eat some meat that had been sacrificed to Beelphegor, the god of lust. Consequently, God sent a plague, which killed 24,000 Israelites before being stopped by Phinehas's slaying Prince Zimri and the Moabite Princess Cozbi. The leaders, as usual, got everybody in trouble.

Notice how Jesus holds the bishop responsible, more so than he does the black sheep in the congregation. He is a "star," a heavenly body, whereas the congregation is a "lampstand," an earthly vessel. The bishop was being too lax and lenient. Some of his flock were probably poor and wanted meat for their pots, occasionally. And, some went to the rituals [probably, Dionysios or Aeskulepios] where other men met to discuss business deals [golf hadn't been invented yet].

But, Jesus makes it perfectly clear he will fight against his enemies and Satan's sly schemes. The Divine Warrior will keep his Church pure, so she can save her members and convert the world. That God is a man of war was first manifested in Exodus 15:3;

> "The Lord is as a man of war, Almighty is his name."

Christ's sword is not the jus gladii [the rule of the sword] of Caesar, but the Thracian battle sword that can strike great gaping wounds unto death, when it is put to work. Jesus is also alluding to the same use of the sword against the "Beast" in 13:3, for there is "a time for war" [Eccles. 3:8].

Well, are you getting the knack of it? Correlate, correlate, correlate!!! If you are patient, you will be able to put the whole apokalypsis into focus—insofar as one can put it into focus. Some parts will remain vague or partly veiled even after one figures out the meanings of symbols. That's OKAY because, if God wanted the reader to have full and exact knowledge, then, He would make every detail perfectly clear.

Make the entire Bible your sole reference as to what God's words ultimately mean. A passage in one book can help illuminate one in another. Always bear in mind the context in which a passage appears. And, correlate!

Now, I said I would BEGIN clarification of the Apocalypse's chronology in this letter. So, I'll begin by identifying approximate dates, two of them, to orient you, in regard to what has already happened. I forgot: there is a third approximate date, namely, the year in which John received the visions. If one doesn't have the starting point, it is very difficult—if not impossible—to figure out what events John symbolically describes in the Sealed Book.

You see, we have an advantage: about 1,900 years have already passed. Since the beginning of the apokalypsis was to happen soon, we can safely deduce that some of the events depicted in the Sealed Book have already happened. Ah, common sense is simple, and, thus, simply beautiful! Come, the game's afoot!

It is historical record that the first imperial persecution against the Christians, under Nero in 64 AD, spread to Asia Minor [now called Turkey]. The second persecution under Domitian in 95 AD was confined to Rome [Domitian was assassinated in 96 AD.]. It was during this second persecution that John was thrown into a cauldron of boiling oil, miraculously spared by God, then was banished to the island of Patmos off the west coast of Asia Minor.

St. Iranaeus [d. 140 AD] was an early Father of the Church, who knew Polycarp, a disciple of St. John. Iranaeus, commenting on John's apocalyptic vision, wrote,

> "For that was seen no very long time since, almost in our day, TOWARDS THE END OF DOMITIAN'S REIGN."

It can be deduced from Christ's seven letters that there was no general persecution at the time Christ dictated them to John. Nerva, who ruled 96-98 AD, was kind to the Christians. But, the third persecution, 112-113 AD under Trajan, did extend to Asia Minor.

Hence, one may reasonably conclude that John received the Apocalypse during 95-96 AD, that he sent the final composition of it 96-97 AD, and that the text was widely circulated by 100 AD. Therefore, the chronology of FUTURE THINGS begins soon after, approximately, the year 100 AD.

Since this letter lengthens like the shadows of evening, prudence admonishes not to presume upon your patience more. The next letter will deal with Chapters 4-9½; it will ascertain two other approximate dates or points in the chronology. This will bring you to the point where the Church is at present. My last letter will deal with the Open Scroll.

I hope my commentary proves helpful. John's vocabulary, grammar, and style are simple, but meaning is conveyed in a subtle manner. I admit there are passages "difficult of interpretation," yet do not think the Apocalypse is just a pretty parable or the like. Its message goes to one who desires to learn it.

Sometimes, it is we who make finding the Truth a difficult, long task, even when it really should be easy, like the time Mary and Joseph searched for Jesus three days and nights: "Did you not know I must be about my Father's business?" People seem to have a penchant for not seeing the obvious.

So, Friends, Two Fingers must betake himself to the refrigerator, now, for some cold chicken. SNACK, GOBBLE, and PLOP on the couch: time to watch the battle of Waterloo.

Your humble exegete,

Steve

CHAPTER 2

—

APOCALYPSE CHAPTERS 4 THROUGH 9½

October, 1997

Dear Friends of the Lord,

I tender these thoughts on Chapters 4 through 9½ of the Apocalypse; hopeful they will be helpful in those spare quarters of an hour, that obligations allot in rare allowance, but into which two-bits of time I would deposit my two-cents worth, in order to compound your interest. Whereas justice and mercy are two sides of the same coin, the former forbids that either cent should sound the mere tinkling of an inkling, for you would spend precious time, unprofitably; and, yet, the latter prohibits ungracious expatiation, for, then, you would counterfeit your own investment. In any case, though I would like you to see an imaginative metamorphosis of this monetary metaphor, aye, I must yield, so that you will pay attention. Aye me! The cost of giving is the cost of living. This was one time a paradox, but now 'tis proved true.

One minute, please: I must bathe my brain, in caffeine. Yo! Is your reason ready? So! Let's go to what's coming.

First, the terms "heaven" and "kingdom" should be defined. In Daniel 7:9-10, the Jews of ancient Israel are called "the army of heaven."

> 9 And out of one of them came forth a little horn: and it became great against the south, and against the east, and against the strength. 10 And it was magnified even unto the strength of heaven: and it threw down of the strength, and of the stars, and trod upon them.

In Isaiah 34:5, God said to the prophet,

> "When my sword has drunk its fill in heaven, lo, it shall come down in judgment upon Edom…"

God was talking about the theocracy; nota bene the expression "come down." Jesus called His Church "the kingdom of heaven" [Mt.16:18-19]. John calls it "the kingdom" in Chapter 1 of the Apocalypse; in Chapter 4 and in many others, he simply calls it "heaven" [7:10; 9:1; 12:1; 13:6; 19:14; 21:7].

Moreover, the "kingdom of heaven" is in two "places." In Dan. 2:31-45, King Nebuchadnezzar had a dream: a stone hewn out of a MOUNTAIN smashed a statue of various metals, beginning with its feet; and, then, the stone became a MOUNTAIN that covered the entire earth. The prophet explained that the "stone" represented the everlasting kingdom, which the "God of heaven" would set up.

Hence, there is the "kingdom of heaven" in eternity, and there is the "kingdom of heaven" on earth. This fact is corroborated in Chapter 10 of the Apocalypse, where a mighty angel comes down from "heaven" into "heaven," and also in Chapter 12, where the male child is "snatched up" from "heaven" into "heaven," and in verse 12 that reads,

> "Rejoice then, you HEAVENS and those who dwell in THEM!"

Therefore, unless context indicates otherwise, the term "heaven" in the Apocalypse means THE CHURCH.

Chapter 4 begins with the phrase, "after these things," which means John has just finished noting down Christ's last dictation. He looks up and sees "a door standing open in heaven." Then, the voice like a trumpet from Chapter 1 commands him,

> "Come up hither, and I will show you what must take place after these things."

The opening and concluding phrases are the same, "μετὰ ταῦτα...μετὰ ταῦτα" [Meta tauta...meta tauta]; the latter alludes to the former, and both allude to Christ's command in verse 19 of Chapter 1. From this point on, the book is future history, the future history of the Church and of the world, insofar as the world will connect with the Church or affect her destiny.

Common sense should see the book will tell about the kingdom of heaven on earth, not in eternity; for, as John himself wrote in his first epistle [4:12], "No one has seen God." Nowhere in the New Testament did any divinely inspired writer even attempt to describe eternity. If any had done so, verily, the comical would have entered, a category all alien to Him who said,

> "The eye has not seen, nor has the ear heard, what awaits those who keep my commandments." [cf. 1 Cor. 2]

Therefore, faith must reject absolutely the view that the Apocalypse is merely a book of parables and consolations.

The description of future history, however, does not begin until Chapter 6, until after Christ opens the sealed scroll in Chapter 5, because something most important must be shown first.

John looked through the door and saw that...

> "a throne stood in heaven, and upon the throne one seated...Around the throne are 24 thrones, and seated on the thrones are 24 elders, clothed in white garments, with golden crowns on their heads...and in front of the throne there is as it were a sea of glass, like crystal. And within the space before the throne and around the throne are four living beings, full of eyes in front and behind. The first living being is like a lion; the second like an ox; the third has a face like that of a man; and the fourth is like an eagle flying."

Regarding the "four living beings," the Greek reads, "καὶ ἐν μέσῳ τοῦ θρόνου" [kai en mesö tou thronou = and in the midst of the throne], described in verse 6. This does not mean the four are sitting in God's lap, for heaven's sake. Rather, the throne is not only the seat at the top where God is, but also the rest of it lower down, perhaps, something like a dais. Hence, the "four living beings" are midway on the dais, between the top and bottom of the whole throne; but, they are, nonetheless, together with God ON THE THRONE.

In a ring around the foot of the throne, but not on it, are the "twenty-four elders," each seated on his own smaller throne. Farthest out is the Crystal Sea.

In 5:11, John wrote that the angels [real ones] surround "the throne and the Four Living Beings and the Elders." It is, thus, a logical deduction that the angels are between the Elders and the Crystal Sea.

What John described is the Church as an organization with a hierarchy. He mentioned God first and the Four Living Beings last, even though the Four Living Beings are second in rank, probably because the first and last positions in a sentence or paragraph are the strongest, psychologically speaking. Euphemistically speaking, his description was circuitous. Rationally speaking, it was meticulously deliberate.

In Chapter 5, John's description of those worshipping proceeds from the Four Living Beings, to the Elders, to the Angels, and to the Crystal Sea. But, in Chapter 7, it proceeds from the Crystal Sea, to the Angels, to the Elders, and to the Four Living Beings.

Likewise, he mentions "lightning" first, then "thunder" in Chapter 4; but, he reverses the order of mention in verse 5 of Chapter 8. In both instances, he altered the order of mention for a specific, concrete reason. His method came neither of madness nor of the intention to occasion it, but of the desire to demonstrate to the reader that, unless God grants a private revelation, faith must reason discursively to find the meaning.

Let common sense absent opinion, for a guess in a brain is like gas in a bubble: the sphere of speculation expands—until the pinhead makes his point. Christ advised, "Be as wise as serpents, but as innocent as doves." It should be no surprise that one of the Four Living Beings has "a face like that of a man," for the "human face" is the symbol of RATIONAL THOUGHT.

Now, many have asserted that the Four Living Beings are the four evangelists. One must bear in mind that the Apocalypse deals with "what is, and what must take place after these things." When John received the visions, all of the other evangelists had been dead long since. John himself would die a few years later and be buried in Ephesus.

The visions are not about them, but about those to whom the Apostles handed down the teachings and authority given by Christ. If one asserts the Four Living Beings are the four Evangelists, then John must be simultaneously both a spectator of the vision and a participant in it. Even worse, the two secretaries, Mark and Luke, would be equal in rank to the two Apostles, Matthew and John, despite the fact that a definite hierarchy is described. A circuitous approach to the identity of the Four Living Beings must be made.

The twenty-four Elders hold lesser positions of spiritual authority in the Church, as shown by the fact that each sits on a throne lower down, and each wears a gold "στεφάνους" [stephanos], the "crown of a regent or subordinate ruler."

In Chapter 5, the Four Living Beings and the twenty-four Elders, but **NOT** the Angels and the Crystal Sea, hold harps and golden bowls full of incense, and they enact worship before God and the Lamb.

The term "elder" is the English translation of "πρεσβυτέρων" [presbyteros]; from that same Greek word is derived the English word "priest." The twenty-four Elders, then, represent the Church's priests.

Since the clergy comprise two principal groups, and since the Four Living Beings hold higher rank, it logically follows that the "Four Living Beings" represent the episcopate—the bishops and cardinals. It is also now clear that the clergy hold higher rank in the Church than the Angels do. The "Crystal Sea" [which includes me!] represents the laity, farthest from the throne and lowest in rank.

Chapters 4 and 5 depict one of the Apocalypse's chief themes: AUTHORITY/POWER. For 5:1, some translations read,

> "Then I saw in the right hand of the one seated on the throne…"

The Westminster version much more accurately reads,

> "And I saw on the right hand of him who sitteth on the throne…"

What John wrote was this,

> "καὶ εἶδον ἐπὶ τὴν δεξιὰν τοῦ καθημένου ἐπὶ τοῦ θρόνου…"
> "Kai eidon epi ten dexian tou kathëmenou epi tou thronou…"
> "And I saw on the right of the one seated on the throne…"

If John had intended to write, "hand," he would have done so, as he did about Christ in 1:16,

> "…καὶ ἔχων ἐν τῇ δεξιᾷ χειρὶ αὐτοῦ…"
> "…Kai ekhön en te dexia kheiri autou…"
> "…And he held in the right hand of him…"

Translators would do best to remember, especially, when they translate, that John was a divinely inspired writer who had an angelical assistant, not Igor. God forbid I condemn the translators, for sure they are all honorable scholars, and I cannot divine their consciences; yet, I cannot condone such vertiginous inadvertence, so slothful sloppiness.

In Chapters 4 and 5, it is most conspicuous that John absented from the text any anthropomorphisms in regard to God the Father. John used the term, "kathemenou," to mean "one who has set or placed himself," not to suggest a human figure in a sitting position. That is why John did not describe a human figure on the throne. Instead, he wrote that,

> "the one seated there appeared like a jasper and a carnelian…,"

which means the colors of jasper and carnelian.

This interpretation is corroborated by the very next words,

> "And around the throne was a rainbow like an emerald."

The rainbow is not an emerald, but light; and the light is the color of an emerald. John saw God the Father as LIGHT, not a solid, human shape.

> "The Father is spirit, and those who worship him must worship in spirit and truth," [Jn. 4:24].

In the New Testament, spirit is symbolized most often by "light." Now, if the Father was a dunce for redundancy, He too would have become a man, just so foggy noggins could make good the proposition of a mistranslated preposition: truly, IN for ON? Well, on the keyboard, "I" does come before "0".

In verse 6, John wrote,

> "And I saw in the midst of the throne and the Four Living Beings, and in the midst of the Elders, a Lamb standing as it were sacrificed..."

But, in verse 9, the Four Living Beings and the Elders sing a new song,

> "Worthy art Thou to take the scroll and to open its seals, for Thou wast sacrificed, and didst redeem to God by thy blood men from every tribe and tongue and people and nation, and hast made them a kingdom and priests to our God, and they shall reign upon the earth."

The Greek terms John used pertain to a creature killed or slaughtered by a priest in worshipping a deity. The term "Lamb" is not a fully accurate translation. Everywhere else in the New Testament, even in John's gospel [1:29], the Greek word "ἀμνὸς" [amnos = lamb] is used to mean Christ. But, the Greek word in Chapter 5 of the Apocalypse, the same in twelve Chapters twenty-nine times, is the diminutive, "τὸ ἀϱνίον" [to arnion], which means THE LITTLE LAMB.

John is telling the reader something important: Jesus Christ, as the Lamb, "was sacrificed," but, as the Little Lamb, he is "as it were sacrificed," and that is why the Four Living Beings and the twenty-four Elders sing a NEW song. Christ's role in the Apocalypse is different from his role before his resurrection. His worthiness to open the scroll and break the seals comes not only from the fact that he "has conquered" but also from the fact that he is the Little Lamb.

Here would arise as many opinions as locusts in a swarm, if John had not provided more details. The Little Lamb is standing <u>between</u> the Father and the Living Beings, while only the Living Beings and the Elders are enacting—indeed, the context suggests REENACTING—some kind of sacrifice to God the Father. Jesus Christ is standing not only in the position of Mediator but also in that of both high priest and VICTIM.

In verse 5, an Elder calls Christ, "the Lion of Judah, the Root of David." This refers to Is.11:10,

> "On that day the root of Jesse…the GENTILES shall seek out, for his DWELLING shall be GLORIOUS."

The Dwelling was the Holy of Holies in the Old Testament. In Ex. 40:33, it reads,

> "Moses could not enter the meeting tent, because the cloud settled down on it and the glory of the Lord filled the Dwelling."

Moses could not enter because God was present, and no man could see God face to face and live.

The meaning of Chapters 4-5 should be clear to anyone who is not "an obtuse spirit": Jesus Christ, Son of God and Son of Man, is the Real Presence Divine and glorified Human, spiritual and corporeal, in His Dwelling, the Church. The Little Lamb is the EUCHARISTIC CHRIST in the UNBLOODIED SACRIFICE of the MASS.

At the Last Supper, Jesus, for the first time, changed bread and wine into his body and blood; and then he declared,

> "Now is the ruler of this world cast out." [Jn. 12:31]

Christ became the Lamb sacrificed on the cross in a bloody manner, so that he could become the Little Lamb sacrificed in the Mass in an unbloody manner. Through him, with him, in him, the Church Militant shall conquer, shall bring the Father's plan to completion. That is why the angels sing in full voice,

> "Worthy is the [Little] Lamb that was sacrificed to receive POWER and RICHES and WISDOM and MIGHT and HONOR and GLORY and BLESSING!"

What else would the angels sing in this context, but the sacred number SEVEN?

So, now you know the most important thing that had to be shown first. By the way, in verse 5, an Elder calls Christ, "The Lion of Judah," because the "lion" is the symbol of royalty, namely, kings. It is also the symbol of the papacy, for the pope is the Vicar of Christ on earth. That is why John wrote in Chapter 4,

> "The first Living Being is like a lion..."

Before showing the next approximate date, a few symbolical numbers need explanation. The number ONE THOUSAND in John's day signified perfection, although it was not necessarily connected with the concept of totality. The world's number of completion or perfection is TEN, a round number that denotes the completion or perfection is not total, but nearly so. The number symbolizing God's completion or perfection in his dealings with the world is TWELVE, which is obtained by multiplying THREE times FOUR, the number of the Holy Trinity times the concept of totality. FOUR usually symbolizes universality, like the four main points of the compass, the four winds, or the Four Corners of the earth; but, totality is the more accurate concept.

For example, there were TWELVE tribes of ancient Israel, because the Savior of the whole world was to come from the Jews. However, God gave them through Moses TEN COMMANDMENTS, because the message and the law were not totally perfect or complete. Jesus Christ, being the fullness of the Truth and the fulfillment of the law, chose TWELVE Apostles to teach the good news to the whole world. As for the number TEN, you will meet it in Chapters 12 and 13. Now, I must keep that date, so to speak.

Chapter 7 begins with...

> "four angels standing at the Four Corners of the earth, holding fast the four winds of the earth, in order that no wind should blow on earth or sea, or against any tree."

Then, John saw…

> "another angel coming up from the east, holding the seal of the living God, and he cried out with a loud voice to the four angels to whom it was given to harm earth and sea, saying, 'Harm not earth or sea or trees, until we have sealed the servants of our God on their foreheads.'"

The first verse mentions the number four three times, thus connoting the number TWELVE.

The four angels are secondary agents whose power and authority over the "winds" have been "given" to them by God. They are not evil angels like the four "bound at the great river Euphrates" in 9:14; for the angel from the east, who holds the seal of the living God, indicates mutuality, in some sense, by the phrase, "the servants of OUR God."

It is evident the four angels were already holding back the "four winds" before the angel from the east addressed them. They will not release the "winds" until God commands them to do so; God will not issue the order until the servants of God have been sealed on their foreheads.

This suggests Ezekiel 9:4, where the order is given to mark a "Thau" on the foreheads of the faithful Jews in Jerusalem, so that they would not be killed by God's agents. A "Thau" has the form of a cross.

The "four winds" symbolize the four judgments, which God will send, of which the first would become operative soon. In the writings of the ancient prophets, "winds" represent revolutions and invading armies. In Daniel 7:2, the "four winds" blowing upon the "sea" [the Gentile nations] brought forth the four "beasts" [pagan empires], and each was a judgment upon the one before it for corrupting or persecuting God's people. In Jeremiah 49:36, the "winds" symbolize great slaughter of both good and bad; and, in 25:32, "whirlwinds" mean revolutions and invasions from nation to nation, and the overthrow of kingdoms.

36 And I will bring upon Elam the four winds from the four quarters of heaven: and I will scatter them into all these winds: and there shall be no nation, to which the fugitives of Elam shall not come. [Jer. 49:36]

32 Thus saith the Lord of hosts: Behold evil shall go forth from nation to nation: and a great whirlwind shall go forth from the ends of the earth. [Jer. 25:32]

Verses 4-8 indicate that the "four winds" are being held back for two main reasons:

(1) to convert that minority of the Jews not so obstinate after the fall of Jerusalem;
(2) especially to strengthen the Church, so that she can cope with the judgments that will affect ALL, BOTH GOOD AND BAD, wherever the Church is.

In the early centuries of the Church, "to seal" meant to administer the sacrament of Confirmation. To "confirm" means to strengthen. Yet, John was not alluding to the administration of the sacrament per se; rather, since the concept of totality is so obvious here, he was alluding to the "sealing" of the whole Church, so that she would be prepared and so that EVERYONE WHO CAN BE SAVED SHALL BE SAVED [are not justice and mercy two sides of the same coin?].

The angel from the east [literally, the rising of the sun: Christ was called the ORIENT by Zachariah.] issues a command/request in a loud voice, which suggests he speaks with authority because his rank is higher than that of the four angels. Add to this the terms angel and "seal" and "living," and it is strongly suggested that he is a member of the episcopate, a very holy bishop who comes and speaks in the name of Christ.

Now, ponder here: the bishop speaks because he knows that, at least, one judgment is due; and he knows this because he knows what has made or is making, at least, one judgment a certainty. He has used his "eyes in front and behind" [Chapter 4], keeping them on the Little Lamb and His flock, and

READING THE SIGNS OF THE TIMES. He does not opine: HE KNOWS. That such a one can hold off a divine judgment is quite clear:

> 6 And now you know what withholdeth, that he may be revealed in his time. 7 For the mystery of iniquity already worketh; only that he who now holdeth, do hold, until he be taken out of the way.
> [2 Thes. 2:6,7]

The transition from verse 3 to the rest of the Chapter is an abrupt leap. The vision changes from the time when some servants are not yet sealed, to when the number of those sealed has reached completion—the Church stands ready. John hears the number of those sealed from the twelve tribes of Israel: it is 144,000 or TWELVE times ONE THOUSAND from each tribe, the number of completion.

However, small is the number of Jews compared to the number of Gentiles; for the former is countable, but the latter is countless. The Gentiles are from "every nation and tribe and people and language"; and these FOUR terms, which John used in Chapter 5, signify the TOTALITY of something, not the universality or CATHOLICITY of the Church to be eventually achieved.

This fact is corroborated by the angels, who sing,

> "Blessing and glory and wisdom and THANKSGIVING and honor and power and might be to our God forever and ever. Amen."

The symbolical SEVEN here means, as it does in Genesis regarding the visible creation, that God has brought a stage of his plan to completion. The scene is a victory celebration. That is why the sealed ones wear white robes and carry palm branches. The victory would not have been possible without the Little Lamb and the active, not passive, participation of the sealed ones; for they have conquered by washing their robes in the blood of the Little Lamb.

In verse 14, an Elder tells John,

> "These are they who have come out of THE GREAT TRIBULATION."

The Elder uses the Greek definite article, which means he is referring to something previously mentioned and presumes John knows it. In 1:9 and 2:10, John stated it and warned the Christians in Asia, of its coming. In 3:10, he called it "the hour of temptation." It is bloody persecution.

Since he emphasizes "τῆς μεγάλης" [tes megalës = the great one], he can be referring only to the imperial persecutions, especially, to the one under Diocletian, which was the last and worst, and which ended everywhere in the spring of 313 AD, after the new emperor, Constantine, was baptized and then decreed religious freedom THROUGHOUT THE EMPIRE.

Chapter 7 depicts the Church just after it has fulfilled the prophecy in Daniel 2: that the "stone" hewn from a "mountain" would smash paganism in all those lands that the "statue" represented.

Even as the Church rejoices in the victory of the Little Lamb, the bishop from the east knows that God will soon send judgment upon the Roman Empire. Why? How? The answer to the first question is found in the latter part of Chapter 6, and the answer to the second, at the first "trumpet" in Chapter 8.

By the way, the scene of Chapter 7 is that of the Church in the fourth century. The bishop from the east comes about 355-360 AD, and the victory celebration is about 400 AD. The latter approximate date [400 AD] is the second one I promised you; but, you have to wait to find out my reasons for saying so. That comes at the beginning of Chapter 8, the time when the number of those sealed is completed by members of a certain institution in the Church, an institution that could not exist during the imperial persecutions.

In 6:9, when he [the Little Lamb] opened the fifth seal, the seer beheld the souls of martyrs under the ALTAR. As final evidence to prove <u>all</u> I have said about Chapters 4 and 5, I point to that verse, because there is no altar in Eternity: every tabernacle in every church on earth is a throne of God. The martyrs ask in verse 10,

> "How long, O Sovereign Lord, holy and true, do you delay to judge and avenge our blood upon them that dwell upon the earth?"

This alludes to the "jasper" and "carnelian," the holiness and justice, mentioned in 4:3. But, the martyrs are told,

> "...they should rest yet a little longer, until the number of their fellow servants and their brethren, who are about to be killed, even as they, should be complete."

Though they are given white robes, one must bear in mind that they are martyrs, whereas those wearing white robes in Chapter 7 are <u>survivors</u> of the great tribulation. The connection, however, is what Tertullian wrote, "The blood of the martyrs is the seed of the Church."

So, there has been persecution before the fifth seal was opened, and there will be more after it. The ultimate number of martyrs will be reached during the reign of the Beast, the very last at the Battle of Armageddon in Chapter 19. Then, they will no longer "rest," but reign with Christ for a "thousand" years.

However, when the number of martyrs sufficed for the overthrow of paganism throughout the empire, then God acted—not out of justice, but mercy. The phrase, "a great earthquake," in verse 12, refers to "them that dwell upon the earth," in verse 10. The Little Lamb did not show the persecutions that followed the fifth seal, because it was enough to tell they would occur; and, more importantly, because He wanted to emphasize that the blood of his martyrs was also the seed of mercy [which will not be the case for the Beast and his followers]; and, most importantly, because He wanted to show that the success of HIS CHURCH was for the sake of HIS HOLY NAME.

Justice and mercy are two sides of the same coin. God did not act out of justice in regard to the Gentiles, because they knew not what they did; but, He did act out of justice for the sake of His Holy Name. The Jews received justice because they could no longer be excused for rejecting God's only Son and persecuting the early Church. The fourth seal tersely tells what God decreed upon them.

As a piece of pedantry, I interject verse 8 from Isaiah 45,

> "Let justice descend, O heaven, like dew from above, like gentle rain let the skies drop it down."

Think about it. Do you recognize it? Now, you will understand what Shakespeare was thinking when he put these words into the mouth of Portia in The Merchant of Venice,

> "The quality of mercy is not strained; it droppeth as the gentle dew from heaven, upon the place beneath."

But, Shylock wanted all of justice; though a merchant, he just couldn't see that justice and mercy are two sides of the same coin. With what measure we measure, so shall it be measured out to us. [cf. Mt. 7:2].

By the way, all of Chapter 7 can be inserted immediately after the phrase, "a great earthquake," in verse 12. Chapter 7 is a flashback. I told you the order of the visions and the order of events were not the same thing. Impetuosity can be excused in the young, but, when scholars with gray or, even, white hair misconstrue the little book about the Little Lamb, whose fault is that? To opine, when it is possible to know, is heinous in a rational being. And, "IN" for "ON", even in the NEW AMERICAN BIBLE? Shudder I do, for I feel the cold breath upon my neck. Reason has fled to brutish beasts. Enough! I must on.

Satan, watching the prophecy in Daniel 2 being fulfilled [the stone hewn from a mountain not on earth smashing paganism represented by the statue], immediately counterattacked from within the Church. In 318 AD, Arius, a priest in Alexandria, began publicly to teach that Christ was merely a man and not also God.

There had been heresies since the Church's earliest years, but Arianism became a spiritual black plague that wreaked pandemic death. After the Council of Rimini in 359 AD, at which almost all of 400 bishops consented to a semi-Arian creed, it is reported that St. Jerome exclaimed, "The whole world groaned to find itself Arian."

This spiritual disaster is aptly described in verse 12, after the "great earthquake." The text reads,

> "…the sun became black as haircloth, and the full moon became as blood, and the stars of heaven fell on earth, as casteth the fig-tree her winter fruit when shaken by a strong wind; and the heaven passed away like a scroll that is rolled up…"

Christ is the Divine Light that the darkness cannot overcome; and, though every priest is alter Christus, another Christ, whose duty is to teach the divine truth by word and act, a priest is not God, and so he can fail in his duty. As a priest's love for Christ grows colder, he teaches less of the divine truth; and thus, it can be said that the "sun," which symbolizes the Divine Light, grows dimmer. And, when priests in large number teach falsehood or consent to it, then it can be said that the "sun" has turned so dark as to seem covered with haircloth woven from a black goat.

Three times, Christ asked Peter,

"Do you love me?"

And three times, He commanded him,

"Feed my sheep." [Jn. 21:15-17]

The Truth is the food for Christ's followers; the Little Lamb is that food.

Arianism denied the divinity of Jesus, and so it sought to starve the "sheep" to death. In Ezekiel 34:8, 12, the Lord says,

> "...and because my shepherds did not look after my sheep, but pastured themselves and did not pasture my sheep...I will rescue them [the sheep] from every place where they were scattered when it was cloudy and dark."

The bishop from the east [Arianism was mostly in the eastern part of the Empire] saw these things happening, and he knew the words, in Joel 2:31, pertained to such times,

> "The sun will be turned to darkness, and the moon to blood, at the coming of the day of the Lord, the great and terrible day."

When love for the Little Lamb grows cold in the hearts of many, especially, the clergy, will Christ find faith on the earth when he comes in judgment? Isaiah in 1:19-20 warned,

> "If you are willing, and obey, you shall eat the good things of the Lord; but if you refuse and resist, the SWORD SHALL CONSUME YOU; for the MOUTH of the Lord has spoken!"

A "scroll" sometimes symbolizes the kingdom of heaven, or its word. In Chapter 10, John is given a very small "scroll" to eat. And, in Isaiah 34:4, it reads,

> "Heaven shall be rolled up like a scroll, and all its host shall wither away, as the leaf wilts on the vine, or as the fig withers on the tree…"

After the Council of Rimini, it seemed the true Church had disappeared, as if it had "rolled up like a scroll." Many of the clergy, symbolized by the "stars," apostatized from the Divine Truth, that is, they "fell on earth" like figs in winter.

By the way, the "kingdom of heaven" in the Old Testament was Israel; the plant that is the national symbol of Israel, is the FIG TREE. This item of information will be important at the conclusion of my commentary.

The rest of the verses in Chapter 6 tersely describe the fall of the Roman Empire. So, verses 12-13 relate to 14-17, as cause to consequence: the reason for the fall of Rome was HERESY.

The Chapter ends with the question, "Who can stand?" This means, "Who can stand in heaven?" Chapter 7 replies,

> "…they who have washed their robes in the blood of the Little Lamb."

And the Little Lamb is the Eucharist, the food of eternal life.

John lists SEVEN classes that represent the Roman population, not only to describe the total subversion of the Roman order, but also to indicate that the fall was the judgment of God and the Little Lamb.

The number "seven," moreover, carries the reader forward to the SEVENTH SEAL. The period of the seventh seal includes that of Chapter 7, and should be extended as far as 400 or 410 AD. It is the brief period of the Church's preparation before the first of the "four winds" will be released.

The first four of the seven trumpets will announce the "four winds"; those "four winds" will be the four major events described in Chapter 8, beginning with the "Hail and fire mixed with blood."

In the beginning of Chapter 8, John sees something that was not before the throne in Chapters 4-6: the GOLD ALTAR.

In the Old Testament, the Holy of Holies was the throne of God; and closest to it was the golden altar of incense [Ex. 40:5]. Only the high priests performed worship there. Gold was the most rare and precious of metals in ancient times.

The context suggests the "altar" is solid gold, unmixed with baser metals. It is different from the other altar mentioned in Chapter 6, in the sense that those who worship at the golden one have a purer, more intimate relationship with God.

What was not present in the Church for two and a half centuries, but appeared and grew after Constantine decreed religious freedom? Only one institution was lacking: the religious orders, especially, the monastic orders that led the contemplative life. Christ said,

> "I have come to cast fire on the earth, and what will I, but that it be kindled?" [Lk.12:49]

That is exactly what the angel did: he...

> "took the censer and filled it with fire of the altar, and cast it towards the earth; and there followed thunderpeals and voices and lightnings and an earthquake." [Apoc. 8:5]

By 400 AD, the religious had carried the "good news," even to the western-most parts of the empire; and they converted many, which is symbolized by the "earthquake" at the end of verse 5. The Church was then ready to convert the barbarians who soon thereafter would begin their invasions; and her monastic orders would preserve in manuscripts any knowledge worth preserving from the old order.

Thus, the second approximate date is 400 AD, and the four major events that follow in Chapter 8 come after it.

The last part of Chapter 6 told why God came in judgment on the empire; the first "wind," announced by the first of the seven trumpets, tells how the judgment was executed: the barbarian invasions. The second "wind," the "burning mountain," would finish the job.

It is historical record that those called barbarians invaded mostly the northern and western parts of the Empire, that is, ONE THIRD of it, just as verse 7 states. The Persians eventually regained much of Mesopotamia. Thus, it is logically deduced that the Burning Mountain will come from the south, that is, from the northern stretch of Africa that touches the Mediterranean Sea.

I will tell you what the other "winds" are, including the Burning Mountain, but only if you cannot figure them out. Remember: they are major events in the history of the Church after the fall of Rome circa 486 AD. It should be obvious to you by now, that numbers "three" and "four" of the winds are spiritual calamities from WITHIN the Church. The third one tells about "a great star," and the fourth one tells about the "sun" and the "moon" again. Now, I must on to the third approximate date. Good sleuthing!

That third date comes in the last verse of Chapter 8: the "eagle" flying in "mid-heaven." An eagle flies higher than any other creature: it flies farthest away from the "earth" and, therefore, closest to the "sun." The "eagle" symbolizes the contemplative life; the one in 8:13 is a member of a contemplative order.

He is obviously delivering a prophecy of warning "to them that dwell upon the earth." Bear in mind that Christ said,

> "There are many inside the Church who are outside, and many outside who are inside."

Those who are not of the Truth "dwell on the earth." Since the "eagle" is flying "in mid-heaven," his direst of warnings is directed mainly at the clergy, aye, especially, the episcopate. Like the bishop from the east in Chapter 7, this "eagle" speaks in the name of Christ, for he cries out in a loud voice, the voice of authority that he wants all to hear.

In view of the description of the fourth "wind" in verse 12, it is clear that the "eagle" is the messenger divinely appointed to deliver the last warning to the Church. If the Church does not heed the warning, then the three woes will overtake many more in their sin than the woes would otherwise. But, understand here: the woes are included in "what must soon befall" in the first verse of Chapter 1.

God knows what men will do, but He warns them anyway, so that none can say that there was no warning. Christ warned the Jews, but they, in general, did not listen. He also said,

> "Offenses must come, but woe to that man by whom the offense comes! Better for him had he never been born." [Mt. 18:7]

Those are strong words from Him Who created man.

Two great saints appear in the first half of the fifteenth century: the Dominican, St. Vincent Ferrer, and the Franciscan, St. Bernadine of Sienna, each a priest in a contemplative order. In 1398 AD, when St. Vincent was dying of a fever, Christ, together with St. Dominic and St. Francis, appeared to him, cured him of his fever, and commissioned him to preach that the Church must repent and do penance, or else judgment would come.

Christ did not tell St. Vincent exactly when the judgment would come or what kind it would be; but, He must have said something thereof, because St. Vincent, on countless occasions, warned that the "Day of Wrath" was to come "quickly, indeed quickly and very shortly" [cito, bene cito et valde breviter]. While preaching to a crowd in 1406, St. Vincent announced that his mantle [commission] would be handed down to someone then listening to him, and that the person would evangelize throughout Italy.

The person was St. Bernadine. The Franciscan priest often used the same words of the "eagle" in 8:13, "woe woe woe!," and he often threatened his listeners with the plague of locusts described in the first half of Chapter 9. He preached from 1417 until he died in 1444.

Of the two men, I would say St. Vincent Ferrer was the "eagle" flying in "mid-heaven" because he, and not St. Bernadine, received a special revelation from Christ Himself. So, the third approximate date is 1450 AD, at verse 13 in Chapter 8.

In the first half of Chapter 9, the fifth angel sounds the trumpet to announce the first of the three woes. This means that Christ's ONE JUDGMENT will come in three stages. The judgment will be the worst, the most terrible, that He will inflict on his Church and the world. Progressively, it will extend until it involves all mankind, and it will intensify until it culminates in the annihilation of all evil agents and agencies on the earth.

John wrote,

> "...and I saw a star which had fallen to the earth, and there was given to him the key of the bottomless pit. And he opened the bottomless pit..."

Here, I must end this letter, not to occasion a sense of suspense, but to rest my two fingers and 13 billion brain cells. By now, you should be able to figure out who the "star" was, and what the "key" symbolizes.

The only major event that comes after, approximately, the year 1450 AD was.... If you can't figure it out, I will tell you. Hint: the first woe is still in progress. Never again can the unique evolvement of the three woes be repeated. The judgment has already begun, and the Little Lamb shall bring it to completion, to THE GREAT DAY OF ALMIGHTY GOD.

I hope this commentary, including its asides, is being helpful. When you are old enough, Friends, I hope the time to come will not surprise you, like a thief in the night.

Well, I have only the Open Scroll left to explain. That will be the third letter. I know John wrote in a subtle manner, but he described what Christ showed him, and, so, the subtlety must be attributed to Christ, as deliberate. That is why I shall not explain everything.

If you were not in the active life, wherein time for such thinking as the Apocalypse requires comes sparely, I would help little, because you have quite more than enough intellectual ability to do the thinking. The meaning goes to those who want it much.

I have demonstrated already, beyond all reasonable doubt, that the message is intelligible and relevant. Many hundreds of millions know how to read and memorize ideas; scarcely one in a million knows how to reason.

Look! The Four Living Beings, and "the fourth is like an eagle flying." Surely, the bishops and cardinals should know the "eagle" flying in the midst of "heaven" is speaking especially to them. If a man cannot see lightning and cannot hear thunder, is he blind and deaf?

Dark, dark, dark, but the moon is on the wane, and the dogs bark, bark, bark. Good night.

Cordially yours,

Steve

Chapter 3

—

Beginning of Part III

Dear Friends of the Lord,

I gave you my word that I would write the last part of the commentary on the Apocalypse, and so here it is for you to keep what I have kept; but, I cannot give you my word that it is my last word on the little book, for, then, I should have to keep what I have never kept: my mouth shut. This statement connotes neither a premise to anything nor a promise to anyone, and it can occasion anxiousness only in those who hope that I, sooner rather than later, will either give or keep my last word on any subject, including myself.

The fact is that my loquacity partially follows my idiosyncratic mind, which has never been an open-and-shut case, regardless of what other kind of case people may have opined of me; yet, from this, my oral reputation notwithstanding, one ought not to draw the silly illation that repetition, which makes reputation, also makes necessity.

Moreover, since God has not anointed me to the office of prophet, it cannot be that He expects me to prophesy with authority unto the people; and since everyone else, including myself, cannot seriously expect He will give me the appointment hereafter, and concomitantly cannot expect I will have the appointment to keep, because it would be silly to expect the unexpected; and since people cannot be necessarily serious regarding disappointment about the appointment, or disappointment about no appointment, because neither appointment nor disappointment was ever the point in the first place; then, also, in keeping with right reason am I in giving no anxiousness whatsoever to whether I will disappoint anyone, or to whether anyone will disappoint me: QUOD ERAT DEMONSTRANDUM. Hence, I presently advise as previously: judge for yourselves!

This part of the Commentary covers the Apocalypse from 9:12 to 22:21; its principal objectives are:

(1) to explain terms.
(2) to clarify the order of events.

Underlining in any excerpt from Scripture will be emphasis mine. I will begin in the classical manner by leaping in medias res, into the middle of things: please read Chapter 11.

Here is a rather literal translation of 11:1-3,

καὶ ἐδόθη μοι κάλαμος ὅμοιος ῥάβδῳ λέγων ἔγειρε καὶ μέτρησον τὸν ναὸν
Kai edothë moi kalamos omoios rabdö, legön, Egeire kai metrëson ton naon
"And was given me a reed like a rod, as he said, "Come and measure the sanctuary

τοῦ θεοῦ καὶ τὸ θυσιαστήριον καὶ τοὺς προσκυνοῦντας ἐν αὐτῷ καὶ τὴν
tou theou kai to thysiastërion kai tous proskynountas en autö. Kai tën
of God and the altar and the ones worshipping in it. And the court the

αὐλὴν τὴν ἔξωθεν τοῦ ναοῦ ἔκβαλε ἔξωθεν καὶ μὴ αὐτὴν μετρήσῃς ὅτι ἐδόθη
aulën tën exöthen tou naou ekbale exothen kai më autën metrësës, oti edothe
outside of the sanctuary cast outside and not it measure, for it was given

τοῖς ἔθνεσιν καὶ τὴν πόλιν τὴν ἁγίαν πατήσουσιν μῆνας τεσσεράκοντα καὶ δύο
tois ethnesin, kai tën polin tën again patësousin mënas tesserakonta dyo.
to the nations, and the city the holy they will be trampling months forty-two.

καὶ δώσω τοῖς δυσὶν μάρτυσίν μου καὶ προφητεύσουσιν ἡμέρας χιλίας
Kai dösö tois dysin martysin mou kai prophëteusousin ëmeras khilias
And I will give to the two witnesses of me and they will be prophesying days thousand

διακοσίας ἑξήκοντα περιβεβλημένοι σάκκους
diakosias exëkonta peribeblëmenoi sakkous
two hundred sixty, all-clothed of sackcloth."

Regarding the above verses, almost every modern edition of the Bible, including the New American Bible, translates the noun "ναὸς" [naos] as "temple," and the imperative "ἔκβαλε" [ekbale] as "omit" or "exclude." Ever and everywhere, it is both prudent and fair not to opine, but rather to seek and find, the meaning of any term or expression that the Bible uses.

A few references out of many will help clarify the term "temple":

> "Destroy this temple, and in three days I will raise it up"...But he [Jesus] was speaking about the temple of his body. [Jn. 2:19, 21]

> You are the body of Christ and individually members of it. [1 Cor. 12:27]

> ...for we are the temple of the living God; as God has said: "I will dwell in them and walk among them, and I will be their God, and they shall be my people." [2 Cor. 6:16] [cf. Lev. 26:11-12]

> It opened its mouth to utter blasphemies against God, blaspheming his name and his dwelling, that is, those who dwell in heaven. [Apoc. 13:6]

Hence, the term "temple" means the Church. For the Church is the Brethren, collectively and individually. The Speaker, however, commands John to omit or to exclude the court outside the temple and measure it not. The command seems redundant and unnecessary, because one does not have to omit or to exclude what is already outside.

The term "ἔκβαλε" [ekbale] is the imperative singular of "ἔκβαλλειν" [ekballein], which is composed of the prefix "ἔκ-" [ek- = out] and the verb "βαλλειν" [ballein = to throw, cast, hurl]. Moreover, the adverb "ἔξωθεν" [exothen], which means "outside" or "on the outside," emphasizes whither the court is to be cast.

Note that the same word is used in apposition with the term “court”: it is thereby intimated that the court outside is, in some sense, already outside. Thus, the command is,

“And the court the one outside the temple cast outside and measure it not.”

The command still seems not to make any sense. But, remember the beginning of Chapter 4: John was suddenly “in the spirit,” and he looked through a door that “stood opened in heaven” and saw “one seated on the throne…” and “the twenty-four elders,” etc. This means John perceived in a spiritual manner the inside court of “heaven,” or the Church. The physical or visible is symbolic of the spiritual or invisible. The description is graphic so that the human imagination has something to grasp more easily.

Now verse 2 begins to make sense, except for the translation “temple.” The New Testament writers consistently used the noun “ναὸς” [naos] instead of “ιερον” [ieron = temple] to denote the Church.

In Acts 17:24, Paul tells the members of the Aeropagus that God does not live “ἐν χειροποιήτοις ναοῖς” [en kheiropoiërois naois = in hand-made shrines]. In Luke 11:51, Christ mentioned,

“Zechariah…who perished between the altar and the house” [τοῦ οἴκου = ton oikon];

but, in Matthew 23:35, He said,

“…between the sanctuary [τοῦ ναοῦ = ton naou] and the altar.”

The term “house” is often translated as “sanctuary,” regarding the Temple of Solomon. A perusal of the New Testament finds that the Temple had a “προανλιον” [proanlion = forecourt], then further inward an “αὐλή” [anlë = court, where beasts were kept overnight], and furthest in, the “μέσουλος” [mesaulos = the inner court behind the “αὐλή,” anlë]. Finally, Christ’s comment in Matthew 23:20-22 sheds light on the matter,

> So whoever swears by the altar swears by it and by everything on it; and whoever swears by the sanctuary swears by it and by the one who dwells in it; and whoever swears by heaven swears by the throne of God and by the one who is seated upon it.

The description John gave in Chapter 4 limits the Church to an inside court, the one in the middle, and an outside court; the "door" implies that there is a wall separating the two courts. If this is compared to a church, the altar and tabernacle [God's throne] are located in the sanctuary. Therefore, the term "ναὸς" [naos] should be translated as "sanctuary," the "μέσουλος" [mesaulos], the one in the middle or midst of the Church. This concept is very important: remember it.

Also, the sanctuary in the Temple of Solomon was sometimes called "the holy place" or, simply, "the place"; but, in a Roman Catholic Church, the sanctuary would be "a holy place," because God is present in each tabernacle.

Thus, the Speaker's command now makes a little more sense: John is to measure the Church's inside court, but its outside court he is to cast outside—the Church. Not yet, not quite yet, is reason fully satisfied, because the text still implies that the outside court is, in some sense, already outside.

The measuring instrument given to John is a "κάλαμος" [kalamos], a kind of reed that grows as high as twenty feet along the Jordan River.

> 24 And when the messengers of John were departed, he began to speak to the multitudes concerning John. What went ye out into the desert to see, a reed shaken with the wind? [Lk. 7:24].

But, ominous is the phrase added to it: "like a rod." The "rod" is a prophetic term that symbolizes authority of divine origin; it signals the terrible severity with which God will separate the good from the bad, the faithful from the unfaithful

> 5 Woe to the Assyrian, he is the rod and the staff of my anger, and my indignation is in their hands. [Is. 10:5].

Since the Speaker commands John to measure only the sanctuary and cast the rest outside, the measuring connotes that those in the sanctuary have a "Thau" on their foreheads and are "sealed," and that they will cooperate with God's grace to persevere to the end of the judgment about to begin; whereas, the rest in the outside court will be cast outside into the spiritual darkness about to flood the world, where, in the end, there will be, as Christ warned, "weeping and the gnashing of teeth" [Mt. 8:12].

So, had John been given a measuring line, an increase in the size of the Church would have been indicated; but the "rod" portends the contrary.

> 1 And I lifted up my eyes, and saw, and behold a man, with a <u>measuring line</u> in his hand. 2 And I said: Whither goest thou? and he said to me: To measure Jerusalem, and to <u>see how great is the breadth thereof, and how great the length thereof.</u> 3 And behold the angel that spoke in me went forth, and another angel went out to meet him. 4 And he said to him: Run, speak to this young man, saying: Jerusalem shall be inhabited without walls, by reason of the multitude of men, and of the beasts in the midst thereof. [Zec. 2:1-4].

> And he brought me in thither, and behold a man, whose appearance was like the appearance of brass, with a <u>line of flax in his hand, and a measuring reed in his hand</u>, and he stood in the gate. [Ez. 40:3].

As a parting comment here, I point out that a reed is not as hard and solid as a rod, for it is tacit that the term "rod" signifies an <u>iron</u> rod. The reed is not for shattering "pottery";

> 9 Thou shalt rule them with a rod of iron, and shalt break them in pieces like a potter's vessel [Ps 2:9];

the iron rod can shatter it, easily and totally

> 31 For at the voice of the Lord the Assyrian <u>shall fear being struck with the rod</u>. 32 And the passage of <u>the rod shall be strongly grounded</u>,

which the Lord shall make to rest upon him with timbrels and harps, and in great battles he shall over throw them. [Is. 30:31, 32].

This means that the most severe part of the judgment will not come during the time of measuring the sanctuary, but after it. God will give to the "nations," as secondary agents, the task of inflicting judgment upon those cast outside the Church. This is only fitting and proper.

But, reason still stands: the text emphasizes the idea that the court is already, in some sense, "outside."

In Greek, the aorist forms of a verb are used to convey the idea that "an action or act is single or simple rather than repeated or prolonged." For example, a present infinitive often indicates a continuous or progressive action or state, while an "aorist infinitive" indicates a single act:

Present Infinitive	Aorist Infinitive
ἐθέλω βλέπειν τὴν πόλιν.	ἐθέλω βλέψαι τὴν πόλιν.
Ethelo blepein ten polin.	Ethelo blepsai ten polin.
I want to see the city.	I want to see the city.
[I want to keep seeing the city.]	[I want to take one look at the city.]

The verb "μέτρησον" [metreson = measure] in verse 1 is a direct positive command in the aorist active voice, second person singular; the direct negative command "μὴ...μετρήσῃς" [me...metreses = not...measure] in verse 2 is the aorist active voice, second person singular, subjunctive mood: each verb conveys the idea that "the command is to be carried out <u>only once</u>."

The present participle "προσκυνοῦντας" [proskynountas = worshipping] near the end of verse 1, though used as a plural noun, nonetheless, conveys the idea of "continuous or repeated action." This means the worshipers at the altar are those who daily keep the commandments of Jesus and often partake of the Eucharist.

The future participle "πατήσουσιν" [patesousin = will be trampling] in verse 2 modifies the noun "nations"; the future participle "προφητεύσουσιν" [propheteusousin = will be prophesying] in verse 3 modifies the noun "witnesses": each participle conveys the idea of "continuous or repeated action."

Finally, note the verb "ἐδόθη" [edothe = was given] at the beginning of verse 1 and also at the start of the dependent clause in verse 2: both are in the aorist passive voice, third person singular; and each indicates a single act or action, which agrees with the aorist sense of the direct commands.

All versions known to me translate the former as "was given," but the latter as "is given" or "has been given." The obvious fact is that the same verb in the same form is used in both places, and, therefore, should be translated the same way: "was given."

Since the future participle "will be trampling" modifies "nations," the outside court, by being given to the nations, is also given to the same tract of time, namely, the forty-two months during which the nations will be trampling the holy city. In other words, the aorist "was given to the nations" can be understood as "will be being given to the nations." The connective "καὶ" [kai = and] after the noun "nations" indicates the synchronism of both "was given" and "will be trampling."

Here, reason again confronts the question of how the court can be outside before it is outside. The answer to the court question comes in verse 3, when the Speaker says,

> "And I will give to the two witnesses of/from me [genitive of possession/origin] and they will be prophesying..."

Obviously, the Speaker is God Himself, for only God can give the office of prophet. Since God is infinite, He is omniscient; therefore, knowing all of the finite creation, He alone can see the future of the present, that the court not yet formally outside the Church is, in spirit, already outside: THOSE IN THE OUTSIDE COURT SHALL NOT STAND BEFORE THE THRONE, BUT APOSTATIZE.

The text is signaling the reader, regarding Christ's letter to the church at Laodicea, the SEVENTH letter [3:16]. The outside court represents those whom Christ will "vomit" out of his mouth. They are the tepid brethren, the half-hearted who do the minimum, at most, to stay within the Church, the timid souls who keep to shadows and will not come full into the light. Spiritually weak, they shall not be able to withstand the storm of evil about to burst over the whole earth. The words of 1 Peter 4:17 apply,

"The time has come for judgment to begin with the house of God."

As the evil grow toward the extreme of evil, so must the good grow toward the extreme of good—just to remain good.

The identity of the Speaker can be logically deduced: it helps one's reasoning, that the phrase, "Ἀποκάλυψις Ἰησοῦ Χριστοῦ" [Apokalypsis Iesou Khristou = The revelation of/from Jesus Christ], dominates the whole prophecy. I will explain more about Greek verbs later, lest your digestion contest its own process.

The Old and the New Testaments make it perfectly clear that "the holy city" in verse 2 is Jerusalem:

> 1 Arise, arise, put on thy strength, O Sion, put on the garments of thy glory, O <u>Jerusalem, the city of the Holy One</u>…[Is. 52:1];
>
> 16 O Lord, against all thy justice: let thy wrath and thy indignation be turned away, I beseech thee, from thy city <u>Jerusalem, and from thy holy mountain</u>. [Dn. 9:16];
>
> 24 Seventy weeks are shortened upon thy people, and upon thy <u>holy city</u>, that transgression may be finished, and sin may have an end, and iniquity may be abolished; and everlasting justice may be brought; and vision and prophecy may be fulfilled; and the saint of saints may be anointed. [Dn. 9:24];
>
> 5 Then the devil took him up into the <u>holy city</u>, and set him upon the pinnacle of the temple, [Mt. 4:5] ;
>
> 53 And coming out of the tombs after his resurrection, came into the <u>holy city</u>, and appeared to many. [Mt. 27:53].

Verse 2 states,

> "For it [the court outside] was given to the nations, and they will be trampling the <u>holy city</u> for forty-two months."

Then, verse 3 states,

> "And I will give to the two witnesses of/from me and they will be prophesying for 1260 days."

These statements, together, constitute a literary device called a "parallelism." Parallelism is employed to show or to emphasize sameness or difference. Here, the parallel construction strongly suggests that the period of 42 months and that of 1260 days will be one and the same period; but, it does not prove it will be so.

To get the proof, this parallelism must be cross-referred with verses 8-14. The city where the two witnesses will be killed by the Beast is also the city "where their Lord was crucified," i.e., Jerusalem, spiritually called "Sodom" because of sins against the flesh, and "Egypt" because of sins against the spirit, most especially, idolatry and persecution against God's dwelling. This will fulfill Christ's words,

> "It is impossible for a prophet to be killed outside Jerusalem." [Lk. 13:33]

The two witnesses' tract of 1260 days ends when the Beast kills them. The tract of 42 months of the nations' "trampling the holy city" ends when the survivors of the earthquake there give glory to God; this event comes 3½ days after the Beast has killed the two prophets, a difference of .277% between the end of one and the end of the other. Hence, for the most part, the 1260 days and the 42 months are the same tract of time.

Nota bene: the conversion of the survivors marks the end of the second woe [11:14]; that is to say, it marks the beginning of the conversion of the Jews, and the beginning of the end for the Beast and his empire.

Before establishing the identities of the two witnesses, I would like to clarify two terms, which appear in this Chapter and in others subsequent. The noun "ἐθνος" [ethnos] means "race, culture, people, nation." In ancient times, separation of religion from government, culture, or business did not exist as it does today in the western democracies; and so, to practice a religion, different from the established one, was regarded as, at least, suspicious, if not outright seditious. Foreigners, of course, often were considered "different."

Thus did the adjective "ἐθνικός" [ethnikos] come to mean "heathen"; and from this word was derived the Late Latin ethnicus, whence the medieval English ethnik, thence the modern word "ethnic" or "ethnical." The modern term has several usages, and among these are:

(1) belonging to or deriving from the cultural, religious, or linguistic traditions of a people or country, especially, a primitive one.
(2) pertaining to non-Christians.

Similarly, the Latin noun gens [plural: gentes] means "family, race, people, nation," and the plural adjective gentiles is derived therefrom. The English adjective "gentile," in some of its usages, is very similar to those of "ethnic":

(1) pertaining to a tribe, clan, people, nation.
(2) heathen or pagan.
(3) pertaining to any people not Jewish.

Thus has it come that the Greek plural "ἐθνη" [ethne] is translated as either the "nations" or the "Gentiles." The New American Bible now uses "Gentiles." Generally, in English, however, the term "Gentiles" has become understood only as "pertaining to any people not Jewish." So, the term less confusing in English is "nations," preferably accompanied by a footnote.

In the Apocalypse, the term "nations," therefore, refers to non-Christian ones, especially, those heathen or pagan. To be most precise, it refers to nations that are not, at least, nominally Roman Catholic. And, sure, the term keeps casting a look at Asia.

Another noun requiring clarification is "ἄβυσσος" [abyssos]. This noun is composed of the prefix "ἄ-" [a- = not, without] and "βυσσός" [byssos = bottom of the sea], and conveys the idea of "bottomlessness."

In ancient cosmogony, it meant "the primal chaos before Creation" or "the infernal regions," that is, "hell," or "the great sea, the primordial ocean beneath the earth," as mentioned in Genesis 7:11 [In the six hundredth year of the life of Noe, in the second month, in the seventeenth day of the month, all the fountains of the great deep were broken up, and the flood gates of heaven were opened…] and 49:25 [25 The God of thy father shall be thy helper, and the

Almighty shall bless thee with the blessings of heaven above, with the blessings of the deep that lieth beneath, with the blessings of the breasts and of the womb.], and in Daniel 7:2 [2 I saw in my vision by night, and behold the four winds of the heaven strove upon the great sea]. This "sea" was thought to contain various monsters

> 1 In that day the Lord with his hard, and great, and strong sword shall visit leviathan the bar serpent, and leviathan the crooked serpent, and shall slay the whale that is in the see. [Is. 27:1];

> 12 Am I a sea, or a whale, that thou hast enclosed me in a prison? [Jb. 7:12],

and especially, "mythological monsters" symbolizing the chaos that God had vanquished in those primeval times;

> 13 God, whose wrath no mall can resist, and under whom they stoop that bear up the world. [Jb. 9:13]

> 13 His spirit hath adorned the heavens, and his obstetric hand brought forth the winding serpent [Jb. 26:13].

In verse 7, John mentions the Beast for the first time in the Apocalypse: it is "the Beast ascending from the abyss…" the same "abyss" that the "fallen star" opened up at the beginning of Chapter 9, and the same "abyss" into which the demons [Legion] begged Jesus not to send them back [Luke 8:31]. John used the term "abyss" to denote the spiritual origin of the Beast, but he also used it to connote the Beast's worldly origin mentioned at the beginning of Chapter 13: the "sea."

The "sea," in the Old Testament, was used to symbolize peoples or nations wicked for their paganism and for their hostility toward God and His people. Isaiah in 17:12 wrote,

> "Ah! The roaring of many peoples that roar like the roar of the seas! The surging of nations that surge like the surging of mighty waves!"

And, in 57:20, 21, he wrote,

> "But the wicked are like the tossing sea which cannot be calmed, and its waters cast up mud and filth. There is no rest for the wicked! says my God."

Therefore, the noun "ἄβυσσος" [abyssos] should not be translated as "the bottomless pit," but as "the abyss," especially, to retain the connotations. With the term "abyss," John conspicuously alludes to "the nations"; but, it must be borne in the brain, at all times, that a term must be interpreted strictly with regard to context. As the commentary proceeds, this rule will become colossally obvious.

CHAPTER 4

THE TWO WITNESSES

It was shown in part two of this commentary that Greek ordinarily uses the definite article when the noun it modifies has been previously mentioned.

Now, the witnesses in verse 3 have not been previously mentioned, but the Speaker designates them as "THE two witnesses," thus indirectly informing the reader that they are definite persons whose identities can easily be ascertained from the Old and the New Testaments.

The angel Gabriel, speaking to Zechariah about the child to be born and named John, said,

> "He will go forth before him [the Lord], in the spirit and power of Elijah, to turn the hearts of parents to their children, and the disobedient to the wisdom of the righteous, to make ready a people prepared for the Lord." [Lk. 1:17]

Speaking about John the Baptist, Jesus said,

> "...And if you will to accept it, he is Elijah who is to come." [Mt. 11:14]

Jesus also said of Elijah,

> "Elijah is indeed coming first to restore all things…But I tell you, Elijah has come, and they did to him [John] whatever they pleased, as it is written of him." [Mk. 9:12]

Finally, people asked John the Baptist, "Are you Elijah?" And, John replied, "I am not" [John 1:21]. The apparent contradiction is cleared away by distinguishing between the office or "spirit" of prophet and the person of the prophet himself, as Jesus and Gabriel make clear enough to those willing to discern it.

One very important point is implied: as John the Baptist preceded Christ's coming, so will Elijah precede the great day of the Lord. Compare what Gabriel said about John, with this citation from Malachi 3:22-24,

> "Remember the law of Moses my servant, which I enjoined upon him on Horeb, the statutes and ordinances <u>for all Israel</u>. Lo! I will send you Elijah, the prophet, before the day of the Lord comes, the great and terrible day, to turn the hearts of the fathers to their children, and the hearts of the children to their fathers, <u>lest I come and strike the land with doom</u>."

Bear in mind that the conversion of the Jews begins with the survivors of the earthquake in Jerusalem [11:13], and that the third woe will come quickly after that [11:14]. The Jews will not be punished in the third woe: God will not come and "strike the land with doom," as is evidenced in Chapter 21 where the names of the Twelve Tribes are included in the New Jerusalem of the Millennium.

The third woe is the seven last plagues [divine punishments] described in Chapter 16; and, in 16:14, John describes the closing event, when demonic spirits have assembled the kings of the earth for battle on "THE GREAT DAY OF ALMIGHTY GOD."

Hence, it is plain and clear that the Two Witnesses will have an important part in the conversion of Israel, just before "the day of the Lord, the great and terrible day." The Two Witnesses will have the authority and power to issue "fire" from their mouths against their enemies, to order droughts, and to inflict every kind of plague upon the earth, during the 3½ years of their prophesying.

Similarly, it was recorded that Elijah summoned "fire" from heaven;

> 12 Elias answering, said: If I be a man of God, let fire come down from heaven, and consume thee and thy fifty. And fire came down from heaven, and consumed him and his fifty. [2 Kgs. 1:12];

and that he ordered a drought for 3½ years during the days of King Ahab;

> 1 And Elias the Thesbite of the inhabitants of Galaad said to Achab: As the Lord liveth the God of Israel, in whose sight I stand, there shall not be dew nor rain these years, but according to the words of my mouth. [1 Kgs. 17:1].

The Two Witnesses will be resurrected after lying dead in a street of Jerusalem for 3½ days, which implies that they had not died on a previous occasion. In agreement with this, it was recorded that Elijah, walking along with the younger man Elisha, was suddenly taken up in a flaming chariot;

> 11 And as they went on, walking and talking together, behold a fiery chariot, and fiery horses parted them both asunder: and Elias went up by a whirlwind into heaven. [2 Kgs. 2:11];

and it was <u>not</u> recorded that he died: therefore, Christ said of him, "Elijah is indeed coming…" In the entire Bible, only one other person was recorded as not having died: Enoch. This is found in Genesis 5:24, which reads,

> "Then Enoch walked with God, and he was no longer here, for God took him."

The passage does not state the usual formula of "then he died," and, thereby, it indicates that Enoch did not die. Saint Paul affirmed this,

> "By faith Enoch was so taken that he did not experience death." [Heb. 11:5].

The future coming of Enoch has been recorded,

> "Enoch pleased God, and was translated into paradise, that he may give repentance to the nations." [Sir. 44:16]

The primary mission of the Two Witnesses will be one of mercy, not condemnation. For 3½ years, they will testify, by word and deed, to the divinity of Christ, and to the divine origin of the Roman Catholic Church alone. They will denounce the teachings of the Beast and his chief henchman, the beast "ascending from the earth" [13:11], later called the False Prophet [19:20]. Clothed in sackcloth, the Two Witnesses will live austerely and preach repentance. They will fulfill Christ's words,

> "And this good news will be proclaimed in the whole world unto the testimony to the nations, and then will come the end."
> [Matthew 24:14].

For their extraordinary service, they will be resurrected and assumed, soul AND body, into heaven. Strictly through the information given in Scripture, I draw the conclusion that the Two Witnesses will be Elijah and Enoch.

As for the rest of Chapter 11, verses 15-18 are sung in anticipation of the beginning of Christ's reign throughout the world; and verse 19 is an abbreviated description of the seventh plague in 16:17-21.

As I said, John "looped" forward and backward several times in the latter half of the Apocalypse; however, this is not as big a problem as it first seems. More comments about this Chapter will appear later, perhaps, ones that will surprise.

CHAPTER 5

INTRODUCTION TO CHAPTERS 9:12-21

November 20, 1998

Dear Friends of the Lord,

The third part of the commentary has been completed. Since the number of its pages is estimated at 130 [260 in typical paperback], the number of weeks to type them at the two-fingered rate is, according to rule of thumb, estimated at four weeks, should vision prove durable for that duration. The assiduity of two forefingers in concert could induce double vision or the sensation of a bicephalous condition; however, a copious supply of coffee and Boston Crèmes, as experience has proved, will undoubtedly sustain single-mindedness throughout.

Notwithstanding this answer to the process goes beforehand, the aftermath of it certainly comes into question. In this case, worry would be an otiose emotion; for anticipation, not seldom, is a false prophet antagonistic toward true advice, "Sufficient for the day is the evil thereof."

Thus, it stands within the prospect of belief that the commentary's third part will depart for your house before December 20, 1998.

On second thought, the relativity of double vision can be an advantage or disadvantage. Once upon a late autumn afternoon, a broom handle of a woman came walking along the street, sweeping the leaves with her feet; and, well....

So thin she was [I speak not in derision],
One had to knock one's head, to double vision,
Which caused this paradox to leap to light:
One sometimes sees things wrong, to see them right.

If you like surprises, you will have some soon. It cannot be claimed that the commentary was written in commendable style, but it can be asserted that it explains a certain number of things unexplained or misunderstood for nineteen centuries, most notably, regarding:

(1) the name of the Beast,
(2) the Woman Clothed with the Sun,
(3) the testimony or "μαρτυρίον" [martyrion] to the nations—as unique and, therefore, differentiated from all other witness or "μαρτυρία" [martyria],
(4) the <u>two</u> kinds of swords,
(5) the approximate time for the battle of Armageddon,
(6) the identification of who/what restrains the "son of lawlessness,"
(7) the "abomination of desolation,"
(8) the identity of the "Great Eagle,"
(9) the confederation of the Ten Kings,
(10) the maximum length of time from the beginning to the end of the second and third woes combined,
(11) and thus, cross-referred with Armageddon, the approximate time for the advent of Antichrist [the season, not the exact year], etc., etc., etc.

In brief, there has not been penned on paper, nor is there now in print, what this third part of the commentary contains. Your request has been requited as best as human brain and grace of God therein could do. The objective has been twofold: to explain terms and to present the order of events. Those objectives have been achieved. Thanks be to God for his permission!

After a weekend for rest, the typing will be commenced in earnest; but, obviously, it just will not do to have fingers crossed.

Hello, to the little ones, individually and collectively, the living proof of the efficacy of Boston Crèmes.

The grace of our Lord Jesus Christ be with all of you.

Yours in Christ, Steve

In 9:13-16, John wrote,

> "Then the sixth angel blew his trumpet, and I heard one voice from the four horns of the golden altar before God, while they were saying to the sixth angel who had the trumpet: 'Loose the four angels who are bound at the great river Euphrates.' So, the four angels were loosed, who had been held ready for the hour, the day, the month, and the year, to kill the third of mankind. The number of the troops of cavalry was twenty thousand ten thousand, I heard the number of them."

Most versions read "a voice" in verse 13, but the Westminster more accurately reads "a single voice." John wrote, "φωνὴν μίαν" [phönën mian], which means "one voice." At the beginning of verse 14, most versions read "saying"; the Westminster reads "it said," thus indicating or referring to "a single voice."

John wrote "λέγοντα" [legonta], which is a circumstantial participle like "λέγων" [legon] in 11:1, and it should be translated, in English, as a temporal clause. But, there is a problem: "λέγοντα" [legonta] can be only one of three possibilities:

(1) the singular masculine accusative case.
(2) the plural neuter nominative.
(3) the plural neuter accusative.

Since the participle functions as the subject and the verb of the clause, it follows that it is in the plural neuter nominative, and, thus, the clause should begin with "as they said" or, more accurately, "while they were saying."

The participle does not refer to "one voice," which is in the singular feminine accusative, but to the only plural neuter noun in the sentence: "κεϱάτων" [kera-ton = horns]. The context corroborates this; for it is obvious that John emphasized the symbolic number "four" by using it four times within three verses.

It is significant that John did not write "a voice," but "one voice." That "one voice" came from the "four horns." John did not mean that four voices together sounded as if they were one voice; rather, he meant that the four speaking "horns" were one voice speaking i.e., they spoke unanimously.

As pointed out in part two of this commentary, the "golden altar" [8:3] symbolizes the religious orders, but, here especially, those congregations contemplative, missionary, charitable, and teaching, established since the "fallen star" unlocked the "abyss" at the beginning of Chapter 9.

In view of the fact that the symbolic number "four" is so heavily emphasized in 9:13-16, the implication is both awesome and ominous: not the totality of something like the Roman Empire is involved here, as was the case in Chapter 7, but the totality of the world. The "one voice" is not only unanimous, but also universal.

The seventh seal marked the completion of the first major phase of the kingdom's revelation or evolvement, that is, the dethronement or decapitation of paganism throughout the totality of the Roman Empire.

Then, in 8:2, SEVEN angels were each given a trumpet; this connoted that another major phase of the Father's plan was about to begin. At that point, the reader could only speculate as to whether another large region would be involved, or whether the whole world: there were only those two possibilities.

In 9:13-16, John begins informing the reader that the objective of the second major phase is indeed the whole world. Then, there can be only one reason why the faithful of the religious orders tell unanimously and universally the "sixth angel" to loose the "four angels" bound at the Euphrates: not that the Church is making very slow progress; not that the Church is temporarily making no progress at all, either merely in a particular region or in the entire world; but that the Church is losing ground everywhere, that evil has grown so great as to have become alarmingly advanced, even in the Church, in its highest ranks.

The faithful of the religious orders will not meet and vote on the matter, obviously; rather, they will desire in their hearts and think in their minds, that God should begin the painful process of removing the many evils on earth and in "heaven," the Church. Even the faithful among the laity will sincerely pray: "...thy kingdom come, thy will be done, on earth as it is in heaven." When the salt is no longer preserving, when corruption is consuming so many, then, it will be time.

God knows all, and He has marked the exact hour and day and month and year for the "four angels" bound at the Euphrates to be loosed upon mankind. No one is more exact than God is. No one. Watch the religious orders: they will be the signal. Already their ranks are thin.

So amazed at the number of "cavalry" was John, that he did not put the connective "καὶ" after it, but only a comma. To make it clear to the reader that the number is to be understood as literal [but approximate, of course], John added: "I heard the number of them."

In John's day, the population of the entire Roman Empire was about 125 million; and one out of every ten could be trained and maintained in the military. The 200 Million Horsemen, therefore, according to the ancient ratio, which has changed little in modern times, suggest a population of TWO BILLION.

John, by human sagacity alone, would have known that the vision was about an event very far in the future. Those who confine the Apocalypse to the Roman Empire are quite in egregious error.

John wrote that...

> "the riders wore breastplates the color of fire and of hyacinth and of sulfur...the heads of the horses were like lions' heads, and fire and smoke and sulfur came out of their mouths." [Apoc 9:17]

The "riders" are the agents who command and direct, and the "horses" are their agencies, especially, those political and military.

The "breastplates" signify that the agents' hearts are hardened against all natural law of reason and supernatural law of God.

The [color of] fire here symbolizes hatred; the [color of] smoke here symbolizes the blasphemies that rise up from their hearts, as the fire burns the sulfur; and the [color of] sulfur symbolizes rebellion against God and the immutable truths He teaches to men, resulting in spiritlessness, generally, in the various forms of carnality or sensuality. With these three things will the Beast and his followers also be tormented: the "fire," the "sulfur," and the "smoke"

> 10 He also shall drink of the wine of the wrath of God, which is mingled with pure wine in the cup of his wrath, and shall be tormented with fire and brimstone in the sight of the holy angels, and in the sight of the Lamb. 11 And the smoke of their torments shall ascend up for ever and ever: neither have they rest day nor night, who have adored the beast, and his image, and whoever receiveth the character of his name. [Apoc. 14:10-11].

The "smoke" here is the same kind of "smoke" that came up out of the "abyss" at the beginning of Chapter 9, and the [color of] fire alludes forward to the Dragon [Satan] in Chapter 12, the Dragon that is not "red," as most translations state, but "flame-colored" or "fire-colored."

Thus, John informs the reader of three things:

(1) The spiritual origin of the 200 Million Horsemen is the "abyss."
(2) The second woe comes as a consequence of the first.
(3) The 200 Million Horsemen are the signal preparation shortly before the advent of the Beast and his empire.

Mark and hark: the second woe begins with the 200 Million Horsemen and culminates in the 3½-year reign of the Beast.

That the "horses" heads are like "lions" heads means that those organizations have the authority and power not only to propagandize, but also to devour, i.e., to kill.

From their mouths issue "fire," "smoke," and "sulfur": from this description, some people have drawn and asserted that John hinted at modern weapons. I do not know whether the Seer intended that hint, if such hint there was, although I understand why some people assert it.

I do not desire to speculate. I certainly do not want to opine, lest I put in John's mouth words that do not belong there, which would be tantamount to telling God that, when I want His "opinion," I will give it to Him.

However, I will assert most boldly and confidently as to what John meant when he wrote,

> "By these three plagues the third of the men was killed, by the fire and the smoke and the sulfur which were issued out of their mouths." [Apoc. 9:18]

John had the spiritual always first and foremost in his mind, and so, by those words, he meant that sin was the root cause that killed "THE third of THE men," i.e., the third of the people, the third of mankind, LIVING AT THAT TIME.

The prophetic term "plague" means a divine judgment or punishment usually carried out by secondary agents. As people sow, so shall they reap; the wages of sin are—death.

However, the Greek noun "πληγὴ" [plëgë] does not mean plague, strictly speaking, but blow, stroke, impact.

The reason this term is translated as plague arises from the fact that, in the Apocalypse, the term connotes the blow or stroke of the "sword" of God, that is, the justice of God applied in the form of punishment to men for their sins. Indirectly, John has told the reader that the proper punishment for sin is sin itself.

The pandemic death and destruction inflicted by the 200 Million Horsemen will be, quite frankly speaking, the externalization of the hearts of billions of people. The very enormity of the event speaks for itself; and, yet, the majority of the people living at that time, like every majority in the past, will fail to perceive the event's significance. In verses 20-21, John conveyed this fact, bluntly,

> "And the rest of the people, who were not killed by these plagues, did not repent."

History repeats itself because human nature does. "It's still the same old story...", as the old song says; and it will continue the same in kind, but worse in degree and extent, until the Little Lamb makes "heaven" new, and so the earth.

Twice directly, once indirectly, John mentioned that "the third of mankind" was killed; this percentage is literal, but approximate. There are now six billion people in the world. If the event of the 200 Million Horsemen began today, TWO BILLION human beings would die. As for the number of the injured, homeless, starving...it is a question.

Until the invention of the train, the horse was the swiftest means of movement for human beings. The symbolism of the "horses" was intended to convey the idea that the combatants will spread violence quickly from nation to nation, from region to region. The implication, then, is that the third of mankind will be killed in a relatively short span of time.

Bear in mind John's use of the definite article: it refers to the people living at that time when the event begins. Indeed, the phrase carries the meaning of "THAT third of THOSE people." Common sense understands that some of the total population will die from natural causes, but also that the total population will increase because of births; this means that demographics is useful more towards reckoning the event's geography, not its duration.

In round numbers, Asia has a population of 3.35 billion, Europe 1.0 billion, Africa 0.65 billion, South America 0.52 billion and North America 0.38 billion: the total human population of the earth is approximately 6.0 billion. The populations of Asia and Africa, combined, account for two thirds, or 4.0 billion; if that of Europe is added, then the amount becomes five sixths, or 5.0 billion.

At present trend, Europe's ratio of births to deaths is -½%; hence, even without compounding the negative rate, it is expected that Europe's population will decrease from 1.0 billion to 0.75 billion by 2050 AD. On the other hand, if the populations in Asia and Africa increase for the next fifty years at only <u>half</u> the rate of the past fifty, then, their populations combined will increase from 3.35 billion to 6.0 billion.

Thus, their total population in ratio to Europe's would be 8 to 1; and, if their historical rate of increase continued for that same period, the ratio would become, at least, 10 to 1.

Whatever set of figures is used, the result points to Asia as the main location for the event. It is most ominous that the four evil angels are bound at the Euphrates River in southwest Asia.

As for the duration of the event, the phrase, "the third of the men," can be fulfilled only if "the third" is killed before more than two thirds "of the men" die from other causes [births after the event begins are irrelevant]; and, so, at this point, the text indicates only that the event cannot last longer than, say, 40-50 years, a piece of information too vague for value in regard to even approximating what the event's actual duration will be. John emphasized something else that, again, gives the spiritual perspective.

The most important point in 9:13-21 is this: the "four horns" of the "golden altar" initiated the second woe. In the beginning of Chapter 7, a very holy bishop commanded four good angels to hold back the "four winds," which, by the end of their succession, would affect the totality of the Church. Here, in contrast, the "four horns" commanded the sixth angel to release the four evil angels, which affected the totality of the world.

The Church incurred the "four winds" [later represented as the first four trumpets] upon herself by the Arian heresy and by the consent to it by the vast majority of bishops at the Council of Rimini in 359 AD; the world incurred the four evil angels upon itself by opposing the Church in her primary mission: to teach and to baptize all nations. The latter half of this last statement requires explanation.

In the book of Daniel, a "horn" symbolized a king or kingdom that belonged to a larger kingdom, as part to whole or quondam whole. For example, in Daniel 7, the fourth "beast" represented the Roman Empire, and the "ten horns" on its head symbolized the kings or kingdoms into which the Roman Empire would become subdivided.

In Daniel 8, the "great horn" on the "he-goat" fell off, and, then, four smaller "horns" grew out of the "goat's head"; the "four horns" symbolized the four Seleucid kings who subdivided the Greek Empire among themselves after the death of Alexander the Great.

To the concept of the "horn" as a part to a larger entity, John added the concept of the "horn" as authority and power subordinate to a higher entity. For example, the "ten horns" on the seventh head of the Beast in Apocalypse 13 and 17 represent the Ten Kings who are subordinate to the Beast.

Secondly, the "seven horns" on the head of the Little Lamb in Chapter 5 symbolize [in indefinite number] the priests subordinate to Christ, who sends the Holy Spirit [seven eyes] through them unto the whole Church by the seven sacraments.

Thirdly, in Chapter 13, the "beast" ascending from the earth [the second beast, identified, in 19:20, as the False Prophet] has "two horns," which symbolize the power and authority in religious and secular agents and agencies subordinate to him.

It is an important point, then, that the command to loose the four evil angels at the Euphrates came from the "golden altar's" "four horns," not directly from the throne of God.

As will be seen later, the Beast will commit offense directly against Christ on the throne, in particular, not just against the Church, in general; and, thus, the command for the Beast's destruction will come directly from Christ on the throne.

It is implicit, therefore, that the "golden altar" has borne the brunt of offense up to the time of 9:13; hence, it is right and fitting that the "four horns" issue their unanimous command to loose the four evil angels.

Nota bene the exactitude of God in His justice and mercy: the "four horns" hold rank higher than that of angels, and so the punishment for offense should have been measured justly so; but, mercifully, only four evil angels were loosed. The evil angels incited the event to a magnitude greater than what man by himself would have done, and this is justice; but, the magnitude of the event was not as great as it could have been, and that is mercy.

When I said that the enormity of the event speaks for itself, I spoke inaccurately, for the event's enormity does not indicate by half what evil men will be doing at that time. The reader should not be shocked at the killing of the "third of the men"; rather, let the reader be shocked that it was [will be] not more than the third. Think, then: the Beast and his followers, who will be of the immense majority, will incur the exactitude of God in full and just measure.

Scripture is definite about the duration of the Beast's global reign of 42 months or 3½ years [Apoc. 13:5], after which comes the third woe; it is vague about the duration of the 200 Million Horsemen; and it offers only a number of hints about the duration of the third woe itself [to be mentioned later].

As for the duration of the second and third woes, combined, Scripture does provide a statement somewhat helpful. To understand that statement, a short lesson in vocabulary is required.

The Greek demonstrative adjective "οὗτος" [outos = this] conveys the idea of "pointing backward," while "ὁδὲ" [ode = this/that] conveys the idea of "pointing forward"; so, forms of these two demonstratives [including their adverbs] often mean more than, simply, this or this/that:

ἐνόμζε δὲ ταῦτα· ἀλλὰ τάδε ἔλεξεν.
enomize de tauta alla tade elexen.
And he was thinking these things: but these things he said.

In Matthew 24:34, Christ stated,

> ἀμὴν λέγω ὑμῖν ὅτι οὐ μὴ παρέλθῃ ἡ γενεὰ αὕτη
> Amën legö ymin oti ou më parelthe ë genea autë
> Amen I say to you that not shall pass away the generation itself
>
> ἕως ἂν πάντα ταῦτα γένηται.
> eös an panta tauta genëtai.
> until all these things have happened.

Juxtapose Matthew 24:34 with Matthew 23:36 in order to understand exactly what Christ meant,

> ἀμὴν λέγω ὑμῖν ἥξει ταῦτα πάντα ἐπὶ τὴν γενεὰν ταύτην.
> Amën legö ymin, ëxei tauta panta epi ten genean tautën.
> Amen I say to you, are coming these things all upon the generation this.

In Matthew 24:34, the phrase, "πάντα ταῦτα" [panta tauta], pointed backward to everything Christ had just told His apostles about the last signs or events before the end of the age; in Matthew 23:36, the phrase, "ταῦτα πάντα" [tauta panta = these things all], pointed backward to everything Christ had just told the crowds, especially, the scribes and Pharisees, about bringing righteous blood upon themselves.

In every English version I have read, both the phrase, "πάντα ταῦτα" [panta tauta], and "ταῦτα πάντα" [tauta panta] have been correctly given the same translation of "all these things." But, both the phrases, "ἡ γενεὰ αὕτη" [ë genea autë] in Matthew 24:34 and "τὴν γενεὰν ταύτην" [tën genean tautën] in Matthew 23:36, have also been treated equally; for, in most versions, both phrases have been given the same translation of "this generation," and, in the NAB, the same translation of "the present generation."

Even at cursory glance, it should have been evident to the translators, that the two phrases do not convey the same meaning, and that their giving the same translation to both would occasion misunderstanding or confusion in the minds of, at least, some readers.

The phrase, "τὴν γενεὰν ταύτην" [tën genean tautën], referred to the crowds, especially, the scribes and Pharisees, to whom Christ had just spoken; hence, the phrase may be translated as "this generation" or "the present generation."

However, the phrase, "ἡ γενεὰ αὕτη" [ë genea autë], did not refer to the apostles or their generation; rather, it referred to the generation of those last signs or events before the end of the age.

The adjective "αὕτη" [autë], in the postpositive, has the reflexive meaning of "-self"; hence, the phrase, "ἡ γενεὰ αὕτη" [ë genea autë], conveys the idea of "the generation itself," i.e., "the selfsame generation" or "that very generation."

Now, a Biblical generation measures forty years

> 9 As in the provocation, according to the day of temptation in the wilderness: where your fathers tempted me, they proved me, and saw my works. 10 Forty years long was I offended with that generation, and I said: These always err in heart.
>
> 11 And these men have not known my ways: so I swore in my wrath that they shall not enter into my rest. [Ps. 94:9-11].

In Matthew 23:36, Christ meant that the Jews would bring righteous blood upon themselves in forty years or less; He was thinking about the destruction of Jerusalem and the Temple in 70 AD. Therefore, Christ did not utter Matthew 23:36 earlier than the year 30 AD.

Whereas Christ died under Pontius Pilate, according to the gospels and the historian Josephus; and whereas history has recorded that Pontius Pilate governed Palestine from 26-36 AD; it follows that Christ uttered Matthew 23:36 sometime during 30-36 AD. It is implicit in Christ's statement that some of the people who heard him say it would live to see Jerusalem and the Temple destroyed.

In Matthew 24:34, Christ referred to those signs or events that the Apocalypse designates as the second and third woes. It is also implicit in Christ's statement that some of those people living, when the second woe begins, will be living when the third woe ends.

The second and the third woes, combined, will have a duration of forty years OR LESS. As far as I know, the Bible does not tell more on this matter of duration.

Matthew 24:4-14 affords additional information about the second woe,

> 4 In reply Jesus said to them, "Watch that someone may not lead you astray: 5 for many will come upon my name, saying, 'I am the Christ', and they will be leading many astray. 6 And you are destined to hear of wars and rumors of wars: see that you are not alarmed: for it is necessary to happen, <u>but</u> <u>it</u> <u>is not</u> <u>yet</u> <u>the</u> <u>end</u>. 7 For nation will rise against nation and kingdom against kingdom and there will be famines <u>and</u> pestilences <u>and</u> earthquakes throughout places: 8 and all these things [πάντα δὲ ταῦτα = panta de tauta] are <u>the</u> <u>beginning</u> <u>of</u> <u>the</u> <u>birth</u> <u>pangs</u>. 9 At this time [τότε = tote] they will be handing you over unto tribulation and will be putting you to death, and you will be hated by all the nations on account of my name. 10 And at this time [τότε = tote] many will be scandalized and they will be betraying one another and will be hating one another: 11 and many false prophets will rise and lead many astray: 12 and on account of the increasing of lawlessness the love of many will grow cold. 13 But the one steadfast until the end is the one who will be saved. 14 And this good news of the kingdom will be proclaimed in the whole world until the proof to the nations, and <u>at</u> <u>this</u> <u>time</u> [τότε = tote] will <u>come</u> <u>the</u> <u>end</u>."

In the Apocalypse, John wrote that…

> "…the whole <u>earth</u> marveled after the beast" [Apoc. 13:3]

and that…

> "…all those dwelling on the <u>earth</u> will be worshipping it" [Apoc. 13:8]

These two verses indicate that the Beast will be the ultimate false messiah during the last 42 months [3½ years] of the second woe; this means, also, that he will be the only false messiah during that time, for <u>everyone</u> except the faithful <u>will</u> <u>be</u> <u>worshipping</u> <u>the</u> <u>Beast</u>.

Hence, in Matthew 24:4-14, Christ indirectly informed the reader that the second woe will have, at least, two phases:

> the tract during which there will be many impersonators of "the Christ" (ὁ Χριστός [o Khristos], the one anointed with chrism, the Messiah: verse 5) and "wars and rumors of wars" [verse 6],
>
> followed by the tract during which "nation will rise against nation" [verse 7] and "many false prophets will rise" [verse 11].

The final clause of verse 6,

"...but it is not yet the end,"

additionally serves to indicate there will be, at least, two distinct, possibly separate, phases of the violence and of the tribulation for the Church; and it indirectly warns the reader against thinking that the period of false messiahs and of "wars and rumors of wars" will be the end of the age.

Similarly, verse 8 directly advises the reader that the period of "false prophets" and "nation...against nation" will also not be the end, but...

"...the beginning of the birth pangs..."

The demonstrative "τότε" [tote], at the start of verse 10, points backward to verse 9; the demonstrative "τότε" [tote], at the start of verse 9, points backward to verse 8; and the phrase, "all these things," in verse 8, in turn, points backward to verses 5, 6 AND 7.

Since the phrase, "all these things," in verse 8, refers to everything mentioned in verses 5-7, it follows that the terms "famines and pestilences and earthquakes" also apply to verses 5 and 6.

Common sense would know, as explained shortly, that the terms "famines and pestilences" also apply to the period of "wars and rumors of wars"; but, verse 8 makes it clear that the term "earthquakes" pertains as well, thus telling the reader about an important sign indicative of the second woe, namely, the extraordinary escalation of seismic activity around the globe.

Furthermore, whereas verses 5-12 constitute a definition of the term "birth pangs," and whereas, at least, some of those things mentioned in them will continue into the third woe, it follows that the term "birth pangs" relates to the tract of the second and third woes, combined.

Note well that verse 12 mentions "the increasing of lawlessness"; this implies that the Church's tribulation will increase in extent and in intensity during the period of "false prophets" and of "nation…against nation", i.e., during the reign of the Beast, when the faithful…

"will be hated by all the nations" [verse 9]

So, let it be clear: the phase of false messiahs and of "wars and rumors of wars" corresponds to the time of the 200 Million Horsemen; and the phase of "false prophets" and of "nation…against nation" corresponds to the reign of the Beast. Obviously, there will be false prophets during the time of false messiahs; but, during the reign of the Beast, when he will be ascending from both the "abyss" and the "sea," there will be only one false messiah: the Beast himself.

The final phase of the "birth pangs" will be the seven last plagues by which Christ will destroy the Beast and his empire; and this statement hints as to what the demonstrative adverb [τότε = tote] in verse 14 factually refers.

Bear in mind, Friends!, as you read verse 14, that the end of the Beast is also the end of the age; for, if you do that, you will unlock your reason and see why I rendered my translation of verse 14 different from all others. Oh, not to worry: I shall return to Matthew 24, in the explanations preparatory to Chapter 14 onward in the Apocalypse.

In Matthew 24:6-7, Jesus alluded to a formula of the Old Testament: sword, famine, and pestilence

> 17 Thus saith the Lord of hosts: Behold I will send upon them the sword, and the famine, and the pestilence: and I will make them like bad figs that cannot be eaten, because they are very bad.
> [Jer. 29:17],

> 18 But since we left off to offer sacrifice to the queen of heaven, and to pour out drink offerings to her, we have wanted all things, and have been consumed by the <u>sword</u>, and by <u>famine</u>. [Jer. 44:18];
>
> 12 A third part of thee shall die with the <u>pestilence</u>, and shall be consumed with <u>famine</u> in the midst of thee: and a third part of thee shall fall by the <u>sword</u> round about thee: and a third part of thee will I scatter into every wind, and I will draw out a <u>sword</u> after them. [Ez. 5:12],
>
> 15 The <u>sword</u> without: and the <u>pestilence</u>, and the <u>famine</u> within: he that is in the field shall die by the <u>sword</u>: and they that are in the city, shall be devoured by the <u>pestilence</u>, and the <u>famine</u>. [Ez. 7:15].

This formula was used in connection with divine judgments, in the sense of punishments, especially, those that were inflicted on Israel. The formula's order of mention follows reality:

(1) The "sword," which was the primary weapon for soldiers until the 17th century, represents warfare.
(2) Warfare disrupts farming and so causes famine.
(3) Both warfare and famine make conditions conducive to pestilence.

The phrases, "wars and rumors of wars" and "nation against nation," are conspicuous substitutions for "sword," the first term in the formula, a formula that Christ knew: for, even as Son of Man, He disclosed on many an occasion immediate knowledge and intimate understanding of the Old Testament. Therefore, the substitutions may be reasonably perceived as a subtle hint, namely, that the signs or events being described would come when the sword would no longer be the soldier's primary weapon. Besides, there was no word for the modern soldier's primary weapon, the rifle or gun, in any ancient language, let alone Greek.

Divine judgments, in the sense of punishments, are almost always carried out by secondary agents—animate or inanimate. That Christ added a fourth term, "earthquakes," to the formula is indeed ominous; that He altered the formula's terms from singular to plural is more ominous.

In most instances, the word "earthquake" is a prophetic term signifying "social upheaval or revolution": the "great earthquake" in Apocalypse 6:12, for example. But, that is not the meaning here, because Jesus already included the idea of "social upheaval or revolution" by mentioning "lawlessness" and "wars." Rather, Jesus meant physical earthquakes.

Since "birth pangs" increase in their frequency and intensity, and since Christ included "earthquakes" in that term, it follows that the second and third woes will be a period of spiritual and physical violence ever increasing in frequency and intensity—including earthquakes.

St. Paul hinted at this,

> "For the creation waits with eager longing for the revelation of the children of God...We know that <u>the whole creation</u> has been groaning <u>in labor pains</u> until now..." [Rom. 8:19, 22]

The Apostle wrote "until now" because he thought, as did many others, that "the day of the Lord" was imminent; he did not know that it would be many centuries in coming.

So, in historical comparison, seismic activity during the second and third woes will be extraordinary; indeed, this activity will culminate at the very last event of this present evil age:

> There came...a great earthquake, such as has not come since man has come on the earth, the violent earthquake was so great. The great city [Jerusalem] was split into three parts and the cities of the nations fell down. [Apoc. 16:17-19]

The meaning of "nations" in that passage is made perfectly clear by the context: "all the nations," even the Great Eagle mentioned in Chapter 12.

It cannot be deduced from Christ's words, however, that the beginning of the second woe and the escalation of seismic activity to the extraordinary will be synchronous; this notwithstanding, it is a safe assumption that said activity will escalate soon after the second woe has commenced, perhaps, within a year or two: for Christ intended that His faithful be informed; and so, lest the information about earthquakes become otiose, Christ's words will be fulfilled soon after the four evil angels are loosed from the Euphrates.

In that way, the faithful, especially, the Four Living Beings, will not mistake other phenomena, such as World War I or World War II, for the second woe. By no means should the reader exclude from mind the possibility that seismic escalation might begin just before the second woe, even as the rumble of thunder warns of the approaching storm.

Those strong in faith will not despair as the 200 Million Horsemen slaughter both good and bad alike; the informed faithful will understand that the event is a divine judgment and a part of God's mysterious plan; and, too, the brethren will not deceive themselves about the eventual decrease in the violence, the decrease implied in Apocalypse 9:20, which reads,

> "And the rest of the men, who were not killed by these plagues, did not repent of the works of their hands, so that they will not be worshipping the demons and the idols the gold [ones] and the silver [ones] and the bronze [ones] and the stone [ones] and the wooden [ones], which cannot see or hear or walk."

Dead men cannot repent; therefore, the general violence will decrease much, but not entirely, so that the men will have a chance to repent. Yet, Apocalypse 9:21 patently states that some forms of lawlessness will continue:

> "And they did not repent of their murders nor of their sorceries nor of their fornications nor of their thefts."

Verse 20 points mainly at nations in Asia, such as China and India; verse 21 points mainly at industrial and technological nations, such as those in Europe and North America.

Thus do the last two verses close Chapter 9, with negative note; hence, to offset their dismal portent, Christ will interrupt the presentation of the order of events by giving the vision of hope in Chapter 10.

Before I commence comment on Chapter 10, I must first mention a little about 9:12, because, if I rightly remember, I did state that the third part of this commentary covers 9:12 to 22:21.

The word intelligent is derived from the Latin verb intelligere, which is a variation of the verb intellegere, "to understand," literally, "to choose between":

inter >> intel, between + legere >> ligere, to choose = intelligere,
to choose between

Derived from the verb is the participle "intelligens, intelligentis," which means "intelligent," in the active sense.

Therefore, ever have I held the principle of juxtaposition as the first example of whether a person is intelligent, much as to slurp the sample of a spoonful tells about the whole pot of soup. To juxtapose objects in the imagination, to set them together, side by side, lets one perceive more easily their relationship to each other, and see the degree or extent of their similitude or dissimilitude.

The principle of juxtaposition is the key to successful thinking, the key to counter a kind of lockjaw of reason, so that a person [including me] may think and SPEAK and write in constant consistency, which is verily a concession from God to such as me: for right reason in man is rather like God in the world, don't you think?

Then, receive two verses, 9:12 and 11:14 in the Apocalypse, two little verses that are a gift to reason from God through His prophet John,

ἡ οὐαὶ ἡ μία ἀπῆλθεν ἰδοὺ ἔρχεται ἔτι δύο οὐαὶ μετὰ ταῦτᾶ.
Ë ouai ë mia apëlthen . idou erkhetai eti dyo ouai meta tauta.
The woe the first has passed: behold are coming yet two woes after these things.

ἡ οὐαὶ ἡ δευτέρα ἀπῆλθεν ἰδοὺ ἡ οὐαὶ ἡ τρίτη ἔρχεται ταχύ.
Ë ouai ë deutera apëlthen . idou e ouai e tritë erkhetai takhy.
The woe the second has passed: behold the woe the third is coming swiftly.

The two verses are each positioned between the descriptions of a preceding and a succeeding woe; they function as interlinks or connectors, suggesting a cause-effect relationship. Both are basically the same in vocabulary and syntax, with exactly twelve Greek words in each: formally speaking, 11:14 is a repetition of 9:12.

Note that every woe was mentioned only once in the singular number, and that the postpositive adjective apposed to it was nominalized by the definite article; in Greek, this kind of apposition is the emphatic form of mention.

The same kind of apposition is used in 9:20 to catch [hopefully] the reader's attention, so that the reader will catch [hopefully] the implication: that the descendent order of the materials for the idols, from "the gold [ones]" to "the wooden [ones]," relates to the descendent order of the people, from the great or rich to the small or poor, who will be worshipping the idols.

Note the colon in each verse. One usage of the colon is to indicate that an initial clause in a sentence will be further explained or illustrated by the material that follows the colon. In effect, the colon substitutes for such expressions as "namely," or "that is [to say]," or "for example."

In each of the two excerpts, the colon acts as a connector, suggesting that what follows it is a development or predication of what preceded it.

Even the vocabulary is psychologically directive. John placed the word "ἰδοὺ" [idou] immediately after each colon; though the word is not as strong as "ἴδετε" [idete], it is, nonetheless, an imperative that directs the reader's attention toward the material that follows: "ἰδοὺ" [idou] is <u>prospective</u>. But, the last word in 9:12 is "ταῦτα" [tauta] that, as has already been explained, is <u>retrospective</u>: it points backward to 9:1-11.

Moreover, John used the definite article with every woe in the singular to refer the reader to the "eagle's" announcement in 8:13, and thus, in turn, to remind the reader that the three woes are the one judgment in three phases.

As John did not put commas when the Four Living Beings sang "Holy holy holy", so he did not put them when the "eagle" repeated "Woe woe woe": the former, to indicate that God is triune; the latter, to indicate that the three-phased judgment will be continuous.

Hence, when John wrote that a woe had passed, he meant that the exact time allotted for certain activity had passed, not that the root cause of the woe[s] had passed; for the root cause will continue "until the end," as Matthew 24:13 implies.

The ascendant order of "the hour and day and month and year" in 9:15, and, likewise, the perfect timing for the "earthquake," in 11:13, plainly punctuate the text with the exactitude of Divine Providence.

Indeed, as the punctuation of the colon has the function of indicating a momentary cessation of speech; so does each brief verse, inserted between much longer sections of material, prompt a pause for reflection. It is conspicuously peculiar that John made both verses interrupt the description of the woes in order to emphasize the continuity of them. I recall another instance of irony in the Apocalypse;

> "...and the court the one on the outside of the sanctuary cast outside and measure it not..." [11:2].

The irony here is that the tacit condition of tepidity, which allows a person feeble membership in the Church, stands potentially as the very condition that disallows it. Since there is not potentiality in the divine nature, the ironical perspective appertains rather to the human, even though God perfectly understands irony.

Excerpts 9:12 and 11:14 evidence intelligent construction; at this point, however, their ultimate purpose is obscure. On the one hand, each seems to act as a connector, like the word "and"; on the other, each seems to function as a divider, like a comma. Consider 1:4-5, which reads,

> "4 John to the seven churches the ones in Asia: grace to you and peace from the one who is and was and is coming and from the seven spirits the ones in the presence of the throne of him <u>and</u> from Jesus Christ, the witness, the one faithful, the firstborn of the dead and the ruler of the kings of the earth."

The phrase, "the throne of him" signifies specifically the throne of [the] God, that is, God the Father. See 11:1, 12:5. The word "comma" came from the Greek noun "κόμμα" [komma], which was derived from the verb "κόπτειν" [koptein] "to strike, chop"; hence, the comma is used for indicating a division in a sentence, for separating items in a list, and for separating types or levels of information.

The Greek word "καὶ" [kai], like the English "and," is used for connecting grammatically coordinate words, phrases, clauses, or sentence to sentence; it is used, also, for denoting or connoting "equality, simultaneity, repetition, and continuation."

The two verses in the excerpt, just given, constitute one sentence, and this grammatical whole has two principal parts: the material prior to the colon and that posterior to it. The posterior material elucidates the prior in only one respect, namely, that John's greeting is also God's, indirectly [humbly] signifying that John speaks or writes in the name of God.

In such a grammatical whole as this, ordinarily, the initial clause contains the main idea; but, here, ironically, the posterior material delivers the more important information, namely, the three distinguishable but inseparable roles, which the three respective persons in God have, in giving grace and peace to the churches.

The construction of the posterior material has two principal parts: the three persons connected by two <u>ands</u> [their description will be epitomized as "Holy holy holy" in 4:8], then the conclusive series of titles punctuated with <u>commas</u>.

John altered the usual order of mention for the three divine persons: from "the Father and the Son and the Holy Spirit" to "the Father and the Holy Spirit and the Son," for two reasons.

First, the Holy Spirit proceeds from <u>both</u> the Father <u>and</u> the Son; John expressed their mutual relationship, their communion, in a <u>syntactical</u> manner by positioning the Holy Spirit as connector between the Father and the Son, in the order of mention.

Secondly, the series of titles appurtenant to Christ is as long as the first part of the posterior material, and thus for clarity and emphasis did John put the Son last in the order of mention. Bear in mind that the little book will tell the Revelation, and so the Seer duly accented Christ as the God-man.

Note that the second part of the posterior material is connected by Christ's "and" to the Father and the Holy Spirit. Christ's series of titles is progressive: He was the witness of the Father; because He was the witness, even unto death, He became the faithful one; and, because He became the faithful one, He rose as the firstborn of the dead, and ruler of the kings of the earth. It was, therefore, logical for John to punctuate this series of titles with commas, but to connect the last two titles with an and.

Apocalypse 1:4-5 reminds me of two examples of symbolism from the works of Charles Dickens, symbolism that the novelist repeated under many guises.

In Our Mutual Friend, his last completed novel, the symbolical scene that predominates is one of a bridge crossing a river. A river rives, i.e., it splits or separates; but the bridge crosses or cancels the separation, i.e., it joins together or connects. The "bridge" symbolizes the novel's title; the title identifies him: Love.

In Great Expectations, Dickens gave to British society the meaning of the word "gentleman," when the principal character, Pip, exclaims to the dying convict who had sacrificed so much for him: "O, thou gentle Christian man!" The adjective "Christian" is the syntactical bridge that conjoins "gentle" and "man" into "gentleman." In the relation between two, only love can so ennoble as to enable even the most lowly to utter "We" and "Us" in actuality: for Love never is but always our mutual friend.

The analysis of 1:4-5 corroborates what the analysis of 9:12 and 11:14 yielded, namely, that John employed punctuation and syntax in a symbolical manner.

As regards 1:4-5, the Seer does not push the grammar at the reader; but, as regards 9:12 and 11:14, he pulls no punches. He deliberately interrupted the flow of description to tell emphatically what has passed and what is coming. Each of the two little verses functions as a separator [a comma] indicating the end of the time allotted for the activity of a woe; and each acts as a connector [an "and"] indicating the continuity of the root cause of the woes: they are like knots on a string.

At first, it seems that 9:12 and 11:14 are unnecessary interpositions. The fifth, sixth, and seventh angels, by their trumpet blasts, denote the beginnings of the first, second, and third woes, respectively; and, so, the temptation is to presume that the sixth and seventh angels will denote the ends of the first and second woes, respectively. This presumption is found correct for the sixth angel, but not for the seventh angel.

Bear in mind that the third woe will be the seven last plagues, by means of which Christ will destroy "...the ones destroying the earth" [11:18].

However, there will be an interval of a few days to, perhaps, a week between the beginning of the general conversion of Israel [11:13], and the beginning of the seven last plagues [16:1]; and, during that interval, the angels sent by God will steadily gather the harvest of wheat, especially, the "first fruits," or "144,000" [symbolical number], mentioned in Chapter 14. This means the Beast and his followers will continue their pogrom against the faithful "...until the testimony [evidence, proof] to the nations"

> 14 And this gospel of the kingdom, shall be preached in the whole world, for a testimony to all nations, and then shall the consummation come. [Mt. 24:14]

> 5 And after these things I looked; and behold, the temple of the tabernacle of the testimony in heaven was opened: [Apoc. 15:5].

To forestall misunderstanding the text and to advise concerning the additional few days or a week of that pogrom, John interposed 11:14 immediately after 11:13, thus designating its function as rather a divider than a connector. Without 11:14, then must the juxtaposer be of the more adroit, to discern the exact order of events in the contexture of Chapters 9-21. That one little verse is a brilliant beacon according to which the ordinary reader can far more easily orient each Chapter or part thereof.

And so, the ulterior purpose of 9:12 is known now: John designed it to be memorable, a psychological preparation for 11:14; and to that end did he ply as many devices as possible: punctuation, textual position, brevity, irony, repetition, prospective and retrospective vocabulary, and apposition, not to mention alliteration and assonance in vehement cadence, such prosody being unusual from the meek Seer.

Take the two little verses, ye Friends, for what they are: a good gift to help you abridge the time and task between asking and receiving, between nescience and knowledge.

If you so juxtapose the here and there, then can you understand: "If I'm all here, then I'm not all there." So saith the idiosyncratic mind.

CHAPTER 6

APOCALYPSE CHAPTER TEN

March 4, 1999

Dear Friends of the Lord,

After numerous delays, yet once more the two fingers ply the keyboard, as if at play. Among the delays was a rather brutal attack by some virus, and this complicated the results of a blood test, to which the doctor responded with vehemence. False alarm, it was: my blood cells returned to normal appearance.

So, now he can add the data and evidence to the studies on leukemia, to wit, a nasty viral infection can present <u>the same symptoms</u>, among cells, as the actual return of leukemia. Believe it or not, this fact has not been demonstrated heretofore. As always, I am a first.

My status among the billions and billions of pseudo-rational bipeds has assumed new measure, for it can now be averred of me: "He was a <u>contributor</u> to science." This statement, out of sympathy and other modes of generosity, should not be qualified by the adverb "involuntarily."

I have expanded the material on Chapter 10 in the Apocalypse, because there was no way for you to perceive the full import of it, unless you could read the original Greek. I did spice it a little with my unconventional sense of humor, especially, in some of the examples, for I know how tedious the reading of technical material can be. It should not surprise you that John employed puns; after all, he was heir to the Old Testament wherein punning appears more often than most people know.

Also, he used syntax and punctuation in a symbolical manner, which places him in a rather rare, small circle of writers. Since the translations are unreliable in that particular, I deemed it worthwhile to point it out to you. These things, the puns and the punctuation and the syntax, militate for a translation that is as literal as possible, preferably accompanied by footnotes.

I have placed many examples, from single words to entire sentences, in Greek. The problem with this is that it takes a long time to print them; but the reward is that you can more easily judge for yourself—or 'selves. The third part of the commentary will keep you busy for years.

When I look at what I have written, I am greeted by evidence of the grace of God, for some of the things explained have not been explained in nineteen centuries. When I was young, I never thought I would write something like this. When it is all typed up, I will not even speculate on what God will do with it. I have not the foggiest idea. I only know I must finish it. And, that is my cue to get back to the typing.

Yours in Christ,

Steve

Chapter 10 may be conveniently seen as having two parts: verses 1-7 and 8-11. In the first part, a mighty angel comes and declares that the "mystery of God" will be fulfilled at the time appointed; in the second part, John receives the very small open [ed] scroll, whose contents relate the manner of fulfillment.

John wrote,

> "And I saw another mighty angel coming down from heaven, clothed with a cloud, and the rainbow upon his head and his face [was] like the sun and his feet [legs] like pillars of fire, and holding in his hand a very small scroll opened. And he set his foot the right [one] upon the sea, and the left [one] upon the earth, and he cried out in a great voice even as a lion roars."

The "cloud" or nimbus, which is the vehicle of celestial spirits, indicates that the angel is not some holy cardinal or bishop, but a real angel. He comes from "heaven," i.e., the Church; in his appearance, he resembles Christ as described in Chapter 1.

That "his face shines like the sun" means that he is illumined with divine knowledge concerning his message and mission; and that "his feet are like pillars of fire" symbolizes his zeal to deliver the message and carry out his task regarding "the earth" and "the sea"; for the servant of God must have both knowledge and zeal, as the proverb suggests,

> "Without knowledge even zeal is not good; and he who acts hastily, blunders." [Prv. 19:2]

The "descent of a cloud" symbolizes divine intervention: that "the angel is clothed with the cloud," and that "he descends to the earth and sea," together convey the idea that "he has been empowered to do God's will and work in the affairs of men."

Being "clothed" with cloud, he himself is like a pillar of cloud, and his feet are "like pillars of fire": this description alludes to the pillar of cloud by day and the pillar of fire by night, which guided and defended the Israelites during their exodus from Egypt; and it alludes to Isaiah 4:5, wherein God promised a cloud by day and fire by night "over all Mount Zion."

The text clearly states the angel has the "rainbow UPON his head," not over it, in the sense of "above." The definite article refers to the emerald "rainbow" around the throne in 4:3; hence, the angel is wearing a "crown of emerald light," which symbolizes his authority. The [color of] emerald symbolizes hope and the promise of peace; however, as the angel's message and the scroll's contents will make clear, peace will not come immediately, but very soon.

His stentorian roar befits his immense size; the reader receives the impression that the angel is quite able to carry out his task. That "he set one foot upon the sea and the other upon the earth" symbolizes superiority so great as to make victory a foregone conclusion. Indeed, the dominant idea of this Chapter's first part is that of POWER AND AUTHORITY.

The description of the angel matches in essentials the description of the "woman clothed with the sun" in 12:1. Let one thing be perfectly clear here: the angel and the "woman" are NOT the same entity.

However, since John used the same perfect participle not only in regard to the "woman" in Chapter 12, but also the TWO Witnesses in Chapter 11, it seems advisable to examine a few examples more of this symbolical term:

> Above all, clothe yourselves with love…[Col. 3:14]

> …and to clothe yourselves with the new self, created according to the likeness of God in true righteousness and holiness. [Eph. 4:24]

> For the marriage of the [Little] Lamb has come, and his bride has made herself ready; to her it has been granted to be clothed with fine linen, bright and pure- for the fine linen is the righteous deeds of the saints. [Apoc. 19:7-8]

> And I will give to the two witnesses of me and they will be prophesying for one thousand two hundred sixty days, clothed of sackcloth. [Apoc. 11:3]

> And a great sign was seen in heaven: a woman clothed with the sun, and the moon under the feet of her and upon the head of her a crown of twelve stars…[Apoc. 12:1]

> And behold, I am sending the promise of my Father upon you. And so stay here in the city until you have been clothed with power from on high. [Lk. 24:49]

Again, the physical symbolizes the spiritual, and I do not think I have to belabor the point [Note well the comma and two <u>ands</u> in Apoc. 12:1]. Now, the first three references pertain to the faithful, in general, but the last three pertain only to certain ones, in particular, even as Saint Paul wrote,

> "For as in one body we have many members, and not all members have the same function, so we, who are many, are one body in Christ, and individually we are members one of another. We have gifts that differ according to the faith given us…" [Rom. 12:4-6]

The two witnesses are "clothed" with sackcloth, and the "sackcloth" indicates their essential message and mission: they will preach repentance and penance to mankind. The angel is "clothed" with the cloud, and the "cloud" indicates his message and mission: the "mystery of God" soon to be fulfilled.

As for the "woman" in Chapter 12, I will comment later. For the nonce, I point out that, as the angel is "clothed" with the cloud, so she is "clothed" with the "sun"; as the angel has the "rainbow" upon his head, so she wears the "crown of twelve stars" upon hers; and, as he stands "upon the sea and the earth," i.e., with them under his feet, so she has the "moon under her feet." "To clothe" means "to empower," "to crown" means "to authorize." Power and Authority are distinguishable but inseparable; each invariably implies the other.

As lightning is to the eye, so thunder is to the ear: the "lightning" represents the charismata of the Church, especially, miracles; and the "thunder" signifies the voice of official authority in the Church, especially, in teaching the Truth to men. In 4:5, John listed "lightning" before "thunder" in the order of mention, because miracles were more common in the infant days of the Church. In 8:5, he listed "thunder" before "lightning," because the Church had grown much by the end of the fourth century, and extraordinary measures were no longer required to gain converts, rapidly.

It is worth noting that the "lightning" and "thunder" come from the throne, where [the] God and the Little Lamb and the Four Living Beings are, but not the twenty-four Elders. This is just one of those little things that mean a lot, like the two little verses, 9:12 and 11:14.

In 10:3, John wrote that when the angel cried out like a lion, "the seven thunders spoke in their own voices." This means the "seven thunders" spoke, even while the angel was still roaring—which implies agreement and readiness upon the part of the "seven thunders." John used the aorist tense for "spoke," so this scene presents an event that will take place <u>only</u> <u>once</u>.

The number "seven" is symbolical. Here, it has not so much to do with indefinite number, quantity, etc.; rather, it alludes to the symbolic "seven" in 8:2, indicating that the Church can now undertake the final phase of the Father's plan. The number "seven" here also means that not just some of the official voices spoke, but all of them to all people.

The definite article designates them as well-known voices. They are the supreme voices of authority in the Church; not the voice of the Supreme Pontiff alone, but "seven" voices, the totality of sacred authority, the voices of an ecumenical council. The time for grave decisions has come. As to what the "seven thunders" said, I will hold that in abeyance, too.

The angel's message should be explained a little. John wrote,

> 5 And the angel, whom I saw standing upon the sea and upon the earth, raised the hand of him the right [one] up to the heaven 6 and swore by the One Living unto the ages of the ages, who created the heaven and the things in it and the earth and the things in it and the sea and the things in it, that time will be not more, 7 but in the days of the sound of the seventh angel, when he is about to trumpet, also will be fulfilled the mystery of [the] God, as He announced to his own servants the prophets.

The seventh angel will blow his trumpet in 11:15, perhaps, no more than a few days after the survivors of the earthquake in Jerusalem give glory to God. Therefore, the days, when the seventh angel IS ABOUT TO TRUMPET, are those days from the deaths of the Two Witnesses to the seventh angel's trumpet peal itself. During that interval, the greatest shedding of innocent blood in the history of the world will take place [this is briefly described in 14:14-16]. At that time, the "mystery of God" will be fulfilled. Saint Paul, referring to his conversion and office of Apostle, wrote,

> "...this grace was given to me to bring to the Gentiles the news of the boundless riches of Christ, and to make everyone see what is the plan of the mystery hidden for ages in God who created all things; so that through the Church the wisdom of God in its rich variety might now be made known to the rulers and authorities in the heavenly places.

> This was in accordance with the eternal purpose that He has carried out in Christ Jesus our Lord." [Eph. 3:8-12]

Again, Paul wrote:

> For I want you to know I am having a tortuous struggle over you and the ones in Laodicea and such as have not seen the face of me in the flesh, so that the hearts of them may be strengthened, uniting in love even unto all wealth of the fullness of assurance, unto the knowledge of the mystery of [the] God, Christ, in whom are hidden all the treasures of wisdom and knowledge. [Col. 2:1-3]

The "mystery of God" is opposed by the "mystery of lawlessness" [2 Thes. 2:7], that is, the "mystery" of iniquity or sin, for "sin is lawlessness" [1 John 3:4]. Christ is the "mystery of God", and the Church is the mystical body of Christ, of which Christ is the head.

It is the Father's plan that Christ and the Church fulfill the Father's purpose for the world; however, it is also His plan that the "mystery of lawlessness" be the antagonist in this great drama of fulfillment.

The two "mysteries" will grow to maturity in the world, and this most surely means that the Church's members, great or small, respectively more or less, will have to endure a "tortuous struggle," as did Saint Paul, who also stated,

> "I am now rejoicing in my sufferings for your sake, and in the flesh I am completing what is lacking in Christ's afflictions for the sake of his body, that is, the Church." [Col. 1:24]

In view of mankind's general lawlessness following the event of the 200 Million Horsemen, and in view of the Church's prime directive, namely, to go and...

> "...make all the nations disciples, baptizing them unto the name of the Father and of the Son and of the Holy Spirit" [Mt. 26:19],

the angel's message, "the mystery of [the] God will be fulfilled," necessarily imports two things:

(1) The climactic struggle between the two "mysteries" is imminent.
(2) That struggle will result in the realization of Christ's and his Church's prime directive.

Thus,

> "From one new moon to another, from one Sabbath to another, all mankind shall come to worship before me, says the Lord." [Is. 66:23]

Not to woe did the angel swear, but to peace. Nonetheless, the price of victory will not come cheap. It never does. A realistic look reveals who has been, is, and will be the cause of those horrors to come with such magnitude as human imagination cannot totally grasp: the world's every person fundamentally lawless, but also the Church's every member tepid and timid. The tribulations of Christ's mystical body are among "the things that must come" [Apoc. 1:1]. They must, on account of God's highest concession to man: freedom.

Ancient cosmogony divided the visible creation into the three principal parts of sky, sea, and earth;

> 9 God also said: Let the waters that are under the heaven, be gathered together into one place: and let the dry land appear. And it was so done. 10 And God called the dry land, Earth; and the gathering together of the waters, he called Seas. And God saw that it was good. [Gn. 1:9-10].

The angel asseverated that "the One Living unto the ages of the ages" [Christ, as in 1:18] made them and everything in them, thus signifying that God is the supreme power and authority, and that all in heaven and sea and earth subserve his purpose. Hence, the angel's message is one of hope, encouragement, and consolation to the Church; and it comes through the angel from Jesus Christ Himself.

Note that the angel makes the gesture of an oath by raising his right hand "unto" [εἰς = eis] the heaven, pointing to the One who has authorized him to swear the oath. Since he speaks for Christ, his oath is actually Christ's oath. This means that Christ has sworn by Himself [God swears only by Himself, and no other]; and, therefore, the text very subtly informs the reader as to who will fulfill the "mystery of God": the mystery of God, Jesus Christ.

To understand the full import here, refer to 15:7 [literally translated],

> "…the seven golden bowls full of the wrath of the God of the One Living unto the ages of the ages."

The Greek wordage means that the Living One, Christ, will be the "wrath of the God"; to wit, the seven last plagues will come directly from the Little Lamb. Thus, the angel's message is also a dire warning to those who intend the Church harm.

Think, then: the Apocalypse, yet once more, witnesses to the ironical perspective of Christ's human mind in the Hypostatic Union of the God-man; for, of the angel, the text states,

> "And he cried out in great voice exactly as a lion roars…"
> [ὥσπερ λέων μυκᾶται = ösper leön mykatai]

The conjunction "ὥσπερ" [ösper = exactly as] indicates the substitutive sense: as the angel's oath represents Christ's oath, so his roar represents Christ's roar, reminding the reader that the Little Lamb is also the victorious Lion of Judah [5:5]; and the irony is that the Lion shall shepherd the flock.

It is not preposterous to imagine, though the text does not say, that the angel's roar reverberated throughout the heaven and the sea and the earth, and, in answer, all creation groaned for the revelation of the children of God.

Who is that mighty angel? I cannot absolutely prove his identity; all I can do is to picture in imagination what John depicted. The angel has the authority to swear by Jesus Christ Himself. Look at his wide stance: he bestrides the "earth" and the "sea" like a Colossus, and his stand declares there shall be no retreat. Listen to his roar: it shakes the "sea" and the "earth," and his roar is a challenge flung fearlessly at Christ's enemies soon to be shouting,

"Who is like to the Beast, and who can fight against it?" [Apoc. 13:4]

That roar is his battle cry, the very same that anciently became his name: "Who is like unto God!" And, this battle cry in Hebrew is Michael. He is St. Michael the Archangel, great warrior of God and the Church.

Although I am, say, experienced in talking, I do not aver I am an expert in the Greek tongue. That notwithstanding, in my idiosyncratic mind perks a penchant for paronomasia, which the principle of juxtaposition has rendered inveterately alert.

Paronomasia belongs to that figure of speech called the pun. Puns are made with words, which are the names man gives to persons and things; words represent meanings; and man spoke words long before he wrote them. This is to say pronunciation represents meaning.

Hence, a pun is the identical or similar pronunciations representing, at least, two different meanings represented by one word or more. If two words or more are involved in the punning [as is always the case for similar pronunciations], it is necessary only for one of the words to be present in the material [text, conversation, etc.], provided that the absent word can be reasonably deduced from the material or from another source [education, culture, experience, etc.].

"Paronomasia" is a Greek word that means "a slight name-change," and, therefore, it always involves two words similar in pronunciation. Punning in Greek, which is a synthetic language, mostly depends on the roots and stems of words, i.e., words minus prefixes and suffixes.

The simplest pun involves only one word: consider the name "Miles." Upon intuiting the term, my penchant for punning perks alert with such alacrity as smacks of laxness in compassion for a fellow so…so affixed. Aye, rare is the person so heartless as to mind this nice name, seriously, as a pun on "miles," covertly cackling over the contradiction— albeit painless—between the designation of an individual and that of a pluralized unit of distance.

Now, let the term come into relationship with a little context, and so be his name "Miles Incher." As the contents of context increase, they corroborate the punning and make it more obvious: "Miles Incher ran the marathon."

A pun is not always for fun, as the ensuing verses testify:

While twilight does compose in hush and hue,
Making a couplement like soft-toned rhyme....

The pun is on the verb "compose," and the context clarifies the meanings intended by the author.

Sometimes, a pun expresses not only meanings but also the sound of a sound:

From bags and boxes set for town collection
This luckless lady plucked the best selection:
Such dusty rags of every weave and hue
As those with nicer noses did eschew.

The pun is on the verb "eschew," and it is also an example of "onomatopoeia," the use of words that imitate sounds, such as, clang, rustle, thump, etc.

Context, if you will, is not merely the words that precede or follow a term, but anything that can be rationally related to it. What would accrue to the pun above, if the names of the bag lady and the town were Spanish? The idea that there can be a Spanish sneeze is not at issue [Gesundheit] with the idiosyncratic mind.

Indubitably, the injudicious will seditiously abuse the prince of principles into antics of semantics. John, however, was not a roguish juxtaposer, not a court jester cleverly juggling words. He was heir to the long tradition of punning in the Old Testament. Divinely inspired, yet, free to set the text with precision and concision.

In 10:3, the Prophet wrote,

"And he cried out in a loud voice even as a lion roars [μυκᾶται = mykatai]. And at the time he cried out, the seven thunders uttered the sounds of themselves."

Compare this with 1 Peter 5:8, which reads,

"And your adversary the devil as a roaring lion [λέων ὠρυόμενος = leön öryomenos] goes about seeking [someone] to devour."

The word "roar" and the stem "öry-" are examples of onomatopoeia, for both are pronounced alike in imitation of the sound, the tone, that a creature, such as, the lion, makes. Whether Peter picked an onomatopoeic verb for emphasis, or whether he was thinking of tomatoes and peas at that particular of composition, is a matter for speculation.

The point here is that the verb "ὠρύειν" [öryein] was available, and others besides; but, John chose else, a verb aesthetically unostensive in a sentence conceptually insistent.

Indeed, I cannot imagine how verse 3, in <u>any</u> language, can be read with attention without some wincing o' the wits, for John's manner of hinting here is about as subtle as pounding a gong: thrice, in the first seven words, and a fourth time more, with the "seven thunders," the reader thinks loud sound, so that the verse redounds as near as possible to a direct communication of the object hinted, i.e., the pun. The wordage induces the mind to the verge of discovery.

If the reader is also a veteran juxtaposer, very high is the probability that he or she, on the first pass, will make that last leap of imagination and interrelate a specific term with the context, and, thus, recognize the pun (in Greek, of course).

John did not care a fig about the aesthetical imitation of the lion's roar; rather, he chose to communicate what the angel cried out.

As heretofore noted, the conjunctive "ὥσπερ" [ösper = exactly as] indicates the substitutive sense. Hence, the <u>pronunciation</u> of the verb "μυκᾶται" [mykatai]—that is, the stem—represents the <u>meaning</u> of what the angel cried out,

> μυκᾶ- [myka-] is similar to Μιχαήλ, to wit, the angel cried out "Mikhael!"

which is Hebrew and has the <u>meaning,</u> "Who is like unto God!" The technical term for this kind of pun is "paronomasia," "a slight name-change."

Context corroborates the pun, and plenty of content is provided here. The angel was described as "all-clothed in cloud" and "his legs as pillars of fire," which alludes to the pillar of cloud by day and the pillar of fire by night, that guided and defended the people of God during their exodus from Egypt; and this suggests a title belonging to Saint Michael the Archangel: Defender of the Church. The angel wore a "rainbow upon his head", which symbolizes the promise of peace; and this suggests another title belonging to Michael: Angel of Peace.

The Bible tells that there are many angels, but it gives the names of only three: Raphael, Gabriel, and Michael; the first two do not fit the role, the very demeanor, of the angel in Chapter 10. Moreover, the noun "φωνῇ" [phönë], in its primary sense, means: a sound, tone, properly, the sound of the voice, mostly of men; like Latin vox, a battle cry.

One recognizes or identifies a person, principally, by sight or sound of the voice, and the "loud sound" of the angel correlates with the pronunciation of the stem in "μυκᾶται" [mykatai]; therefore, the "great voice" may be translated as "loud battle cry", the sound "Mikhael!"

The phrase, "great/loud voice," alludes to Jesus Christ, in 1:10, which reads,

> "I became in the Spirit on the Lord's day and heard behind me a loud voice as a trumpet…"

This, in turn, alludes to the voice of God, as described in the Old Testament,

> "These words, and nothing more, the Lord spoke with a loud voice to your entire assembly on the mountain [Horeb] from the midst of the fire and dense cloud." [Dt. 5:22]

John indicated in 1:10, as in many other passages, that Christ is not only human [Son of Man] but also divine [Son of God]. Hence, in the Apocalypse, the phrase, "great/loud voice," signifies that the voice is of divine authority, and that the speaker is either Christ or someone who speaks in his name [almost always the case will be the latter].

But, in 1:10, John added "ώς σάλπιγγος" [ös salpiggos], "as a trumpet," to the phrase. In the Old Testament, Divine judgments were announced with trumpet blasts. Note the little word "ώς" [ös], which indicates the substitutive sense. Therefore, the mention of a great voice or a trumpet refers to a Divine judgment. This means that Christ comes many times in judgment, through secondary agents, and these are not to be confused with his Second Coming at the end of human history.

As I pondered 10:3, I was puzzled at the relationship between two verbs: "κϱάζω" [krazein], "to cry out, shout loudly, scream, shriek," and "λαλέω" [lalein], "to talk, chat, prattle, chirp [birds], to speak, utter."

The verb krazein indicates that the angel issued his battle cry with great vehemence, but the verb lalein does not convey that vehemence, despite the fact that the "seven thunders" uttered their sounds at the time [ὅτε = ote] the angel cried out. The situation suggests there should be agreement in regard to ardor for battle. Bear in mind that the "seven thunders" are members of the episcopate, i.e., the Four Living Beings, as shown by 4:5, which reads,

> "And from the throne [are] coming lightnings and sounds [phonai] and thunders…"

in cross-reference with 6:1, which reads,

> "…and I heard one of the Four Living Beings speaking as [ώς = ös] a sound [phone] of thunder…"

So, the verb "ἐλάλησαν" [elalësan] should not be translated as "chatted/prattled/talked," but as "uttered," making the second sentence, in verse 3, read,

> "And at the time he cried out, the seven thunders uttered the sounds of themselves."

The sense here is not that the "seven thunders" added their battle cries to the angel's, but that they spoke in their official capacity, i.e., they uttered decrees, exhortations, teachings, etc. This particular usage of the verb lalein is found, for example, in 13:5, which states,

> "And there was given to it (the beast ascending from the sea] a mouth uttering great things…"

and it is found in 13:15, where the image of the Beast, like a judge, issues death sentences,

> "And there was given to it [the beast ascending from the earth] to give a spirit [an evil one, naturally] to the image of the Beast, so that the image of the Beast might both speak and do, so that such as they, if they will not be worshipping the image of the Beast, will be being condemned to death."

Having taken these things into account, I was puzzled at the difference between the official utterances of the "seven thunders" and the vehement battle cry of the angel, because they were issued at the same time.

The number "seven" here does convey the idea of "indefinite number," in that it represents many members of the episcopate gathered together; but, as said earlier, it has not so much to do with "indefinite number" as it does with the Church's readiness to undertake and complete, by patient endurance, the seventh and final phase of the second major part of the Father's plan. This is indicated by the angel's oath,

> "…that time will not be more [i.e., there will be no more delay], but in the days of the sound of the seventh angel, when he is about to trumpet, also will be fulfilled the mystery of the God, as He announced to his own servants the prophets."

The "seven thunders" symbolize the totality of sacred authority in the "heaven," or Church; they are the voices of an ecumenical council: in modern times [since 1059 AD], this has meant the Supreme Pontiff and, mainly, the faithful members of the Sacred College of Cardinals. Most of the other members of the episcopate, or Four Living Beings, namely, the bishops, will not be present at the council, but in their native countries.

The difference between krazein and lalein suggests that the "seven thunders" will not physically participate in the culminative conflict between the "mystery of God" and the "mystery of lawlessness," the conflict that is imminent, as indicated by the angel's setting his right foot upon the "sea" and his left upon the "earth," then roaring forth his battle cry.

Be it noted, however, that the angel did these things AFTER he descended from heaven. As Defender of the Church, Saint Michael would not leave the Church, at that time, except for one reason: God's enemies are not inside the Church, but outside.

If there are no enemies inside the Church, then, either they were never inside in the first place, or, if they were inside, then, they have already been cast out. If they are already cast out, then, the "seven thunders" are the pope and those cardinals faithful to him, who cast Christ's enemies out of the Church. The question, then, is whether the Apocalypse contains an account of that expulsion.

The verb krazein appears in 6:10, 7:2, 10:3, 12:2, 14:15, 18:2, and 19:17; in every instance, it is somewhere accompanied by the phrase, "loud/great voice," except in 18:2, which has "mighty voice."

Only the first two instances are not directly related to the second or third woe; instead, 6:10 is related to the eventual dethronement of paganism throughout the Roman Empire, and 7:2 is related to the eventual judgment upon the Empire for the Arian heresy.

The last three instances relate to the seventh plague of the third woe, which is the very end of the end of this present evil age.

Both 10:3 and 12:2 have something in common: both relate to that time immediately before the last 3½ years of the second woe begin, that is, the 42 months during which the nations will trample Jerusalem, and the Beast [from the "sea," Chapter 13] will wage war against the Little Lamb and His Church.

In 12:2, John wrote,

> "…And while holding in womb, also she is crying out [krazei] while having birth pangs and being put to the test/torture to bear/bring forth."

The "woman clothed with the sun" is a great sign: she is herself and portends or points to something else, namely, "the Great Day of Almighty God" [16:14]. But, the proximal result of this "great sign" is that Saint Michael and his angels [angelic and human] cast out Satan and his angels [angelic and human] from heaven "unto the earth"; and in 12:12 a "loud voice in heaven" declares the time of this event,

> "Woe to the earth and to the sea, for the devil has come down to you, having great wrath, knowing that he has a short time."

This implies that, as Satan was cast out of the Church, so he will be cast out of the world [the earth and sea]. Therefore, the term "a short time" can refer to only one period: the last 3½ years of the second woe.

Hence, the vision of Chapter 10 may be placed immediately after 12:9, because the war inside heaven is over, and so Michael has come down from it on the offensive against the "earth" and the "sea."

The "woman clothed with the sun" and the "seven thunders" are one and the same entity, basically speaking: the "woman" is, initially, the entire Sacred College [12:1], but after the war in heaven, she is the faithful surviving members [excepting the pope, of course].

At the time the cardinals will be "put to the test," it will be irrelevant whether they know that God has prepared for their escape to safety [12:6 and 12:14], for none will know beforehand who will escape and who will "...not love their life even unto death" [12:11]. Having proved their quality or mettle, the Cardinals will, with clear conscience and authority, exhort the bishops, priests, and laity to remain faithful, even while they themselves, for the sake of preserving the official authority of the Church, flee to safety in the "wilderness."

This, then, explains why John, by the verbs krazein and lalein, indicated a difference between Michael and the "seven thunders."

To shed more light on Chapters 10 and 12, I proffer some passages from the Old Testament. As you read them, remember the mighty angel who swore the oath in the name of the Living One, as well as the "woman" who cries out in "birth pangs":

> Learn then that I, I alone, am God, and there is no god besides me. It is I who bring forth death and life, I who inflict wounds and heal them, and from my hand there is no rescue. To the heavens I raise my hand and swear: as surely as I live forever, I will sharpen my flashing sword, and my hand shall lay hold of my quiver. [Dt. 32:39-41]

> To whom can you liken me as an equal says the Holy One.
> [Is. 40:25]

> The Lord goes forth like a hero, like a warrior he stirs up his ardor; he shouts out his battle cry, against his enemies he shows his might: I have looked away, and kept silence, I have said nothing, holding myself in; but now, I cry out as a woman in labor...[Is. 42:13-14]

> By myself I swear, uttering my just decree and my unalterable word...[Is. 45:23]

> I am God, there is no other; I am God, there is none like me. [Is. 46:9]

To human reason, I cannot prove absolutely, by the text of Chapter 10, that the mighty angel is Michael. I did not say that I could not prove it to faith. God does not mislead: the angel is indeed Michael.

He is that archangel who, in ancient time, opposed, like David against Goliath, the highest of the seraphim, Lucifer his name; and he is that archangel who, yet once more, and for the final time, will sound the battle cry for the King of kings and Lord of lords: "Who is like unto God!" His name is Michael. If, dear reader, you were given that name, remember what it means.

Pursuant to the tradition of the Old Testament prophets, John utilized the divisions of "heaven," "earth," and "sea" as symbols of certain peoples and places, as well as the spiritual states or conditions that would predominate in them. To discern the exact meanings of these three terms throughout the text, it helps to keep in mind these thoughts:

(1) The primary purpose of the Apocalypse is to relate the evolvement of the "mystery of God," and, therefore, it tells about the world only insofar as the world connects with the Church, or affects her destiny.
(2) The spiritual perspective preponderates.

It is important to note that the three divisions can be reduced to two: the heaven as that which is "above," and the earth and sea as that which is "below." It is more important to note that these two major divisions can be reduced to one category: the visible creation. This is to say that the Apocalypse does not describe the "mystery of God" in eternity, but in the temporal order. When last I checked, the vast majority of mankind still lived on the surface of the planet; and, so, common sense alone should suffice to understand that John did not restrict the term "heaven" to people who live in space stations.

The term "earth" can mean the planet itself, as in 16:18, which states,

> "...and there came a great earthquake, such as did not come since man came upon the earth..."

Generally, however, it signifies human society, the world in regard to things of this life, not the next such as, business, government, marrying, and being given in marriage, etc. Take, for example, 20:11, which comes at the Last Judgment,

> "...from the presence of which the earth and the heaven fled and a place was not found for them."

This statement indicates the fulfillment of what Christ said,

> "The heaven and the earth will pass away, but my words shall not pass away." [Mt. 24:35]

Clearly, Apocalypse 20:11 and Matthew 24:35 refer to that "heaven" that exists in the temporal order and that is, therefore, temporary, i.e., they refer to the visible institution called the Church, the kingdom of heaven on earth. In Chapter 6, begins the account of things that "...must come into existence" [4:1]; so, here are the first five instances of the term "earth":

> And out came another horse flame-colored, and to the one riding on it there was given to him to seize peace from the earth and so that they will be killing one another there was also given to him a great sword [μάχαιϱα = makhaira]. [Apoc. 6:4]

> And there was given to them authority upon the fourth of the earth to kill with sword [ῥομφαίᾳ = rhomphaia] and with famine and with pestilence and by the beasts of the earth. [Apoc. 6:8]

> "Will you not ever, O Sovereign holy and true, judge and avenge our blood from the ones dwelling upon the earth?" [Apoc. 6:10]

> And a great earthquake...[Apoc. 6:12]

Patently, in these four excerpts, the term "earth" does not simply mean the planet or the crust thereof, nor merely man in his daily, mundane affairs; rather, it symbolizes a certain category of people. At first, it seems enough to confine that category to pagans, here meaning the pagan peoples in the Roman Empire, for virtually nowhere else did the Church spend her first four or five centuries; but, in view of the "great earthquake" in verse 12, namely, the dethronement of paganism throughout the empire [but not annihilation, note], the definition "pagan peoples" will not do.

That category, designated by the term "earth," is comprehensively defined as those who, for whatever reason or reasons, are not members of the visible Church founded by Jesus Christ, the Church whose birthday was the first Pentecost, and whose life has since continued to this very day: the Roman Catholic Church. Obviously, the spiritual perspective preponderates in that definition, for it includes even those who hold appearance of membership, but not the actuality of it.

So, the Roman world became predominantly Christian, which is to say that the term "earth" changes from designating the general pagan population per se to designating a specific spiritual condition.

However, the term does not change from designating all the territory of the Roman Empire—temporarily, that is. And, therein lies the key to understanding the term "earth" in later Chapters, most especially, in 10, 11, 12, 13, & 17.

Undoubtedly, O Friends, ye have suspected that when Michael set his right foot on the "sea" and his left on the "earth," he was not placing each on just a spiritual condition.

The term "the sea" appears, for the first time [As symbol, actually 5:13; not to be confused with "the Sea of glass like crystal"; in Chapter 4, which symbolizes all the faithful laity], in the forepart of Chapter 7, but note sharply how John introduced it:

> 1 After this I saw four angels having taken their positions upon the four corners of the earth, controlling the four winds of the earth so that [a] wind might blow not upon the earth nor upon the sea nor upon every tree. 2 and I saw another angel ascending from the rising of the sun [,] holding the seal of the living God, and he cried out in [a] loud voice to the four angels the ones to whom it was given to harm the earth and the sea [,] 3 saying, "Harm not the earth nor the sea nor the trees, until we have sealed the servants of our God upon their foreheads."

The "four angels" are real angels, and the "angel ascending [the participle connotes a continuous state of power and authority] from the rising of the sun" is a very holy bishop from the east [most likely, Caesarea in Palestine], as I have already explained in part two of this commentary.

The bishop referred to "the servants of our God," clearly indicating that the command to harm not "the earth nor the sea nor the trees" concerned the Church's faithful members inhabiting the territory of the Roman Empire.

In verse 2, John mentioned that the four angels were given authority to harm "the earth and the sea" [the Church cannot be harmed unless God permits]; then, in verse 3, he recorded the bishop as saying,

> "Harm not the earth nor the sea nor the trees…"

By adding the phrase, "nor the trees," John signaled the reader that he was emphasizing a difference in aspect, but not in fundamental meaning, between the mention of "earth" and "sea" in verse 2, and the mention of them in verse 3 [or 1].

The term "trees" is the symbol for prominent members in a society; the taller or bigger the "trees," the higher the positions of wealth, power and authority of those members. In contrast to the "trees" is man, in general, symbolized as "the grass."

These symbols, the "trees" and the "grass," are found in 9:4, which reads,

> And it was told to them so that they will be harming not the grass of the earth nor every green thing nor every tree if not the men the

> ones who [are] not having the seal of the God upon the forehead. [Translation: "…so that they will be harming not the people who have God's seal on their foreheads"]

The "trees" and "grass" are symbols from the Old Testament,

> So the Lord severs from Israel head and tail, palm branch and reed in one day. [The elder and the noble are the head, the prophet who teaches falsehood is the tail] [Is. 9:13-14]

Likewise, the elder and the noble are the palm branch, and the prophet who teaches falsehood is the reed.

> The very cypresses rejoice over you [King Nebuchadnezzar], and the cedars of Lebanon: "Now that you are laid to rest, there will be none to cut us down." [Is. 14:8]

> All mankind is grass, and all their glory like the flower of the field. The grass withers, the flower wilts, when the breath of the Lord blows upon it. [So, then, the people is the grass.] [Is. 40:6-7]

The term "trees" was added to the "earth and the sea" in verse 3 [or 1], in order to clarify and emphasize to the reader that "earth" and "sea" symbolize people—in this case, the common people, the "trees" being those prominent in society.

Absent the addition of "trees," the phrase, "the earth and the sea," emphasizes the aspect of territory. In other words, the term earth as the totality of Roman territory, at this point in the Apocalypse, is regarded as differentiated into two major parts: the "earth" and the "sea."

This portends that one part will remain the "earth," i.e., territory inhabited by God's people, but that the other part will undergo a "sea-change," if you will, i.e., it will not continue as territory inhabited by the Church: for the "sea" symbolizes the wicked, the people hostile toward God, as has already been explained earlier in the section on the "abyss." I say "portends," because the words of the holy bishop indicate that the part now being called "the sea" is still territory inhabited by "the servants of our God."

Bear in mind that the forepart of Chapter 7 is synchronous with the "great earthquake" AND with the "stars" falling onto the earth, in 6:12-14 [circa 360 AD]. Even as the Church is dethroning paganism and becoming victorious throughout the Empire, she is being attacked from within by the horrible heresy of Arianism.

The holy bishop knows that Christ will come in judgment, that "the breath of the Lord" [Is. 40:7 above] will blow four times upon all; but, first, he and the other faithful members of the episcopate, and elders, as well, must "seal," must confirm or strengthen the faithful laity.

The "four winds" become the first four trumpets in the next Chapter; it will be the second trumpet in 8:8-9 when the "Burning Mountain" will be "cast out unto the sea," and the "sea" will be lost to it. Indeed, this will be the "sea" punished by the second plague of the third woe in 16:3.

To this day, what was once the territory of the Roman Empire remains divided into two large parts differentiated by two religions: Christianity, in Europe, and Islam, in North Africa and the Middle East. In 13:1, John wrote,

"I saw a beast ascending from the sea…"

and, in 13:11, wrote,

"I saw another beast ascending from the earth…"

Just so will these things come into existence.

The term "the heaven" is an abbreviation of the phrase, "the kingdom of heaven" [Mt. 23:13, 25:1]; and this kingdom is also called "the kingdom of God" [Luke 13:18, 11:20]. In almost every instance throughout the Bible, this term symbolizes the visible organization or body, composed of the people of God: in the Old Testament, Israel; in the New Testament, the Church. It can also symbolize the spiritual condition or state that qualifies a person as one of God's people. Since there are those who, by "invincible ignorance," are outside the visible Church but who qualify, by spiritual condition or state, for membership therein, the term "the heaven" must be discerned most carefully according to its context in the Bible.

Whereas:

(1) Christ commanded John to write the seven letters to the seven churches, and, thereby, symbolically indicated that he intended the Apocalypse for the whole Church;

(2) Christ, in 1:19, stated the format of the Apocalypse, i.e.,

> "Write now the things you saw [the seven lampstands and seven stars, Chapter 1] and the things that exist [the seven letters, Chapters 2 & 3, plus Chapter 4 on the Church as an organization, and 5 on the Eucharistic celebration of the Mass] and the things destined to come into existence [future events, even to the Last Judgment, Chapters 6-21],

and thereby indicated that he intended the message for the whole Church for all time;

(3) there can be only one true Church, since Christ is not a dunce for redundancy, nor an adulterer having more than one bride;

it is clear and plain that the term "the heaven," in the Apocalypse, means strictly the Church founded by Christ, and no other founded by mere man.

The citation of Apocalypse 20:11 cross-referred with Matthew 24:35, plus several references at the beginning of part two of this commentary, additionally demonstrate that "the heaven" in the New Testament means the Church. Notwithstanding this information provided by the Bible, it is fact that some still do not accept it.

Therefore, let a few more passages be proffered, in the hope this will help such to right reception of the text.

Consider Apocalypse 19:6-8,

> And I heard as the sound of a great multitude [the laity or Sea of Glass like crystal] <u>and</u> as the sound of many waters [the elders, who most often dispense the waters of life to the laity] <u>and</u> as the sound of mighty thunders [the episcopate, who hold the highest power and authority after Christ, and who ordain men as elders] saying, "Hallelujah! that the Lord our God the Almighty began reigning. Let us rejoice and exult and give the glory to him, that the marriage of the Little Lamb came and the bride of him made herself ready and it was given to her so that she may be clothed with bright, clean linen": for the linen is the righteous deeds of the holy ones [the saints].

In this passage, the people of God are presented in the collective sense, and their order of mention is ascendant, according to rank. The angels are not mentioned because they do not have bodies; and therefore, though God permits them to participate in his divine nature, in the strictly spiritual sense, they cannot participate in it, bodily, through Jesus Christ.

St. Paul wrote,

> If there is a body of the soul [σῶμα ψυχικόν = söma psykhikon, i.e., the psychosomatic], there is a body of the spirit [σῶμα πνευματικόν = söma pneumatikon, i.e., the pneumatosomatic]. And thus is it written, "The first <u>man</u> Adam <u>became</u> <u>unto</u> <u>a</u> <u>living</u> <u>soul</u>, the last Adam unto a life-giving spirit. But not first [is] the one of the spirit but the one of the soul, then the one of the spirit. The first man [was] dust from the earth, the second man from heaven. [1 Cor. 15:44-47]

The bride is clothed in "bright, clean linen," and the "linen" is the righteous deeds of the saints; ergo, the saints, collectively, are the bride of the Little Lamb, Jesus Christ. Clearly, the saints are the Church, the mystical <u>body</u> of Christ, <u>the</u> bride, as St. Paul repeats what Christ said,

> "For this reason a man will leave his father and mother and be joined to his wife, and the two will become one flesh." This is a great mystery, and I am applying it to Christ and his Church. [Eph. 5:31-32]

Again, St. Paul indicated that the bride of Christ is the members of the Church,

> For I am jealous with God's jealousy toward you, for I promised you to one husband, to be presented as a chaste virgin to Christ. [2 Cor. 11:2]

As it was in the beginning, is now, and ever shall be, even to the end of the world, Christ cannot have more than one bride, lest he commit the sin of adultery; and yet, in this last year of the twentieth century, some 2500 denominations individually aver, "I am the bride of Christ!" Judge for yourselves, ye Friends, the signs of these times, when hundreds and hundreds of millions testify, "You, Jesus Christ, are a fornicator, like us!" Contemplate earnestly, therefore, what is coming, and make ready.

Consider 19:14, which reads,

> And the armies the ones in the heaven follow him [the Word of the God] upon white horses [,] wearing white, clean linen.

The armies mentioned here are "wearing white, clean linen"; this unmistakably alludes to the "bright, clean linen" of the saints in 19:8. Obviously, not every individual member of the whole Church will be in those armies. Hence, to indicate the whole of the Church, the term "the heaven" is used; and to indicate a part of the Church, the phrase, "in the heaven," is used.

Verse 14 is also an apt example of spiritual condition or state. In the Old Testament, there was only one army of heaven, the nation of Israel; but, in the New Testament, there will be "the armies" of heaven, going into battle at Armageddon.

It is most doubtful that every soldier will be formally a member of the Roman Catholic Church. Though some will not be already baptized with water, all will have the baptism of desire, and many will receive the baptism of blood.

Therefore will those armies be only one army in spirit, and that is the reason John used the singular in verse 19,

> And I saw the beast and the kings of the earth and their armies gathered to make war against the one riding upon the horse and against his army.

Apocalypse 7:14-17 describes those who wear the white robes of fine linen,

> 14 And he said to me, "These are the ones come out of the tribulation the great one and they washed their robes and made them white in the blood of the Little Lamb. 15 Because of this are they in the presence of the throne of the God and are worshipping him day and night in the sanctuary of him, and the One seated upon the throne will pitch his tent over them. 16 They will not be hungering still nor will they be thirsting still nor will the sun strike upon them nor every scorching heat, 17 for the Little Lamb the one at the center of the throne [ἀνὰ μέσον τοῦ θρόνου = ana meson ton thronou] will shepherd them and he will guide them to springs of waters of life, and the God will wipe away every tear from their eyes."

The ones who wear white, clean robes of fine linen are those who live in the middle court, the "μέσauloς" [mesaulos] or "ναός" [naos], THE SANCTUARY. Their deeds are holy or righteous, because they are done in the blood of the Little Lamb, i.e., in the spirit and body of Christ who obeyed the will of the Father, even to death on the cross. One word denotes the Father's will and the Son's obedience: love. The saints, then, are those who keep the two great commandments,

> "'You shall love the Lord your God with all your heart and with all your soul and with all your mind': this is the great and first commandment. And the second is like to it, 'You shall love your neighbor as yourself.' On these two commandments depend all the law and the prophets." [Mt. 22:37-40]

In the letter to the angel of the church at Ephesus, Apocalypse 2:4-5, Jesus said,

> "But I hold against you that your love the first one you have abandoned. Remember whence you fell and repent and do the first works..."

The bishop has fallen from keeping the first great commandment; in symbolic terms, he has fallen from the "ναός" [naos] down, at least, into the "αὐλή" [aulë], the outer court, the "place" where the tepid and timid are.

Recall the symbolical description at the beginning of Chapter 4. John saw an opened door in the heaven, and a voice commanded him, "Come up here..." [literally, "Ascend hither..."]. The wordage implies that there is a wall separating the "ναός" [naos] from the "αὐλή" [aulë], and that the "ναός" [naos] is higher up, i.e., spiritually superior.

The reason for these symbolical expressions is that the "temple" stands atop the "mountain," God's "holy mountain." The intimation is that the "ναός" [naos], with its surrounding wall, will become the city called the New Jerusalem described in Chapter 21, verses 9-27.

Those who wear white robes have "conquered" or "overcome," for the color "white" symbolizes victory. They shall inherit the "kingdom of the heaven" in the Millennium, and they shall inherit also the earth.

Consider what Christ said, in 3:15-17, to the bishop at Laodicea,

> "I know your works [,] that you are neither cold nor hot. I wish you were cold or hot. So, because you are lukewarm and neither hot nor cold, I am about to vomit you out of my mouth. For you say that 'I am rich and I have prospered and I have need of nothing,' and you do not know that you are the one wretched and pitiable and poor and blind and naked..."

In ancient times, the "αὐλή" [aulë] was where the beasts were kept at night. Beasts do not wear clothes. From Christ's point of view, the bishop at Laodicea is spiritually naked because he, like the bishop at Ephesus, no longer keeps the first great commandment: to love God with all one's heart and all one's soul and all one's mind. Half-heartedness will not do. Moreover, a human being, by means of self alone, cannot keep the first great commandment, and, consequently, not the second, a point pellucidly made in the citation from Chapter 7,

> "...they washed their robes and made them white in the blood of the Little Lamb."

The individual must become clothed in the new creation, clothed most of all with love [as St. Paul wrote], in order to be properly attired for the sanctuary, in the presence of the God on his throne, where one may come to God's table, the altar, to partake of the Eucharistic Christ. Strictly speaking, the lukewarm are still within the Church, but their position is perilous; for Christ warned in strong, blunt language,

> "I am about to vomit you out of my mouth."

This means He will expel them from his body, that is, He will cast them out of his Church. In other symbolic terms, they will be cast out of "the heaven" and fall onto the earth. This symbolism should be familiar to more than a few, for, historically, it is long from new; indeed, the very first violation by man against the first great commandment has always been called—the Fall.

I have written enough, for the nonce, about "the heaven" and "the earth" and "the sea." One short paragraph more will wrap the chapter up. After that, I will comment on Christ's letter to the bishop of Laodicea, in adumbration of the material to follow concerning Chapters 17, 12, & 13, for it is important to know the signs that will precede even the "birth pangs" of the second and third woes. It seems those signs are already in their incipience.

John used the word "βιβλαρίδιον" [biblaridion] to designate the scroll he took from the angel. The Greek noun is the diminutive of a diminutive, and that is why it should be translated as "very small scroll." Its size indicates a very short period of time, to wit, the 1,260 days, or 42 months.

That it is already "opened" and not "sealed" means that its contents can be understood with complete certainty before its contents "come into existence."

When John ate the very small scroll, it tasted sweet; but, when he digested it, his stomach turned sour: this simply means that the news of total triumph about to be achieved by Christ and his Church delighted him; but, after he had thought about the loss of everlasting life for so many people, the news upset him very much.

Then, he was told he must…

"prophesy again about many peoples and nations and tongues and kings."

John did not use the definite article, which means that the very little scroll is for the generation that will be living during the second woe. Had he used the definite article, he would have meant the peoples and nations of his own day. In spite of this clue and many such, there are commentators who insist that Chapter 9:13-19 pertains to the days of ancient Rome.

Chapter 10's point of time in the sequence of events comes after Satan has been cast out of the Church in Chapter 12; perhaps, the most precise point is when Satan takes his stand upon the sand of "the sea" after he has left the region termed "the earth": I say this, because John did write that the mighty angel [Michael] set his right foot on the "sea" and his left foot on the "earth." It is logical, to me, that Michael would leave the "seven thunders" only after they were safe in the "wilderness." Indeed, this adds support to my explanation as to why the "seven thunders" issued official statements instead of battle cries. One thing is certain: the other members "in the sanctuary" will be ready to do battle with the "angel of the abyss" [9:11], with Satan—and his pet, the Beast.

Chapter 7

—

The Letter to Laodicea

Laodicea was a principal city of Asia Minor for banking, commerce, and industries, with specialties in sandals, eye salve, and woolen goods from black sheep. Six miles across the Lycos valley were the hot springs of Hierapolis [the name means "sacred city"], whose waters flowed down from Mt. Salbacos, became lukewarm as they crossed a plateau, then fell down a cliff, depositing a white crust of lime on its face.

The Laodiceans had a spirit of independence and self-sufficiency on account of their wealth. When an earthquake destroyed the city in 60 AD, the rich citizenry turned down an imperial offer of help and by themselves built the city anew.

Laodicea received from the emperor the title of free city, and Roman authorities were under orders not to trouble the Jewish community there; for the Jews contributed annually to the imperial coffers. Hence, the financial importance of Laodicea forfended persecution against the local church, also.

It would be naive to think the members of the Christian community, including the bishop, did not directly or indirectly participate in the city's prosperity. It would also be naive to think that the wealth and the long sense of self-sufficiency did not affect the Christians in their relationship with God. So, Christ's words to the bishop apply as fully to his flock, and those words are to be understood in both the material and spiritual senses.

It is a point of historical interest that St. Paul ordered his letter to Colossae be read in Laodicea, and his letter to Laodicea be read in Colassae [Colossians

4:16]. His letters clearly indicate that the Christians in the three neighboring cities of Colossae, Hierapolis, and Laodicea were secure.

Christ began his address to the bishop with the phrase, "Thus saith the Amen," which refers to the Old Testament formula, "Thus saith the Lord," a formula used by the prophets to introduce a message, which would contain, at least, in part, statements from God about his activity in the future. The Church ends a prayer, creed, or other formal statement, with the term "Amen" to express solemn ratification [so be it] or agreement [it is so].

The Hebrew word "amen" literally means "certainly" or "certainty." By the time John received the Apocalypse in 95-96 AD, the Amen was familiar to anyone who had read the gospels or had heard them read, because, as is recorded in the gospels, Jesus used it, frequently. Indeed, he made the Amen personal to himself, as he did the "stone" or "rock" in Daniel 2; therefore, the term is inseparable from him as the Mystery of the God, whose purpose is to bring the "kingdom of the heaven" over the whole earth.

The Amen points backward, for example, to Isaiah 65, especially, verses 16-17,

> He who takes an oath in the land shall swear by the God of truth; for the hardships of the past shall be forgotten, and hidden from my eyes. Behold! I am about to create a new heaven and a new earth; the things of the past shall not be remembered or come to mind.

The term also points forward to the Millennium and the New Jerusalem, in Apocalypse 21:1-2,

> And I saw a new heaven and a new earth. For the first heaven and the first earth passed away and the sea is no more. And I saw the city the holy [one] New Jerusalem coming down from the heaven from the God, prepared as a bride adorned for her husband.

Thus, the term "Amen" connotes the renewal of all things; and the phrase, "Thus saith the Amen," means that Christ swore by himself: for he is the new Adam, "the witness faithful and true," and "the beginning/origin of the creation of the God," who has all power and authority to bring the Father's plan to fulfillment.

Hence, Christ immediately intimated to the bishop:

(1) that the words to follow would be absolutely true and certain;
(2) that they would concern the bishop's urgent need of renewal;
(3) that they would tell the consequence of failure to repent:
- (a) especially, for the bishop and his congregation, in the near future,
- (b) more especially, for the general Church in the time of the seventh seal,
- (c) and, most especially, for the Church in the time of the seventh trumpet.

Bear in mind that Christ deliberately made the message to Laodicea letter number SEVEN. His words were most solemn; the Eternal Truth and Certainty uttered them to Laodicea and, in fact, to the Whole Church for all generations to come. To the bishop, to everyone, Christ has delivered the ultimatum of either life or death, with little time left to choose—forever.

Persecution under the Emperor Trajan came to Asia Minor in 113 AD. Trajan was famous for riding a white horse; he was the first of the "four horsemen" mentioned in Chapter 6: for thus had said the Amen,

"I am about to vomit you out of my mouth."

It is obvious that Christ used symbolical terms when he informed the bishop,

"You are lukewarm and neither hot nor cold."

The three adjectives are each to be understood as indicial of spiritual condition or state

> He had been instructed in the Way of the Lord and with ardent spirit, spoke and taught accurately about Jesus, although he knew only the baptism of John. [Acts 18:25];

> Do not grow slack in zeal, be fervent in spirit, serve the Lord. [Rom. 12:11];

and, in turn, the condition or state is to be understood as measured according to only one model or standard: Jesus Christ. He is the exemplar omnibus [the example for all], the one who persevered perfectly in obedient love, who faithfully and truly kept the two great commandants, even to death on the cross.

It is plausible that Christ had in mind the nearby city of Hierapolis, for the descendent temperature of the waters of its springs, from hot to lukewarm to cold, corresponds with the descendent terrain: from Hierapolis on the mountain of Salbacos, to the plateau lower down, to the cliff; and these things aptly represent the bishop's situation.

In the Bible, "water" symbolizes spiritual life. Lukewarm "water" can provoke nausea; hence, the tepid bishop is nauseous to Christ. The bishop is midway between the "sacred city" higher up on the "mountain" and the "fall" over the cliff.

He has reached a plateau in his spiritual life, in the sense that he does not seek to advance in sanctity. He regards himself as levelheaded; and, what Christ considers nauseatingly neither "hot" nor "cold," the bishop deems well-balanced and comfortable and not fanatical, but reasonable.

He has deluded himself into thinking his life is perfect and does not need any change; indeed, he thinks himself rich and secure. He is free from the troubles and weaknesses in other churches: there are no Nicolaites or Jezebels or heretics or other bothers among his people. All goes well and, he reckons, will continue so. Thus does he say in his heart, "I am rich and I have prospered and I have need of nothing."

How unaccommodating is his memory to what Christ said on this matter,

> "Amen I say to you that a rich man will enter with difficulty into the kingdom of the heaven. And again I say to you, it is easier for a camel to go through the eye of a needle [metaphor: one of the low, arched entrances in the wall around Jerusalem] than for a rich man to enter into the kingdom of the God." [Mt. 19:23-24]

> And seeing the crowds, he went up onto a mountain, and as he was seating himself they came close to him the ones being taught by him: and opening his mouth he instructed them, saying, "Blessed are the poor in spirit, for of them is the kingdom of the heaven."
> [Mt. 5:1-3]

Like the water flowing across the plateau, the bishop is falling little by little—toward the cliff. His prince of principles is *ne quid nimis*, "nothing to excess"; and that is the maxim of the world, the typically human. "There is some good and some bad in every man," saith he, as he continues falling, falling, falling. It is true that a man can be *both* good *and* bad, at any particular point in life; but, it is not true that a man can *become* both good and bad, at the same time. The spiritual life has a motto, "Grow or die," like that of the French Foreign Legion, "March or die."

In the bishop's heart is secret pride and arrogance: that the riches he has are HIS; that the prosperity he enjoys was achieved by HIM; and, therefore, nothing is needed by HIM. Thrice did Christ repeat the idea of "I," hinting that the bishop is not God, and that he has no authority to give the name "good" to anyone or anything. Adam and Eve tried that.

A man, by means of himself alone, cannot be or become good. The bishop's words, "I have need of nothing," express what Christ abhors: self-exaltation. The insolence, the insult, of that word "nothing"!!! For such is the speech of sin, that Christ is—nothing.

I think the rest of the letter is clear enough, certainly Christ's loving and kind counsel to the bishop, on how to correct his condition. Christ saved until last his admonition to the Church, for all its future history,

> "Let the one having an ear hear what the Spirit is saying to the churches!"

The letter's contents, emphatically, the phrase, "at the door," and the clause, "I am about to vomit you out of my mouth," are most especially applicable to the Church in the generation or two or three before the advent of the Beast of Chapter 13. Only the spiritually ignorant think that so much scientific knowledge, being used to make so much material wealth in the world, is not dangerous. Indeed, it will give rise to Babylon the Great.

As the letter to Laodicea intimates, and, as later Chapters will show, a major sign preceding the "birth pangs" will be a period of ever increasing wealth, much greater than the human race has ever known; correspondingly, faith will decrease and charity will grow colder. Why, look there and here: it has, already, made its initial appearance.

So, this section of the commentary's third part ended where it began,

> And there was given to me a reed like a rod, as he was saying, "Come and measure the sanctuary of the God and the altar and the ones worshipping in it. And the court the one on the outside of the sanctuary cast outside and measure it not, for it was given to the nations, and the city the holy one they will be trampling for forty-two months.

In relation to 11:1-2, and in adumbration of Chapters 17, 12, & 13, a statement from Moses is appropriate,

> If there arises among you a prophet or a dreamer who promises a sign or wonder, urging you to follow other gods, whom you have not known, or to serve them: even though the sign or wonder he has foretold you comes to pass, pay no attention to the words of that prophet or dreamer; for the Lord, your God, is testing you, to learn whether you truly love him with all your heart and with all your soul. [Dt.13:2-4]

It has been shown that the second woe will unfold in three phases:

(1) the 200 Million Horsemen,
(2) the measuring of the sanctuary in the Church, and
(3) the tract of 42 months or 1260 days, during which the nations will be trampling Jerusalem and the Two Witnesses will be evangelizing throughout the world.

The measuring of the sanctuary and the coming of the Beast are subjects too important to be confined within a few verses in Chapter 11. Hence, it should not surprise, at all, that the former and the latter are expanded in Chapters 12 and 13, respectively: as 11:1-2 relates to 11:3-13, so all of Chapter 12 relates to all of Chapter 13. However, to abbreviate the commentary and to alleviate the task of typing with two fingers, I will leap ahead to Chapter 17, wherein an angel explains the chief symbols wherewith to make brief and relief of Chapters 12 and 13. I will do this after demonstrating that the Beast in Chapter 17 is the same Beast in 13:1 and in 11, and that Chapter 13 chronologically, not just numerically, follows 12.

Chapter 8

—

Preparation for Chapters 17, 12, & 13

The chronological question concerning Chapters 12 and 13 will be answered first.

John wrote,

> And they [the Dragon and his angels] were not strong and not a place was found of them still in the heaven. And he was cast out the dragon the great one, the serpent the ancient one, the one called Diabolos and the Satanas, the one leading astray the whole world, he was cast out unto the earth, and the angels of him with him were cast out. [Apoc. 12:8-9]

John described the action of casting out Satan and his angels [demonic and human] from the Church, in the aorist tense, thus indicating that the event will happen only once. Although Satan and his followers will no longer be "still in the heaven," they will still be in the world for "a short time," as 12:12 states.

This expulsion of Satan from the Church will be effected after the event of the 200 Million Horsemen, and before the 3½-year reign of the Beast, the last 3½ years of the second woe: for John did not record that Satan and his own will have to be cast out of the Church again during that period of 42 months;

instead, he recorded that Satan will try to destroy the Church from outside. The text is pellucid of the point that this casting out will be complete and entire.

The third woe, which will come swiftly after the second woe, will effect the expulsion of Satan from the whole world; and the text is pellucid of the point that Christ will not have to do that twice, either. The emphasis is on the completeness or entirety, of Christ's casting out Satan and his angels, first, from the Church, then, from the world.

In the past, Christ has not cast out Satan and his followers from his Father's house, completely and entirely, in any particular judgment; hence, the judgment in Chapter 12 will be unique for its thoroughness. Like Father, like Son: the Father is not a dunce for redundancy, and neither is Jesus Christ.

For emphasis and unequivocality, thrice did the meek Seer express in 12:9 the aorist tense of the verb ekballein, "to cast out"; plus, he mentioned five names or titles, for the Archenemy of God; and, therefore, a valid excuse for missing or messing the message is an utter impossibility for any adult in possession of average mind or better.

So, let the principal point here be committed to fixed remembrance: the war in "the heaven" will be fought immediately before the reign of the Beast begins, and Michael and his angels [angelic and human] shall cast out Satan and his to "the earth and the sea," as 12:12 indicates.

In 13:5, John wrote,

> "There was given to it [the Beast] authority to do for forty-two months,"

and those 42 months are the "short time," or "little time," also mentioned in 12:12. Hence, Chapter 13 follows 12, chronologically, in the sense of next: quod erat demonstrandum.

Consider 12:4-5, which reads,

> 4 And the tail of it [of the dragon] dragged by force [σύϱει = surei]
> the third of the stars of the heaven and cast out [ἔβαλεν = ebalen]
> them unto the earth, and the dragon took his stand [aorist] in the
> presence of the woman the one about to bear so that when she bore
> he might devour the thing born of/from her [τὸ τέκνον αὐτῆς = to
> tekhnon autës]. 5 And she bore [aorist] a son virile, who is about to

> shepherd all the nations with an iron rod. And snatched away was [aorist] the thing born of/from her [τὸ τέκνον αὐτῆς = to tekhnon autës] to the God and to the throne of him.

John recorded the short sequence of activities, in the aorist tense, indicating that this sequence will happen only once, just before the war in "the heaven." Regarding the dragon, the term, "the heaven," here means the Church as the visible organization, for, obviously, the dragon is not "in the heaven," in the sense of spiritual condition or state. Regarding the "stars," the term "the heaven" in 12:4 signifies mainly the spiritual condition or state necessary for membership in the Church, which does not exclude the sense of the Church as visible organization.

The phrase, "the third of the stars," is the same, in form, as "the third of the men" in Chapter 9, and it conveys the idea of "that third of those stars" living at that time. Subtle is the statement that the "third of the stars" was cast out "unto the earth"; for, though it plainly tells that those "stars" lost, at the very least, the spiritual condition or state for membership in "the heaven," it does not necessarily signal that they were cast out of "the heaven," in the sense of visible organization. To discern here a difference between "heaven," as visible organization, and "heaven," as condition or state, is not to split hairs.

Remember 8:13, in which the "eagle," flying "in midheaven," directed his three cries of woe to "the ones dwelling upon the earth," and proximal to the warning were the Four Living Beings first, the Twenty-four Elders second. The idea of 12:4 is that the dragon, by means of his "tail," dragged the "stars," irresistibly, and cast them "unto the earth," i.e., to the kingdom of this world, Satan's kingdom, whose capital criterion for membership therein is spiritual condition or state. The "stars" will still be members of the Church, according to appearances only.

Now, the dragon is Satan, as 12:9 states; and Satan qua angel is INVISIBLE. But, 12:3 states,

> "And there was seen another sign in the heaven, and behold a great flame/fire-colored dragon having seven heads and ten horns and upon the heads of it seven diadems,…"

A "sign" is something that can be seen by means of physical eyes. Since the dragon, Satan, is, most certainly, not in the spiritual condition or state for genuine membership in the Church, the phrase, "in the heaven," modifying the "dragon" in 12:3, must mean the visible organization called the Church.

The terms "seen" and "sign" and "behold," taken together, compel the deduction that the dragon is Satan in his political aspect, i.e., that the "head and tail" of the dragon are visible "in the heaven," and that, therefore, the "head and tail" symbolize human agents who serve Satan. Only at the very end of Chapter 12 does the "dragon" symbolize Satan, in person. Satan is, indeed, present throughout the Chapter, but, for most of it, he is behind the scenes, so to speak.

Clearly, the "tail" of the dragon will be irresistible only to the "third of the stars"; conversely, the other two-thirds will be stronger than the "tail." Hence, it is the other two-thirds who will prove the stronger in the struggle coming, and they will visibly rid the Church of Satan and his agents,

> "And they were not strong and not a place was found of them in the heaven." [Apoc. 12:8]

The "third of the stars" will succumb to the dragon's "tail," for only one reason: it will be those "stars" who are tepid and timid. Bear in mind that, in 12:2, the "woman" was "being put to the test," i.e., her spiritual mettle was being measured.

Let, then, three major items of information be weighed:

(1) Both 11:1-3 and 12:4-12 are in the aorist tense.
(2) Both passages involve a term that symbolizes a false prophet [reed/tail].
(3) Both tell what will happen immediately before the last 42 months of the second woe begin.

Since it would be preposterous to propose Christ will conduct two complete purgations of his mystical body, simultaneously, it stands to reason that the two passages are depictions of the same, unique sequence of events.

Moreover, since the "reed" and the "tail" are each mentioned in the singular number; and since each is instrumental in measuring the mettle of the Church, most especially, the "woman clothed with the sun"; and that measuring is part of the unique sequence of events; it stands to faith, that the "reed" and the "tail" symbolize only one and the same false prophet in Satan's service. It stands to faith, I say, because, at this point, it cannot be cogently shown that there are not two false prophets involved in the same, unique operation.

To help the reader reason to the conclusion that the "reed" and the "tail" represent the same false prophet, John provided the following:

> And I saw [come] out of the mouth of the dragon and out of the mouth of the beast and out of the mouth of <u>the</u> pseudoprophet three unclean spirits as frogs…[Apoc. 16:13]

This verse tells:

(1) that the "dragon" is neither the "beast" nor the pseudoprophet [ψευδοπροφήτου = pseudoprophëtës],
(2) that the "beast" is neither the "dragon" nor the pseudoprophet,
(3) that the pseudoprophet is neither the "dragon" nor the "beast."

Henceforth, I will refer to these three as: the "Dragon" or "Satan," the "Beast," and the "False Prophet."

The use of the definite article "the," with each of the three, signals to the reader:

(1) that each has been previously mentioned, or
(2) that each can be identified by conning the text.

Now, the Dragon presents no problem, for John first used the term in 12:3 and identified it, in 12:9, as "…the serpent, etc." Each of the other two terms, the "Beast" and the "False Prophet," does present a problem, for John described two "beasts" in Chapter 13, and he did not previously use the term "ψευδοπροφήτου" [pseudoprophëtës], at all. The latter will be treated first.

The term "ψευδοπροφήτου" has not been previously used; however, two symbolical terms for "false prophet," namely, the "reed," in 11:1, and the "tail," in 12:4, have been used; and their meanings were established in the Old Testament,

> So the Lord severs from Israel head and tail, palm branch and reed in one day. [The elder and the noble are the head; the prophet who teaches falsehood is the tail.] [Is. 9:13-14]

Since the terms "head and tail" and "palm branch and reed" are in apposition, what Isaiah said of the former applies to the latter, respectively.

So, the definite article, modifying the term "False Prophet" in 16:13, cannot be grammatically correct and accurate, unless it refers to either the "reed" or the "tail," or to both the "reed" and the "tail," because there is NO OTHER TERM, in the text of Chapters 10-16:2, that per se signifies a false prophet. The very expression of "the False Prophet" indicates that John was referring to THE False Prophet, but, at this point, reason still cannot judge, from the evidence, that there are not two false prophets involved.

John clarified the identity of the False Prophet even more in the following:

> And the Beast was captured, and with it the False Prophet the one that performed the signs in the presence of it, by which he led astray the ones receiving the mark of the Beast and the ones worshipping the image of it. [Apoc. 19:20]

The juxtaposition of 19:20 and the following excerpt, will help confirm the identity of the False Prophet,

> And I saw another beast ascending from the earth, and it had two horns like to a little lamb and spoke as a dragon. And all the authority of the first beast he exercised in the presence of it, and he made the earth and the ones dwelling in it so that they will be worshipping the beast the first one, of whom the blow of its death had been healed. And he did great signs, so that he made even fire come down from the sky unto the earth before men, and was leading astray the ones

> dwelling upon the earth by the <u>signs</u> which were given to him to do <u>in the presence of the beast</u>, telling the ones dwelling upon the earth to make an image to the beast, that had the blow of the sword [μάχαιρα = makhaira] and lived. [Apoc. 13:11-14]

From the aforegiven excerpts, three deductions can be securely made:

(1) The False Prophet and the "beast ascending from the earth" is one and the same agent.
(2) The False Prophet will be the right-hand man of the Beast.
(3) The term "the Beast" refers to "the beast ascending from the sea" in Chapter 13.

The order of mention in 16:13, namely, the Dragon <u>and</u> the Beast <u>and</u> the False Prophet, can now be explained: it is descendent, according to rank, from highest to lowest, as determined by power and authority. Bear in mind that the Apocalypse relates only major events and principal persons involved in them, to wit, that John did not write about what every Tom, Dick, and Harry would do or say. Hence, notwithstanding that Matthew 24:11 states,

> "…many false prophets will arise and will be leading astray many,"

it is clear that John was concerned about describing only one of them, the principal one, the chief henchman of the Beast. Satan and the Beast and the False Prophet are the fulsome threesome, the three most evil antagonists against the operation of the Holy Trinity. Now, therefore, does it stand to reason, that the "reed," in 11:1, and the Dragon's "tail," in 12:4, are one and the same entity, <u>the</u> False Prophet: <u>quod erat demonstrandum</u>.

So, attention now turns to that entity whom John designated simply as THE BEAST. Consider these two excerpts,

> Come, I will show you the judgment of the harlot the great one <u>the one seated upon many waters</u>….And he carried me away unto a wilderness in spirit. And I saw a woman <u>seated upon a scarlet beast</u>

> covered with blasphemous names, while <u>he</u> was having [ἔχων = ekhön] seven heads and ten horns. [Apoc. 17:1-3]
>
> And I saw a beast ascending from the sea, while <u>it</u> was having [ἔχον = ekhon] ten horns and seven heads and upon the horns of it ten diadems and upon the heads of it blasphemous names. [Apoc. 13:1]

Note the circumstantial participle "ἔχων" [ekhön] in 17:3; like "λέγων" [legön], in 11:1, and "λέγοντα" [legonta], in 9:14, it is in the <u>nominative</u> case and functions as both subject and verb, for what should be, in English, a subordinate temporal clause. It is in the <u>masculine</u> gender, despite the fact that it modifies the <u>neuter</u> noun "θηρίον" [thërion, beast]; and, thus, John begins the process of informing the reader, that Chapter 17 will describe the Beast as both a man and a thing, as a king and a kingdom.

Now look at the participle "ἔχον" [ekhon] in 13:1. In view of 17:3, it, too, should be translated as a subordinate temporal clause. The special reason for translating both participles as temporal clauses is that each governs a direct compound object whose <u>order of mention</u> indicates the Beast <u>at a specific time</u> in the overall sequence of events. I will comment on this aspect in greater detail, later.

The important point here is that John's description of the Beast is a verbal photograph, so to speak: the Beast, in 17, has "seven heads and ten horns," and the Beast, in 13, has "ten horns and seven heads"—a figure or physique, not exactly nondescript. Therefore, they are one and the same: <u>the</u> Beast? Aye, the Dragon has "seven heads and ten horns," and, if one reflects a moment, one realizes that it, too, is a beast.

The Dragon, however, is "πυρρός" [pyrros], i.e., "flame-colored" or "fire-colored" [not "red," as some English versions state]; whereas, the Beast in 17 is "κόκκινον" [kokkinon], <u>scarlet</u>. The problem is that John did not tell the color of the Beast in 13, and so, both faith and reason must prudently dispose of the possibility that the Beast in 13 and the one in 17 are twins.

A conning of the following two excerpts will confirm the identity of the Beast:

> The beast that [ὃ, relative pronoun in neuter accusative] you saw was and now is and is about to ascend from the abyss and unto destruction is going. [Apoc. 17:8]

> ...and the dragon gave [aorist] to it [the Beast] its [the Dragon's] power and its throne and great authority. [Apoc. 13:2]

Note that, in 17:8, the angel refers to the Beast as a thing. Now, the juxtaposition of 17:1 & 3 makes it clear that the Great Harlot is not immediately seated upon "the many waters" [which term includes "the sea"], but immediately upon the Beast. She is seated upon "the many waters," indirectly, i.e., through him or by means of him; to wit, he is the one seated directly or immediately upon "the many waters."

The Beast, then, in Chapter 17 is the Beast in that state or status, designated by John, of "ascending from the sea," and in that time when he/it is "about to ascend from the abyss." The term "to ascend" means "to rise in power and authority," and, by using the present participle, John indicated a continuous state or status of being in the ascendancy.

In 13:2, John wrote that Satan gave his own personal power and throne and great authority to the Beast with "ten horns and seven heads." It is pellucid that the Beast in 13 is no longer "ascending" only "from the sea" but also "from the abyss": for the Dragon is Satan, and Satan is the king or ruler, of the "abyss" by his natural or inherent power.

Mark him in 9:11, which reads,

> They [the locusts] are having over them a king the angel of the abyss, a name for him with Hebrew [is] Abaddon, and, in the Greek, he has a name: Apollyon.

The usual translations for the names "Abaddon" and "Apollyon" are "destruction" and "destroyer," respectively; but the more accurate translations for them are "annihilation" and "annihilator." The two names refer to Satan's spiritual condition or state, and to him qua secondary agent, not to his finite being [essence-existence].

Since Satan seriously, if not absolutely, rejected God and thereby rendered his own condition or state, a permanent deprivation of Love naturally unselfish, he now, of necessity, acts by means of himself alone, in naturally selfish love of his own will, and, thus, seeks to deceive other rational creatures into choosing the same condition or state for themselves.

That is Satan's motive in the act John described,

> "And the dragon gave to it [to the Beast] its power and throne and great authority." [Apoc. 13:2]

Aye, he gave, but he gave ONLY ONCE, he gave to ONLY ONE PERSON: the Beast with "ten horns and seven heads."

The verb "ἔδωκεν" [edöken = gave] is in the aorist tense. Upon that verb depends all other parts of this argument for identifying the Beast. In Chapter 17, the Beast is "ascending" from the "sea" and is about to ascend from the "abyss"; in Chapter 13, the Beast is "ascending" from the "sea" and is ascending from the "abyss." Ergo, they are one and the same Beast at two different times in the order of events.

Finally, consider this excerpt:

> And when they [the Two Witnesses] will be ending the testimony of them, the Beast ascending from the abyss will do with them battle and overcome them and kill them. [Apoc. 11:7]

The participial phrase, "ascending from the abyss," patently and plainly denotes that the Beast in Chapter 11 is also the Beast in 13:1, and, therefore, also the Beast in Chapters 16, 17, 19, & 20: quod erat demonstrandum.

The preceding argument about the Beast also shows that the 42 months of his victorious reign, and the 42 months during which the nations will be trampling the "city the holy one," will be one and the same period of time. There will not be two periods of 3½ years each, as some have asserted. Indeed, mere common sense understands that the Beast and the Two Witnesses will have to be contemporaneous, in order for the Beast to kill them.

Here, Friends, ends the preparation for Chapters 17, 12, & 13. However, if you have the feeling of being somewhat disoriented, understand that it has come as a matter of course, the course of an idiosyncratic mind, of whose motions the meanderings of an ant give visible similitude. However the manner may work on you, it works for me. In fact, were my mind ever to evidence the incipience of system, I would interpret that as a symptom of insidious illness, for a system is a closed thing. Ah! Life does have problems, but my cheerful reminder is that people do not solve many of life's problems: they survive them.

Besides, life's quite acquainted with paradox, and, ultimately, life is the Absolute Paradox, as every Christian knows. Then, comparably very easy should this commentary prove, whose primary paradox is as the ant's: that indirection finds direction out. Sooner or later, the ant partakes of the picnic.

Chapter 9

—

Apocalypse Chapter 17

This chapter is a little like a jigsaw puzzle: its sentences are like the printed pieces, which need only to be assembled, and, then, they will present an intelligible picture. However, during the tract of 1,900 years since written, the chapter has proved paradoxically intractable, in that it has both kept its pieces to itself and yet given them in a strange impression on its readers: for many an intellect has met it, read it, and left it in pieces. Yes, in spite of many an opinion given to its every piece, the chapter has kept its peace every time, all because, I suspect, the readers did not like to slurp soup.

At first, it seems a discrepancy arises from the description of the "woman," the "beast," and the "many waters":

> Come, I will show you the judgment of <u>the</u> <u>harlot</u> the great one the one <u>seated</u> <u>upon</u> <u>many</u> <u>waters</u>...[Apoc. 17:1]

> ...and I saw a woman <u>seated</u> <u>upon a</u> <u>scarlet</u> <u>beast</u>..., while he was having seven heads and ten horns...[Apoc. 17:3]

> ...I will tell you the mystery of the woman and of <u>the</u> beast [of] <u>the</u> one carrying her [of] <u>the</u> one having <u>the</u> seven heads and <u>the</u> ten horns. [Apoc. 17:7]

> …The seven heads are seven mountains, where the woman is seated upon them. They are also seven kings. [Apoc. 17:9]

> …The waters that you saw where the harlot is seated, are peoples and multitudes and nations and languages. [Apoc. 17:15]

> And the woman whom you saw is the city the great one the one having dominion upon the kings of the earth. [Apoc. 17:18]

Except for 17:4-6, the aforegiven six excerpts comprise everything that Chapter 17 states concerning the relationship between the woman and the Beast, with the emphasis here being on the woman first, as accords with a gentleman's observance of courtesy, even toward the fallen and the fell.

I will begin by leaping into the middle of things, upon an interesting little item in 17:15. Though, at first, it will seem that my thoughts digress from the subject of the woman, it will be seen that she is their object. In Chapter 17, the pieces of information come in so random a manner that reason must go the way of the ant. Let's go picnicking.

The text relates that the woman is seated upon "many waters" [17:1 & 15], and it also tells that she is seated upon the Beast's "seven heads" [17:9]. The ineluctable inference here is that the "many waters" and the "seven heads" symbolize the same object, in some sense.

To induce the reader into sleuthing for that sense, the angel gives a clue,

> "The waters…are peoples and multitudes and nations and languages." [Apoc. 17:15]

This statement alludes to what John wrote about the Beast,

> "…There was given to it authority upon every tribe and people and language and nation." [Apoc. 13:7]

This, in turn, alludes to what the Seer was told earlier,

> "It is necessary for you to prophesy again upon many peoples and nations and languages and kings." [Apoc. 10:11]

Finally, in turn, this alludes to the forepart of the second woe, where John introduced the symbolical number "four," i.e., the "four horns" of the "golden altar," the four angels bound at the Euphrates River, etc. [9:13-15]. Whereby, he began informing the reader that the second major part of the Father's plan would involve the whole world.

Three times [in 10:11 and 13:7 and 17:15] are four terms used in order to convey the symbolical numbers "three" and "four," respectively, whose sum is seven. In each instance, three of the four terms are the same, and thus did John constitute a little item called a formula. In Chapter 10, the formula expresses the general theme of the scroll, which John got from Saint Michael. However, the scroll is very small, and the scene of Chapter 10 comes just after Satan and his followers have been cast out of the Church. Those two facts modify the formula into a particular allusion to the "little/short time" [12:12], which will be the 42 months of the Beast's victorious reign, and, so, modify it into a particular allusion to the Beast [13:7].

As 9:12 was a psychological preparation for 11:14, so 10:11 and 13:7 will [hopefully] help the reader recognize the formula in 17:15 and thereby understand in what sense the "many waters" and the "seven heads" symbolize the same object. The numerical adjective "seven" in the term "seven heads" [17:9] symbolizes an indefinite number, and the adjective "many" in the term "many waters" [17:1] indicates that the indefinite number is large. Here, the meaning of the term "heads" is that of the term "waters", namely,

> "...peoples and multitudes and nations and languages" [Apoc. 17:15]

It is this meaning, and only this one meaning, which pertains to the seating of the woman. Ergo, <u>nota bene</u>: the woman is seated upon the "beast," in the sense of the thing, the global kingdom, or empire extant, not in the sense of the man, the king or emperor who rules the "seven heads"/"many waters." The angel again expresses, in 17:9, that the woman is seated only upon the empire extant. The relative clause that begins with "where" has been translated variously:

"on which the woman is seated" [NRSV];

"on which the woman sits" [NIV];

"whereon the woman sitteth" [WV];

"on which the woman sits enthroned" [NAB].

But, John recorded this,

"...ὅπου ἡ γυνὴ κάθηται ἐπ' αὐτῶν"
"...opon ë gynë kathëtai ep autön"

The fragment means,

"where the woman is seated upon them."

The text does not read that the woman "sits/sitteth," rather, that she "is seated," which preserves the idea of "passive voice" expressed in 17:3, wherein John used the perfect participle "καθημένην" [kathëmenën] to describe her as "seated upon a scarlet beast." That she is "seated" does, most certainly, not mean that she is "enthroned," even as a regent.

Note that each of the four versions quoted reduces the two terms, "where" and "upon them," to "on which/whereon." The translators fudged, and I suspect they fudged because they opined the term "upon them" redundant. I have said it a few times already, but I will say it again: God is not a dunce for redundancy. The word "where" relates to the term "seven mountains," and the phrase, "upon them," refers to "the seven heads." The sentence can be worded thus,

"The seven heads are seven mountains, where the woman is seated upon the seven heads." PERIOD.

Only after that "period" comes the brief statement: "They are also seven kings," i.e., the "seven heads" are also "seven kings." The angel was explicating to John that the term "heads" has two meanings: "mountains" and "kings"; and he, for a good reason, separated the statement about the "heads' being "kings," from the statement about their being "mountains": to avoid the ambiguity of whether the word "where" relates to "mountains," or to "kings," or to both. This becomes obvious if the two statements about "mountains" and "kings" are combined thus:

> "The seven heads are seven mountains and seven kings, where the woman is seated upon them."

The angel deliberately separated the two meanings of the symbol, "heads," into two sentences, so that the word "where" could grammatically refer to only one of the two meanings: the "seven mountains." The phrase, "upon them," is not a redundancy but an important differentiation from the word "where"; for "where" and "upon them" cannot both refer to the "seven mountains," nor can they both refer to the "seven heads," without effecting a redundancy. Had the term "heads" involved only one meaning, one definition, or usage, then, the angel would have worded the relative clause in 17:9, exactly as he worded the clause in 17:15, which reads thus,

> "where the harlot is seated,..."

There was no need to add "upon them."

Now, the angel uses 17:9-11 for a short lesson about the long history behind the Beast, a history that pertains to the Beast only, but excepting the seventh head, which represents the extant Beast, the one having the "seven heads and the ten horns." In this sense, that seventh part equals the whole, and the whole equals that seventh part; the seventh head on the Beast is the seven-headed Beast, and the seven-headed Beast is the seventh head. It is the whole seven-headed Beast, the one contemporary or extant, upon which the woman is seated; and the "seven mountains" are where she is seated upon those "seven heads" of the seven-headed Beast.

As will later be shown, the prophetic term "mountain" symbolizes a kingdom, especially, in the sense of an empire; and, so, for the nonce, I will simply say that a man cannot be a king unless he has a kingdom, and, therefore, it is the man, not the woman, who is king of the "mountain."

In regard to where the woman is seated, the term "seven mountains" has the same meaning as does the term "many waters," namely,

"peoples and multitudes and nations and languages";

and conspicuous by its absence from that formula is the term "kings." Ah, by indirection find direction out!

In Greek, capital letters [majuscules] are used:

(1) to indicate proper names,
(2) to begin direct quotations,
(3) to begin a long section in a literary work, such as, a chapter.

Hence, miniscules, not majuscules, are used at the beginnings of most words and sentences.

John adhered to Greek usage. Therefore, in order to differentiate between emperor and empire, I will indicate the former and the latter by using majuscule and minuscule, i.e., "Beast" and "beast," respectively, yet altering not by one dot or jot the Apocalyptic text.

It is the cause, that the weft of petty contradiction be unraveled: for, although, in the warp and woof of the human mind, it is possible for some people to fabricate pleasure out of pain, I am not one of them; and, so, I will not continue weaving through this commentary such phrasings as "the Beast, in the sense of the man," or, "the Beast, in the sense of the thing," lest a sensible man do a senseless thing. Frankly, I think such phrasings droll, as if uttered by a nitwit, and I have no intention of so keeping my mind, or that of my reader, in stitches.

The angel enclosed in Chapter 17 a terse description of the Beast's relationship to the "seven mountains"/"many waters," and thence to the woman, so that the matter would not be left open to speculation and opinion, which, in respect to the Scriptures, are disrespect to their author, the Amen.

So then, consider 17:7; specifically, the following three terms:

(1) "the beast."
(2) "the one carrying her."
(3) "the one having the seven heads and the ten horns."

Note that the angel nominalized the participles in terms (2) and (3) by using the definite article, so rendering them apposed to the first term, "the beast," and setting, so, those three in the emphatic form of mention. Hence, if the nominalized terms are substituted for "the beast," then, the sentence should not lose any of its meaning, thus:

"I will tell you the mystery of the woman and of the one carrying her the one having the seven heads and the ten horns."

Evidently, the angel referred to the scarlet beast mentioned in 17:3.

The crux of 17:7 is whether the term "the beast" signifies the emperor or signifies the empire extant; but, the problem is that, as regards Greek participles and the definite article, the form of the masculine genitive singular reads the same as that of the neuter genitive singular. To assert the neuter form, because of the neuter noun "τοῦ θηρίου" [tou thëriou, of the beast], would be myopic, for, in Chapters 11, 13, 16, 19, & 20, John used "τὸ θηρίον" [to thërion] to signify the man.

The second term contains the verb "βαστάζειν" [bastazein], meaning:

(1) to lift, lift up, raise.
(2) to carry, bear, support.
(3) to hold in one's hands.

The meaning of the term, "the one carrying her," is clear enough: "the beast" has raised her to pre-eminence and continuously supports her there, so that she is "the city the great one" [17:18], i.e., the wealthiest city in the world, as her description in 17:4-6 indicates. She is seated upon the "seven mountains"/ "many waters" by action of "the beast," not by means of herself alone.

At this point, it can be reasonably suspected, but not cogently argued, that the term "the beast" signifies the man, since it is quite implausible that so many "peoples and multitudes," etc., have acted in concert to exalt her to pre-eminence in wealth: that, rather, seems the doing of an emperor.

The first and second terms are finally clarified by the third: "[of] the one having the seven heads and the ten horns." The Beast, not the woman, is the one who has those heads and horns. They are his possessions; they belong to him.

That the angel meant the man and not the thing is evident for two reasons:

(1) Basically, in structure and, essentially, in content, the nominalized third term in 17:7 is the same as the participial phrase in 17:3, namely, "while he was having seven heads and ten horns."

(2) The use of the definite article in the third term of 17:7.

As for the first reason, I point out that the participle "ἔχων" [ekhön] in 17:3 is in the nominative masculine singular as subject, and that it conveys the active voice, governing the compound object, "seven heads and ten horns"; whereas, the perfect participle "καθημένην" [kathëmenën = seated], modifying the "woman," conveys the sense of the "passive voice." The idea of this contrast or difference between the woman [the city] and the man, as regards "the beast," is repeated in 17:7, but with a twist: the woman "seated" becomes shown as the woman "carried/supported." Indeed, 17:3 and 17:7 illuminate and elucidate each other.

As for the second reason, the use of the definite article makes the third term in 17:7 a direct, unambiguous allusion to the basically and essentially same participial phrase in 17:3, and, therefore, to the masculine singular of the governing participle. Textually speaking, the term "the beast" was first mentioned with the definite article in 11:7; but, chronologically speaking, the term "beast" is first mentioned without the definite article in 17:3, despite the fact that the term had been previously mentioned in Chapters 11, 13, & 16.

Chronologically, the definite article first appears with the term "beast" in 17:7, and, therefore, the nominalized third term in 17:7 can refer only to the participial phrase, "while he was having seven heads and ten horns," in 17:3. Hence, the term "the beast" in 17:7 signifies the emperor, not his empire.

The verb, "καθησθαι" [kathesthai: note the passive form], means, "to be seated," as a judge in a court, for example. This verb is derived from the noun "καθέδϱα" [kathedra], a seat or chair, whence came the Latin cathedra, the ancient Roman copy of the Greek klismos, which was used by women, and also used to designate the chair or seat of office or authority: hence the phrase, ex cathedra, meaning "from the chair," i.e., "from the seat of authority" or "with authority."

Now, the text clearly tells that the woman is seated upon the "seven mountains"/"many waters," which means that she exercises authority upon them; and, in this regard, it may be said that she is seated immediately or directly upon them. But, authority comes by power: no power, no authority. The text also tells that the Beast is the one carrying her, which means that she does not seat herself upon the "many waters," but is seated there by power of the Beast, because he, not she, is the one having the "seven heads and ten horns"; and, in that regard, it may be said that she is seated mediately or indirectly upon them.

The principal point of 17:9 cannot be overemphasized: the woman is seated upon the empire extant, but neither upon its emperor nor upon the many kings under him. That is why the term "kings" is absent from the formula in 17:15.

In contrast to this, 17:18 states,

> "the woman…is the city the great one the one having dominion upon the kings of the earth."

So, the woman herself has power. She rules that territory designated as "the earth," and the Beast rules those territories designated as "the many waters." When the Beast ascends from the abyss, he will rule also "the earth" through his regent, the False Prophet; and, thus, he will become the supreme head of both the "earth" and "many waters," which term includes the "sea."

When the Beast has reunited "the earth" and "the sea," and has re-enthroned paganism thereto, he will, then, have healed "the blow of the death," [13:3] that "blow of the sword" [13:14], which Christ and his Church inflicted on the sixth historical head: the ancient Roman Empire. And, all those who are not in the "kingdom of the heaven" will marvel after the Beast.

Chapter 10

—

The Description of the Great Harlot

John recorded,

> 4 and the woman was clothed of purple and scarlet <u>and</u> adorned with gold and precious stone and pearls, <u>holding</u> in her hand a gold cup full of abominations and the impurities of her fornication 5 and upon her forehead [was] a name written,
>
> MYSTERY,
> BABYLON THE GREAT,
> THE MOTHER OF THE HARLOTS
> AND OF THE ABOMINATIONS OF THE EARTH.
>
> 6 and I saw the woman drunken with the blood of the holy ones and with the blood of the witnesses of Jesus. And seeing her, I wondered great wonder. [Apoc. 17:4-6]

The woman's name is obviously too long to have been written in a single line across her forehead, unless her head was shaped like that of a hammerhead shark. Therefore, as John's use of two commas suggested, I stacked the three titles in her name, according to descendent order of power and authority; but, I kept the two commas to remind the reader of how John used them, as in 1:5.

Note the nominative participle "ἔχουσα" [holding] in 17:4, then relate it to the nominalized participle "ἔχουσα" in 17:18; only in those two instances is the woman described in terms of the active voice. Now, juxtapose that pair with the nominative participle and the second nominalized participle referring to the Beast in 17:3 and 17:7 respectively. This parallelism of the two pairs of participles is additional corroboration of all that has been said, so far, about the woman and the Beast, as regards who rules what. The Apocalypse was written in fourth-grade grammar and vocabulary, but simplicity does not necessarily exclude subtlety.

The woman is adorned in proofs of her greatness:

(1) "Gold" is for royalty, and it signifies her power to command the commerce of the world;
(2) The "precious stone" [jewelry] and "pearls" are possessions of the rich; and
(3) The "jewels" are obtained from the earth, and "pearls" from the sea.

Unlike the "woman" in Chapter 12, who is clothed with heavenly simplicity; unlike the Two Witnesses in Chapter 11, who are austerely clothed with sackcloth; the Great Harlot is clothed with purple and scarlet. The color "purple," like the metal, gold, indicates her royal status; the color "scarlet," however, symbolizes serious sinfulness, as it is written [Is. 1:18]

Though your sins be as scarlet,
they may become white as snow;
Though they be crimson red,
they may become white as wool.

The woman, obviously, is not as pure as the driven snow, but of the sundry sins she commits John specifies only what is surely her worst: that she…

"…is drunken with the blood of the holy ones and with the blood of the ones witnessing of Jesus." [Apoc. 17:6]

The color "scarlet," then, alludes to the blood of the saints and the witnesses of Jesus, i.e., those in the "kingdom of the heaven" as a spiritual condition or state, and those in it as both a spiritual condition or state, and a visible organization. The color "scarlet" also alludes to the "beast."

So, the color "purple" signifies that she is "...the one having dominion upon the kings of the earth"; the color "scarlet" signifies that she is "...seated upon a scarlet beast." It is irrelevant whether the woman is wearing two articles of clothing, one purple and the other scarlet, or whether she is wearing only one article of clothing with the two colors; for there remains the fact that both colors are joined together regarding her, so that her status and wealth, in part, at least, are not separate from the blood of the saints.

Her two relationships, signified by "precious stone and pearls" and by "purple and scarlet," are connoted a third time in the latter half of verse 4:

(1) The term "abominations" relates to "the earth," as the third title in her name indicates.
(2) The term "the impurities of her fornication" relates to the "many waters," but, especially, to the Beast himself, as the second title in her name indicates [a matter I will explicate later].

The question, now, is whether the woman is directly responsible for the blood of the saints, in the sense that she is conducting a general, bloody persecution in her own domain, or whether she is indirectly responsible because she abets the Beast/beast. Bear in mind that the whole Beast/beast is "solid scarlet," and this signifies that he is persecuting God's own throughout the "many waters."

The answer waits about thirteen inches in front of the reader's eyes: verse 4 contains three instances of coupled terms, namely, "purple" and "scarlet," "stone" and "pearls," "abominations" and "impurities of fornication"; and this fact evidences that John knowingly emphasized the woman's relationships.

Hence, that she is "clothed of...scarlet" serves primarily to indicate her relationship to the "beast," and thereby serves secondarily to indicate her relationship to the blood of the saints; to wit, she is indirectly but, nonetheless, actually responsible for their blood, because she abets the Beast/beast by doing business mutually remunerative. In the kingdom of this world, money is the first power; and the woman and the Beast do not mind that it comes with sums of blood on it.

To some, it may seem that the idea of the three couplets, each indicial of the woman's two relationships, is an opinion imposed upon the text, because, for example, it is obvious that there are three adornments, not two. Remember, however, that the Great Harlot is the composite symbol of a city, and that, therefore, the components of her description are symbolical. Also, it has a few times been shown that the very order of mention for terms conveys additional meaning; and terms are, of course, to be understood according to context.

Now, as was noted in Chapter 10, "clothing" is the symbol for power. In John's day, the color "purple" was for royalty. Hence, the purple part of the woman's clothing, in the context of Chapter 17, can signify only one fact: that she has "...dominion upon the kings of the earth." By logical consistency, then, the scarlet part of her clothing means that the Beast rules the "many waters" and the kings therein. The "two colors," therefore, signify the Great Harlot's two relationships concerning political power.

Having indicated that, John next described her financial and commercial power. It is obvious that the woman can, in reality, obtain jewels from the "many waters" and pearls from the "earth." Thus, the terms "precious stone" and "pearls" serve to signify the woman's relationships to the "earth" and the "many waters," respectively. The term "gold," however, refers to both the "earth" and the "many waters"; indeed, the terms "precious stone" and "pearls" elucidate and define the significance of the term "gold": her power of the finances and commerce of both the "earth" and the "many waters." Thus, the term "gold" represents her royal status in the economic sense, not the political.

The three terms, "gold and precious stone and pearls," are adornments; and this fact signifies that the woman spends her wealth, mainly, for luxurious living, as 18:11-14 makes perfectly clear. The Great Harlot is a hedonist; her political and economic powers are two means to one end: carnal pleasure.

Finally, John described the woman's activities: the "abominations" are sins that she alone commits, and the "impurities of her fornication" are sins she commits with the Beast/beast, the former having long since become conducive to the latter. Hence, her "abominations" and "impurities of her fornication" are together in the "gold cup" she is holding.

So then, John's description of the woman contains three major parts: her clothing, adornments, and activities. The term "was clothed" comprises "purple and scarlet," which make a couplet. The term "was adorned" comprises "gold and precious stone and pearls," but the term "gold," in turn, comprises "precious stone and pearls," which make a couplet. The term "[while she was] holding" comprises the "gold cup," but the "gold cup," in turn, comprises "abominations and the impurities of her fornication," which make a couplet.

Note the order of mention in each couplet: the woman has priority over the Beast [who, being not a gentleman, naturally has a different idea of proper priority]. Hence, the first couplet of "purple and scarlet" subsumes the two subsequent: the "gold" by which she obtains every kind of thing for her pleasure, and the "gold cup" full of those activities by which she obtains the gold. It is tacit that the Great Harlot drinks the blood of the saints from the "gold cup."

The description of the woman has also these two major aspects: the terms, "clothed" and "adorned," express the passive voice, whereas the term "holding" expresses the active voice. This differentiation between passive and active is a subtle allusion to the first title in the woman's name: MYSTERY. John did not mean "the mystery of lawlessness," but "the mystery of the God" [10:7], Jesus Christ; for, supremely speaking, it is through Him that power and authority are given to her [and to the Beast], but she, and only she, freely wills to perform her sinful activities. That is why John connected "clothed" and "adorned" with the word kai, but separated "holding" from them, with a comma [refer, for example, to 1:4-5 and 12:1].

It is Christ who gave John the vision, and it is Christ who gave the woman her name. "To give a name" is a Biblical idiom meaning, "to have dominion over," and the Apocalypse is pellucid about who is the King of kings and Lord of lords.

So, the point has come to begin explaining the woman's name.

Chapter 11

The Woman's Name

Whereas, Seneca mentioned that prostitutes in the city of Rome wore their names on their foreheads ["Contro. V, i"], St. Peter referred to Rome as Babylon

> 13 The church that is in Babylon, elected together with you, saluteth you: and so doth my son Mark. [1 Pt. 5:13],

and the Apocalypse tells that the Great Harlot is seated upon "seven mountains" [17:9], many people have concluded that Rome will become Babylon the Great.

As for the first point, it does not exclude the possibility that prostitutes elsewhere did likewise. As for the second point, it cannot be demonstrated that Peter had [knowledge of] the Babylon of the Apocalypse in mind [John himself was amazed at the woman]. As for the third point, it is irrelevant; indeed, to use it in arguing for Rome as Babylon the Great would be an egregious error, one indicative of inattention to the words of the Amen: for the city is located in the region termed "the earth," not in any of the regions termed the "seven mountains," i.e., the "many waters." In brief, the "seven mountains" have nothing to do with the geographical location of the Great Harlot.

On the other hand, Rome stands within the region termed "the earth," and, for that fact, the city must be kept in the question. So, having shown, up front, the irrelevance of the three points aforestated, I have prevented their nagging the examination of the three titles in the woman's name. The angel said to John:

> "I will tell you the mystery of the woman and of the beast." [Apoc. 17:7]

The terms, "woman" and "beast," are in the genitive case and, thus, modify or define "mystery." This is to say that the single term "mystery" comprises immediately both the woman and the Beast, rendering them particular, concrete examples of "the mystery." Since the woman and the Beast come under the rubric of lawlessness, the term "mystery," in this case, connotes "the mystery of lawlessness," the same that St. Paul mentioned;

> 7 For the mystery of iniquity [lawlessness] already worketh; only that he who now holdeth, do hold, until he be taken out of the way. [2 Thes. 2:7].

The term, then, is an abbreviation, just as "the heaven" is an abbreviation for "the kingdom of the heaven." A "mystery" is a person or thing not yet revealed, either in part or in entirety, especially because the person or thing has not fully "come into existence" [see 1:19 and 4:1]. Note that the angel tells many things about the woman and the Beast, but he does not tell their real names. Those names will remain a mystery until the political and economic state of affairs in Chapter 17 comes into existence.

Now, it has already been shown that the Beast, politically speaking, rules the "seven mountains," and that the woman, economically speaking, is "seated" upon them; hence, the symbolical number "seven" pertains to both the woman and the Beast. The number "seven" here indicates not only indefinite number, but also the final phase of the second major part of the Father's mysterious plan, even as the number "seven" does in "the seven thunders" of Chapter 10.

Bear in mind that the Beast of Chapter 17 is "about to ascend from the abyss" [17:8]; and, so, it is the time when the sequence of events in Chapter 12 will happen; and at the end of that sequence is the time when the scene of Chapter 10 will take place, wherein Saint Michael swears by the One Living unto the ages of the ages, Jesus Christ, that

> "...in the days of the seventh angel, when he is about to trumpet, also will be fulfilled the mystery of the God, as announced to his own servants the prophets." [Apoc. 10:7]

Clearly, the term "mystery" in 17:7 immediately connotes and emphasizes "the mystery of lawlessness"; however, since it also comprises the symbolical number "seven," pertinent to the woman and the Beast, it indirectly refers to "the mystery of the God." The question now is whether the signification of the term "mystery" in 17:5 is the same as that in 17:7.

The woman rules merely the "earth," whereas the Beast rules the "many waters"; and, thus, he is the greater in political power. The woman, however, commands the commerce of both the "earth" and the "many waters"; and, thus, she is the greater in economic power. This [temporary] state of affairs is symbolized by her being seated upon the "beast."

Her economic superiority is indicated also by the order of mention throughout the chapter:

(1) The first half of the chapter is mostly a description of the woman, and the second half mostly of the "beast" and, then, of the Ten Kings.
(2) In each of the three couplets in 17:4, the term concerning the woman's relationship to the "earth" comes first.
(3) In the phrase, "the mystery of the woman and of the beast," the woman comes first.

John used order of mention elsewhere to convey the idea of "a scale of power and authority." Take, for example, the phrase,

> "out of the mouth of the dragon and [καὶ] of the beast and [καὶ] of the pseudoprophet" [16:13]

The Dragon, or Satan, is superior to the Beast, and the Beast is superior to the False Prophet. But, note the use of the connective "καὶ" [and], just like that in the phrase, "of the woman and of the beast" [17:7]: it conveys the idea of "equality or sameness" because the terms belong to a certain kind or category.

Indeed, IF John had written somewhere the phrase, “the mystery of the dragon and of the beast and of the pseudoprophet,” his meaning would have been as clear as it is in the phrase, “the mystery of the woman and of the beast.”

For another example of kai, take the phrase:

> “from the one who is and was and is coming and from the seven spirits the ones in the presence of the throne of him and from Jesus Christ” [Apoc. 1:4-5]

In this instance, the order of mention does not convey a scale of power, because the Three Persons are in the same divine nature; and, to express their co-equality, John used the word “kai.” Note the relative clause [in the Greek, three nominalized participles: “from the existing one and the was-existing one and the is-coming one,” in literal translation.],

“from the one who is and was and is coming”

The clause expresses the fact that the present and the past and the future are equally known by the eternal Father AS WELL AS the Holy Spirit and the Son, i.e., by the God who creates them in one and the same act.

So, the woman’s name will be analyzed according to such considerations as:

(1) her greatness by economic power.
(2) the order in which her titles are mentioned.
(3) the absence of the word “καὶ” [and] in her name.

The three titles are not connected by two ands; instead, they are separated by two commas. As was stated earlier, the comma is used for indicating divisions in a sentence, for separating items in a list, and for separating types or levels of information.

Take, for example, the following excerpt:

> “a woman clothed of the sun, and the moon under her feet and upon her head a crown of twelve stars” [Apoc. 12:1]

Note the comma after the word "sun." It separates the one kind of power from the two kinds of authority. Note the and after the word "feet": it connects the two kinds of authority.

Finally, note the and after the comma: it connects the one kind of power and the two kinds of authority. Anyone who has power also has authority, but anyone, who has authority, does not necessarily also have the power that sustains the authority; and, therefore, John mentioned power first, authority second. In fact, the and after the comma may be translated as "with" or "also." The question, then, is whether the woman's name of three titles indicates a scale of power. To answer it, I will yet again leap into the middle of things.

The second title, BABYLON THE GREAT, is an unmistakable, direct reference to that city of the same name, which stood beside the Euphrates twenty-six centuries ago. As the Babylon of the past was the center of finance and commerce in the Babylonian Empire, so will the Babylon of the future be in the Beast's empire; and, as the former persecuted Israel, so the latter will persecute the Church.

Bear in mind that the four-part formula in 17:15, namely, "peoples and multitudes and nations and languages," not only pertains to the woman and the Beast/beast, but also alludes all the way back to "the four angels the ones bound at the river the great Euphrates." [9:14]

Now, ancient Babylon stood beside the Euphrates, which flows through the Middle East; the Middle East is part of that quondam Roman territory designated as "the sea"; the "sea" is part of the "many waters"; and both the "many waters" and the "seven mountains" mean the same thing,

"peoples and multitudes and nations and languages."

Since it has already been shown that the "seven mountains" have nothing to do with the woman's geographical location, it logically follows that the formula in 17:15 does not allude to it, either. Therefore, the second title, BABYLON THE GREAT, though it refers directly to the ancient Babylon, does not allude to that ancient city's location. Hence, the second title in the woman's name can signify only one thing: her economic relationship to the Beast/beast.

Aye, the four-part formula and the second title, taken together, strongly suggest that the woman's relationship to the "beast" goes as far back as the beginning of the second woe, which, in turn, suggests that she and he participated in fomenting the event of the 200 Million Horsemen.

In any case, the principal point here is that the Babylon of the past is a prefigurement of the Babylon of the future; and, in the Old Testament prophecies, against the former can be found many passages relating to the latter, for so the mighty angel Michael swore,

> "...also will be fulfilled the mystery of the God, AS ANNOUNCED TO HIS OWN SERVANTS THE PROPHETS." [Apoc. 10:7]

So then, the second title signifies the woman's economic relationship to the "beast," and that relationship accounts for the greater part of her total power.

The third title,

THE MOTHER OF THE HARLOTS AND OF
THE ABOMINATIONS OF THE EARTH

signifies the woman's political and economic relationship to the "earth." Note the noun "earth" in the genitive case at the end of the title; it modifies the terms, "the harlots" and "the abominations," so that the title may be understood thus,

> "the mother of the earth's harlots and of the earth's abominations."

The term "the harlots" refers to the "kings" in 17:18, and the term "the abominations" refers to the "abominations" in 17:4, but <u>not</u> to "the impurities of her fornication" with the "beast." Therefore, the third title signifies only the woman's relationship to the "earth," and that relationship accounts for the lesser part of her total power.

It is now evident that the second title to the third is as greater to lesser in power, to wit, their order of mention indicates a descendent scale of power and authority. The second and third titles have the same theme: worldly power.

John could have placed a "καὶ" [and] between them without changing their order of mention, and, thus, without losing the descendent scale of power; yet, he chose to put a comma. In each of the three couplets in 17:4, the term concerning the woman's relationship to the "earth" came before that to the "beast"; here, in 17:5, it comes after. This is to say, the two titles' order of mention is the reverse of each couplet's order of mention, which can be indicated thus:

from "earth" + "many waters" to "many waters" – "earth,"
from "καὶ" [and] to comma,
from connection to separation.

Since the word "and" between the second and third titles would not have nullified their descendent scale of power, the second comma is, therefore, a repetition emphasizing the function of the first comma: to separate the titles, and most especially, to separate the first from the second and the third, so that the term "mystery" in 17:5 cannot, grammatically speaking, comprise them, as it does the woman and the Beast in 17:7. Hence, the first title does not have the same, exact signification of the term "mystery" in 17:7; rather, it is an abbreviation for, and, primarily, a direct reference to, "the mystery of the God," Jesus Christ.

The three titles in the woman's name correspond to the three divisions in the ancient cosmogony: the heaven, the sea, and the earth. As pointed out earlier, these can be reduced to two: the heaven above, the sea and the earth below. But, John did not reduce them so. The second comma, therefore, together with order of mention, makes it perfectly clear that the woman's name is to be understood as a descendent scale of power and authority. Christ, not the woman [or the Beast], is the Supreme Power; he, and no other, is King of kings and Lord of lords, as St. Paul wrote of him,

> "He is [the] image of the invisible God, [the] firstborn of all creation; for in him were created all the things in the heavens and upon the earth, the things visible and the things invisible, whether thrones or dominions or rulers or powers: all things are created through him and unto him: he himself is before all things, and in him all things hold together." [Col. 1:15-17]

Christ is the one having dominion upon the woman: it is he who gave the name to her, he who wrote the name UPON HER FORHEAD. Since the woman's name is appropriate to her, and since she comes under the rubric, "the mystery of lawlessness," it follows that her first title, MYSTERY, is secondarily an indirect reference to the "mystery of lawlessness." This apparently opposes what has just been shown previously. Since the three titles constitute a descendent scale of power, and since "the heaven" is the power above the "sea" and the "earth," it follows that her first title is, primarily, a direct reference to the "mystery of the God."

This is to say: in 17:5, the woman is under the rubric, "the mystery of the God," and, in 17:7, she is under the rubric, "the mystery of lawlessness." The text is pellucid of the point that she comes under BOTH MYSTERIES. Since reason, even illumined by faith, cannot here intuit why both "mysteries" are appropriate to her, it must resume its discursive analysis. The picnic is not over yet. By indirection find direction out!

The second title, "BABYLON THE GREAT," is a direct, explicit reference to the ancient city of Babylon, but not to the "beast." In order to show that the second title signifies the woman's relationship to the "beast," one must first demonstrate that the "many waters" [which term includes "the sea"] and the four-part formula and the "seven mountains" [extant] have the same meaning.

The second title expresses and emphasizes a specific aspect of the woman: that she is the wealthiest city in the world, the center of finance and commerce, just as Babylon was in its ancient day. Hence, the second title pertains only to the woman; it makes no direct reference to, no explicit mention of, the "beast." Indeed, it induces the reader to restrict perception to her, so that the "beast" is excluded. In the third title,

THE MOTHER OF THE HARLOTS AND OF
THE ABOMINATIONS OF THE EARTH,

the term "the abominations" refers to "abominations" in the third couplet. Note that, in the third couplet, the term "abominations" is connected by an and to the term, "the impurities of her fornication" [both are together in the gold cup], but, in the third title, the former is separated from the latter by simply not mentioning the latter. Hence, the wordage of the third title restricts the reader's perception to a specific aspect of the woman, and excludes any direct, explicit mention of the "beast," or her relationship thereto.

Neither the second title nor the third denies the fact of the woman's relationship to the "beast"; rather, the two titles, taken together, constitute a very subtle instruction to the reader: that the first title, likewise, pertains only to the woman, that it is appropriate only to her and not to the "beast."

So, the "mystery of lawlessness" pertains to both her and the "beast," yet the "mystery of the God" pertains only to her and not to the "beast"; the name of Christ is upon her forehead, yet not in the sense of a "Thau." There is only one way that this can be a fact: the woman bears the indelible mark of baptism upon her soul, but she has apostatized from her Lord. The bride has abandoned her bridegroom or husband; and, therefore, spiritually speaking, the term "harlot" is to be understood as "adulteress." The Beast is fell, but the woman is fallen.

So, the term "the earth" in Chapter 17 is actually a pun: it designates the spiritual condition or state of lawlessness into which the woman has fallen down from "the heaven"; and it designates, as it has done since Chapter 5, the European part of the ancient Roman Empire. The evidence, the objective evidence, compels the conclusion that a Roman Catholic city will sometime become Babylon the Great.

Some announcements that God's own servants, the prophets, made against ancient Babylon will be fulfilled in the days of the Apocalyptic Babylon. This imports that the reader must reason in fine manner through those prophecies, so as to discern what passages pertain not only to which city but also to which emperor or empire, and what to both. Success in this undertaking requires a modicum of historical knowledge about Babylon.

For now, I will juxtapose excerpts from the Apocalypse and from the Old Testament, which excerpts will aid toward a more adequate understanding of the text, noteworthily, the woman's name and her gold cup.

	APOCALYPSE		THE OLD TESTAMENT
A.	Fallen, fallen is Babylon the Great! [Apoc. 18:2]	A.	The wall of Babylon falls!
B.	Come out of her, my people, so that you do not take part in her sins, and so you do not share in her plagues. [Apoc. 18:4]	B1.	Leave her, my people; let each one save himself from the burning wrath of the Lord. [Jer. 51:44-45]
		B2.	Flee out of Babylon, let each one save his life, perish not for her guilt. [Jer. 51:6]
C.	And the kings of the earth… will weep and wail over her when they see the smoke of her burning…[Apoc. 18:9]	C.	Babylon suddenly falls and is crushed: howl over her! [Jer. 51:8]
D.	For her sins are heaped as high as heaven… [Apoc. 18:5]	D.	Her judgment reaches heaven, it touches the clouds. [Jer. 51:9]
E.	It has become a dwelling place of demons, a haunt of every foul spirit, a haunt of every foul bird, a haunt of every foul and hateful beast. [Apoc. 18:2]	E.	Babylon shall become a heap of ruins, a haunt of jackals, a place of horror and ridicule where no one lives. [Jer. 51:37]
Fl.	The woman…holding in her hand a gold cup full of abominations and the impurities of her fornication… [Apoc. 17:4]	F.	Babylon was a golden cup in the hand of the Lord which made the whole earth drunk; the nations drank its wine, and with this they have become mad. [Jer. 51:7]
F2.	For all the nations have drunk of the wine of the wrath [great madness or anger] of her fornication…[Apoc. 18:3]		

	APOCALYPSE		THE OLD TESTAMENT
G.	Since in her heart she says, "I rule as queen, and I am no widow, and I will never see grief," therefore her plagues will come in a single day...and she will be burned with fire; for mighty is the Lord who judges her. [Apoc. 18:7-8]	G.	Hear now this, voluptuous one, enthroned securely, saying to yourself, "I, and no other! I shall never be a widow, or suffer the loss of my children"—Both these things shall come to you in a single day... [Is. 47:8-9]
H.	Then the angel raised his right hand unto the heaven and swore by the One Living unto the ages of the ages, who created the heaven and the things in it and the earth and the things in it and the sea and the things in it...[Apoc. 10:6]	H.	The Lord of hosts has sworn by himself...sworn has he who made the earth by his power, and established the world by his wisdom, and stretched out the heaven by his skill...He is the creator of all things... [Jer: 51:14-19]

Some people think that the Great Harlot's "gold cup" with blood in it suggests the kind used for libations in idolatrous rituals, through which the votaries of paganism honored the gods and communicated with demons. In support of this view, they adduce the noun "βδέλυγμα" [bdelygma], which basically means a loathsome thing, an abomination, and, therefore, was used generally to denote any sinful activity, but, especially, to signify an IDOL.

They proffer a valid view, if they hold it prospectively toward the forty-two months of Chapter 13, at the beginning of which time the False Prophet will seduce the inhabitants of "the earth" into worshipping the icon of the Beast. They do not have a valid view, if they hold it toward the time of Chapter 17.

Relate hereto the fact that bloody persecution is being waged throughout those regions designated as the "many waters," where non-Christians are the large majority and Roman Catholics a very small minority [this statement implies the assumption that statistics stable for the past 1,300 years will continue so for the next 100 or 200 years].

It logically follows that most of the blood in the Great Harlot's cup has come from non-Christian peoples, those of whom Christ said,

> "I have other sheep that are not from this fold: I must bring them and they will listen to my voice, and there will be one flock, one shepherd." [Jn. 10:15-16]

It is, therefore, fitting and proper that John put the blood of the non-Catholic "holy ones" <u>first</u> in the order of mention in 17:6; and this corroborates what has been said about the fact that the <u>whole</u> beast is <u>scarlet</u>, the beast that will comprise many, if not all, of "the nations" in Asia and Africa.

Every serious sin, at bottom, is an act of idolatry; and, thus, tacit to the passage of 17:4-6 is Christ's adage, "As you sow, so shall you reap." Europe is the region designated as "the earth" in Chapter 17, and open idolatry and bloody persecution will come to it immediately after the Beast appoints the False Prophet as his regent thereof.

It has been shown that the Great Harlot's name is a scale of power and authority, and highest in that scale is the "mystery of the God," the Lord Jesus Christ. Then, it is Christ who has dominion upon the woman; it is he who gave her the financial and commercial power symbolized by the "gold cup." Bearing these things in mind, it may be said that, although the Great Harlot is "holding a gold cup in her hand" [Apoc. 17:4], she is actually "a gold cup in the hand of the Lord" [Jer. 51:7]. Hence, what Christ said about himself to Pontius Pilate is what Christ's holy ones can say to the Great Harlot and the Beast,

> "You would not have power upon me if it were not, given to you from above." [Jn. 19:11]

But, there is more. Recall from 17:7 the verb "βαστάζειν" [bastazein], which means:

(1) to lift, lift up, raise;
(2) to carry, bear, support;
(3) to hold in one's hand(s).

This is the same verb used in Luke 14:27, which reads,

> "Whoever does not carry his own cross and come after me cannot be my disciple."

The message of 17:4-6 is clear: As Christ was lifted up in bloody sacrifice by his enemies, so will his holy ones be offered up by the woman and the Beast; for the saints complete

> "...what is lacking in Christ's afflictions for the sake of his body, which is the Church." [Col.1:24]

The Amen has promised that there will be one flock, one shepherd; he has forewarned his followers of how "the words of the God shall be fulfilled." [Apoc. 17:17], for

> "Indeed, the Lord God does nothing without revealing his plan to his servants, the prophets." [Am. 3:7]

It is left to the reader to profit from what the prophets have written, to know beforehand what the cost of that one flock will be, and so to make prudent preparation. As one sows, so shall one reap.

I have written enough, ye Friends, to help you toward an adequate understanding of the Great Harlot. Judge for yourselves, most rigorously, what I have written! Now to the man who would be King of kings, the one whom the Apostle called the Beast.

CHAPTER 12

THE "BEAST"

Consider the "angel's" description of the "beast":

> 8 The beast which you saw was and is not and is about to ascend from the abyss and unto annihilation is going, And they will be marveling—the ones dwelling upon the earth, of whom was not written the name upon the scroll of the life from foundation of world—when they see the beast because it was and is not and is to come. 9 Thus [is] the mind the one having wisdom. The seven heads are seven mountains, where the woman is seated upon them. They are also seven kings: 10 the five fell, the one is, the other did not yet come, and when he comes it is necessary for him to remain a little while. 11 and the beast which was and is not is himself also eighth and is from the seven, and unto annihilation is going.

The following excerpts, taken from the writings of God's "own servants the prophets," give the signification of the symbolical term "mountain":

> Then he [the angel] said to me, "This is the Lord's message to Zerubbabel: Not by an army, nor by might, but by my spirit, says the Lord of hosts. What are you, O great mountain? Before Zerubbabel you are but a plain." [Zech. 4:6-7]

> I will help you, says the Lord; your redeemer is the Holy One of Israel. I will make of you a threshing sledge, sharp, new and double-edged, to thresh the mountains and crush them, to make the hills like chaff. [Is. 41:14-15]

> While you [Nebuchadnezzar] looked at the statue, a stone which was hewn from a mountain without a hand's being put to it, struck its iron and tile feet, breaking them in pieces. The iron, tile, bronze, silver, and gold all crumbled at once, fine as the chaff on the threshing floor in summer, and the wind blew them away without leaving a trace. But the stone that struck the statue became a great mountain and filled the whole earth…The God of heaven will set up a kingdom that shall never be destroyed or delivered up to another people; rather, it shall break in pieces all these kingdoms and put an end to them, and it shall stand forever. That is the meaning of the stone you saw hewn from the mountain without a hand's being put to it, which broke in pieces the tile, iron, bronze, silver, and gold.
> [Dn. 2:34-35 & 44-45]

> Behold! I come against you, destroying mountain, destroyer of the entire earth, says the Lord; I will stretch forth my hand against you, roll you down over the cliffs, and make you a burnt mountain.
> [Jer. 51:25]

In the excerpts from Zechariah and Jeremiah, the Lord addresses Babylon as "mountain." In Jeremiah, the term, "burnt mountain," according to the context, may be understood as "destroyed mountain"; and the term, "destroying mountain" may be understood as "burning mountain."

This "burning mountain," which arose in the Middle East, is a subtle allusion to the "great mountain burning with fire" in Apocalypse 8:8, the one which was "cast out [meaning, "cast out from the heaven"] unto the sea"; and that "sea" is the one from which the "beast" will arise in the future, the same "sea" that was once territory of the Roman empire, namely, the regions of North Africa and the Middle East. For this reason, the color of the seven-headed dragon in Chapter 12 should be translated not as "red," but as "flame-colored" or “fire-colored”; for the “dragon” symbolizes not only the ruler of this world, but also his kingdom, which will be the culmination of the “burning mountain” in Chapter 8.

Please note and remember the underlined parts in the excerpts from Isaiah and Daniel, because they allude ultimately to the “harvest” during the third woe, especially, that of Armageddon on the day of the Lord, the great and terrible day. The main point here is that the term “mountain” symbolizes a kingdom, either the eventually universal kingdom of the God, or a pagan multinational kingdom, which, in English, is called an empire. Having respectfully ascertained the Amen’s signification of the symbolical term “mountain,” I proceed to the description of the “beast.”

The angel begins by saying to John, “The beast that you saw…”; later, in 17:18, he says about the Great Harlot, “the woman whom you saw…” In this way, the reader is informed that the beast and the woman have vanished from the vision, and only the angel remains. Such is not new. In 1:11, Christ told John,

“Write onto a scroll what you are seeing…”

Then, in 1:19, he said,

> “Now write the things that you saw [aorist] and the things that are and the things that are about to come into existence.” [This statement indicates the format of the Apocalypse.]

In 1:20, the very next verse, Jesus clarified the meaning of the phrase, “the things that you saw,” by saying,

> “The mystery of the seven stars that you saw [aorist]…and the seven lampstands the gold ones…”

In other words, the “seven stars” and the “seven lampstands the gold ones” had vanished from the vision, and only Christ remained. So, after John had adequately scrutinized the woman and the beast [and probably written notes], the angel removed them from the vision, so that the Seer could concentrate fully on what the angel would subsequently say.

The term "θηρίον" [thërion], strictly speaking, means "little beast," for it is the diminutive of "θήρ" [thër], but was, in ancient usage, equivalent to it. It is not accidental that the strict meaning of the diminutive agrees with the term "little horn" in Daniel 7. Thus, by the similitude of diminutive terms for protagonist and antagonist, namely, the "Little Lamb" and the "little Beast/ little horn," the text emphasizes their dissimilitude or opposition; indeed, this commentary will show that the "little Beast/little horn" is the Antichrist. It has already been pointed out that the term "θηρίον" [thërion], i.e., "little beast," although of neuter gender, is used for denoting either the emperor or his empire; and the reader must keep this in mind.

In verse 8, the angel tells John that the beast "unto annihilation is going," thereby alluding to one of Satan's names in 9:11. To say that the beast "is going" is to connote the fundamental fact that the beast "is existing," to wit, that the beast IS; and, yet, the angel patently states that the beast "is not," i.e., that he/it "is not existing." However, he also tells John that the beast…

> "was and is not and is to come [literally, it will arrive, will become present]." [Apoc. 12:11]

The angel did not say that the beast simultaneously "was and was not," nor did he say that the beast simultaneously "would come and would not come."

Hence, to understand when the beast can be described as simply "is" or "is existing," one must understand when the beast simply "was" or "was existing," or when the beast simply "will be" or "will be existing"; and, thus, one will be able to understand the angel's definition of the term "beast," and why he says in verse 8 that the beast simultaneously "is and is not." The angel wastes neither time nor words: he immediately begins the brief history lesson about the beast, verses 9-11.

In order for the angel to speak about the beast as simply "is" or "is existing," without contradicting or canceling his statement in verse 8 that he/it simultaneously "is and is not," the angel must shift the temporal point of reference from the time of the vision to the time of John; and, so, he says about the kings [and their kingdoms, bear in mind] in verse 10,

> "The five fell [aorist], THE ONE IS, the other did not yet come [aorist], and when he comes it is necessary for him to remain a little while."

The clause, "the one is," meaning the king/kingdom in John's day, can denote only the Roman Empire. The fallen five in historical order were: the Egyptian, the Assyrian, the Babylonian, the Medo-Persian, and the Greek empires; and the first five heads on the beast represent them. The sixth head is the Roman Empire, and the "seventh head" represents the whole seventh beast, i.e., the beast in the vision of Chapter 17, but only in the sense of "when he comes" [verse 10].

The first six beasts had one thing in common: each afflicted all or almost all the members of God's visible organization. That organization in the Old Testament was Israel, and in the New Testament was and is and will be the Church, the Roman Catholic Church, for it is the only church whose history can be traced back to the first Pentecost.

The "little while" in verse 10 is the same "little while" or "short time" mentioned in 12:12, the 42 months, which will be the last 3½ years of the second woe.

Hence, what the angel is saying about the "other," the seventh beast, in effect is this: the beast in Chapter 17 will become and then remain a beast for the 42 months, i.e., simply "will be/will be existing" as a beast; and this implies that the seventh beast will afflict God's visible organization on a great scale during those 3½ years.

There stands the difference between the beast in Chapter 17 and the same later [chronologically] in Chapter 13: the beast in Chapter 17 is NOT YET afflicting the Church on a great scale, but, in Chapter 13, he will, because, at that time, he will have the Roman Catholic nations in the "earth" under his rule, and, through the financial and commercial power of Babylon the Great, he will impose his policies upon the Catholic nations in South America.

A "beast," then, in the full sense of the prophetic term, is a king who uses his kingdom to afflict all or almost all the members in God's visible organization; and that is the meaning the angel has in mind, as he explains the beast to John. Dearest to Christ is the Church, his beloved bride; and, when the Beast, "the little horn," attempts to annihilate her, he AND HIS ENTIRE EMPIRE shall go "unto annihilation."

Nota bene: it is impossible to argue cogently that the angel does not shift the temporal point of reference from the time of the vision to the time of John, and, thus, cogently to hold that the clause, "the one is," in verse 10 denotes the beast carrying the woman, simply because there will come no "other" after the beast having the "seven heads and the ten horns."

Therefore, also is it impossible to conclude rationally that the whole beast in Chapter 17 is the Roman Empire, because the universal reign of Christ did not begin immediately after Rome fell, indeed, did not begin when Christ and his Church dethroned paganism in the Roman Empire, even before it fell!

Rome lasted a thousand years: it did not remain merely a "little while" or a "short time"; and yet, some people persist in the opinion that the beast, in Chapter 17, and the Roman Empire are one and the same entity. Such are not perusers.

In verse 8, the angel states,

> "They will be marveling—the ones dwelling upon the earth, whose name was not written upon the scroll of the life from [the] foundation of [the] world—seeing the beast that it was and it is not and it will arrive."

This statement is the combination of 13:3 and 13:8, which read,

> "And the whole earth marveled after the beast...and all the ones dwelling upon the earth will be worshipping it, [they] whose name was not written on the scroll of the life of the Little Lamb slaughtered from [the] foundation of [the] world."

These constitute another proof that both the Beast in Chapter 17 and the Beast in Chapter 13 are one and the same man.

As for the term "σοφία" [sophia] in verse 9, the Greek noun has these meanings:

> (1) skill, knowledge of, acquaintance with.
> (2) sound judgment, intelligence, practical wisdom.
> (3) cunning, shrewdness [in bad sense].

To John and to every future reader, the angel is saying that an intelligent thinker, a person who perceives the least motions of his or her own intellect and will, can come to understand the message. Sound judgment implies patience, of course, and practice in discursive REASONING, not just logic. But then, why would love not be patient, though the God has chosen fourth-grade grammar and vocabulary through which to give his message? The reader does not need a special revelation concerning what is already a revelation. What the reader needs is to let the words of the Word of God say what they say. This conduct toward a rational being is called common courtesy, and, by example, it was one time commonly taught in school and home.

Consider verse 11:

> καὶ τὸ θηρίον ὃ ἦν καὶ οὐκ ἔστιν καὶ αὐτὸς ὄγδοός ἐστιν καὶ ἐκ τῶν
> kai to thërion o en kai ouk estin kai autos ogdoos estin kai ek tön
> and the beast that was and not is also himself eighth is and of the
>
> ἑπτά ἐστιν καὶ εἰς ἀπώλειαν ὑπάγει.
> epta estin, kai eis apöleian ypagei.
> seven is, and unto annihilation is going.

The angel repeats in verse 11 specific elements of verse 8, namely, that "the beast…was and is not…and unto annihilation is going." In this way, he signals that he is <u>again</u> <u>speaking</u> <u>only</u> <u>about</u> <u>the</u> <u>seventh</u> <u>emperor</u>, at whom the inhabitants upon the earth will be marveling, and whom they will be worshipping. However, this does <u>not</u> mean that the angel has shifted the temporal point of reference back to the time of the vision. Bear in mind that the angel is continuing the explanation that he began, with the words,

> "They are also seven kings:…" [Note the colon after the word "kings."]

In verse 11, he is speaking <u>only</u> about the <u>seventh</u> emperor, and is speaking about him <u>in</u> <u>the</u> <u>present</u> <u>tense</u>, thus,

> "and the beast…also himself eighth is and of the seven is…".

In order for the angel to speak about the seventh Beast as simply "is," he shifts the temporal point of reference from the time of John, when the sixth one simply "is," to the time when the seventh Beast will be simply "is," i.e., to the time "when he comes" [verse 10].

In other words, the temporal point of reference has shifted not to when the Beast is about to ascend from the abyss [verse 8], but to when he has ascended from the abyss; the shift is from the time of John to the time of Chapter 13. Recall what was said earlier: To understand when the Beast can be described as simply "is" or "is existing," one must understand when the Beast simply "was" or "was existing," or when the Beast simply "will be" or "will be existing."

In Chapter 17, the Beast is ascending [rising in power and authority] only from the "many waters," which includes "the sea"; but, in Chapter 13, the Beast is not only ascending from "the sea," he is also ascending from the abyss, which is to say,

> "And the dragon gave to it [to the Beast] its power and its throne and great authority." [Apoc. 13:2]

That explains the two terms connected by και in verse 11,

> "…is himself also eighth AND is of the seven [,]…"

All seven kings derive power from their visible empires, and, in that sense, the seventh king is just like the six kings before him: he is "of the seven." But, the seventh king is different from the previous six in one important respect: he also derives power from the invisible Satan. The angel worded verse 11, carefully and precisely; he did not say that the Beast is also himself THE eighth, because, if he had nominalized the adjective "ὄγδοός" [ogdoos = eigth], he would have contradicted the statement that "the seven heads are…also seven kings" [verse 9], and contradicted verse 10, and contradicted the phrase, "of the seven" [verse 11].

The adjectives, "αὐτὸς" and "ὄγδοός," are in the masculine nominative singular, even though they modify the neuter noun "θηρίον," the subject of the sentence [see: ekhon in 17:3]. The term αὐτὸς is reflexive and emphasizes the person of the seventh king, the little Beast himself; and, thus, the term "ὄγδοός" becomes personal to him and has nothing to do with the previous six kings.

Let it be clearly understood that verse 10 deals, strictly speaking, with the seven kings and not their empires; but, it sounded better to mention empires, which implies that each of the first six kings actually represents a series of kings. The text is pellucid of the point that the seventh Beast will not have a successor.

As for the clause, "and unto annihilation is going," in 17:8 AND 17:11, it does not restrict the temporal point of reference in verse 11 to the time of the vision, for it is equally applicable to the Beast in Chapters 17 and 13.

The noun "ὄρος" [oros] can signify either a mountain OR a hill, according to the dictionary. According to Isaiah 41:15, God differentiates between threshing mountains and making hills like chaff, which is to say that God knows the difference between a mountain and a hill, just as he knows there are big fish and little fish. In this case, therefore, it is neither otiose nor odd to note how others differentiate between "ὄρος" and "ὄρος." Some translators, like those for The New American Bible, have rendered "ἑπτὰ ὄρη" [epta orë], in verse 9, as "seven hills" instead of "seven mountains." This is strange, passing strange, because, as far as I could find, those translators for the NAB, in all other instances throughout the New Testament, rendered the very same noun as "mountain"—aye, aye, even in Apocalypse 8:8. The last time I saw, Apocalypse 13:7 stated,

> "…It was given authority over every tribe and people and language and nation…"

That spells out "emperor" and tells about an "empire." This situation reminds me of what the chain gang warden in the movie, "Cool Hand Luke," said, "What we've got here, is—failure to communicate." The Great Harlot and the Beast are separate entities; the Beast's seven heads epitomize the Beast's history, not hers. The "ἑπτὰ ὄρη" are SYMBOLICAL; relative to the Great Harlot, they represent…

"peoples and multitudes and nations and languages."

It is recklessness to render "ἑπτὰ ὄρη" as "seven hills" simply because the city of Rome sits on seven hills. John himself wondered with great wonder, mainly, on account of the name Babylon. But, as it sat then, regarding the real names of both the seventh Beast and the Great Harlot, so it sits now: only Time will tell, for John did not tattle, and that he someday will stands not within the prospect of belief. Yet, it seems some people cannot stand sitting.

Apparently, latitude in the noun's definition admitted the attitude of the translators to an alteration in altitude. I do not know whether the translators, when they trampled down the little big noun, acted out of nescience or acted out of knowledge: if the former be the case, I would offer them each a box of soft, sweet raisins as food for thought, but I do not think that they, as yet, believe in cannibalism; and, if the latter be the case, they have already long indulged in the vile practice; whilst, in either case, I remind them of the final warning in 22:18-19.

They moved "mountains" to Babylon the Great—aye, seven of them, simultaneously!— notwithstanding that six existed in auld lang syne, noncontemporaneously: a feat of transition with such attrition as reduced them to "hills," instantaneously. I think the little Beast himself, when he comes with many signs and wonders, shall not be able to perform the like.

I will speak bluntly: To opine regarding Scripture is to assert the words of one's own heart and substitute them for the words of the God. This act reveals such contumacy and contumely as should shock even a weak conscience; it is an act of blasphemy, a violation of the First Great Commandment, and the sin against the Holy Spirit. The Apocalypse is a gift from above, and every gift from above is good. Therefore, if one is having a bad time with the Apocalypse, it is not the Apocalypse that is giving one a bad time, but oneself that is giving a bad time to the Apocalypse. Originally and ultimately speaking, the Apocalypse and the parables in the gospels have the same Author; that Author gave them in the same symbolical manner, for the same reason. If the reader is interested in knowing that reason, I refer him or her to Matthew 13:

> 10 And his disciples came and said to him: Why speakest thou to them in parables? 11 Who answered and said to them: Because to you it is given to know the mysteries of the kingdom of heaven: but to them it is not given. 12 For he that hath, to him shall be given, and

> he shall abound: but he that hath not, from him shall be taken away that also which he hath. 13 Therefore do I speak to them in parables: because seeing they see not, and hearing they hear not, neither do they understand. 14 And the prophecy of Isaias is fulfilled in them, who saith: By hearing you shall hear, and shall not understand: and seeing you shall see, and shall not perceive. 15 For the heart of this people is grown gross, and with their ears they have been dull of hearing, and their eyes they have shut: lest at any time they should see with their eyes, and hear with their ears, and understand with their heart, and be converted, and I should heal them.

Then and now, but not just now and then, can it be said, "What we've got here, is—failure to communicate." And, it is eternally certain that the failure comes not on the part of the Amen. If my words have stung, then I am a good gadfly.

The seven heads on the "beast" present the symbolical number "seven" with two special connotations here:

(1) The kingdom of the Beast will be the maximum in collective evil that God will permit Satan to develop by the bonds of Adam.
(2) The Beast himself will be the maximum in individual evil that God will permit one man only to reach.

The "head" signifies that an evil person occupies the highest seat or office in the worldly kingdom, and it follows that he has put agents like himself in control of social agencies, such as those political, military, educational, and religious. He will control every public means of communication, and the financial and commercial resources of nearly the whole world will be his treasury. Indeed, he will have it all—for all of three and a half years.

Verse 17 indicates that the Beast will become the head of the Confederation of Ten Kings,

> ...for the God gave unto the hearts of them to do his mind and to make one mind and give [aorist infinitive] their kingdom to the beast until the words of the God will be fulfilled.

John recorded the second aorist infinitive "δοῦναι" [dounai = to give], and by this is the reader informed that the event will happen only once. It would be a noteworthy event if ten good men agreed on a specific course of action; but, when ten evil rulers, each selfishly ambitious, agree to give their own power and authority to an eleventh man, it will be an event so unusual as to catch the attention of any informed member of the faithful, who keeps abreast of affairs in the Middle East. The transfer of power from the Ten Kings to that one man will be an unmistakable sign that the final 3½ years of the second woe are about to begin; more importantly, it will serve to identify the man who is about to become Satan's champion of evil: the Antichrist.

That the Ten Kings GIVE their kingdom to the Beast is impressive testimony as to how extraordinary a person the Beast will be, even before he becomes the Antichrist; and that Satan also gives his own power and throne and great authority to him implies not only the Beast's qualification of malice, but also Satan's, toward Christ and his Church: for Satan so hates them, that he is willing to put himself at the beck and call of a mere man, an inversion of the scale of being comparable to a man's subserving a slug. Thus, by having a visible head, can Satan deceive a greater number of souls to annihilation.

Contrary to the opinion asserted about twenty-five years ago in The Late Great Planet Earth, by Hal Lindsay, the Ten Kings will not have their confederation in Europe, but in southwest Asia, the region that includes the lands around the Black Sea and the Caspian, and those of Iran, Oman, Kuwait, and Saudi Arabia; this region holds 70% of the world's known oil reserves and is predominantly Islamic. That the Confederation of the Ten Kings will not arise in Europe is shown by one salient fact: the Great Harlot will have dominion over "the earth" until the Beast annexes it to his "many waters," and, thereafter, the False Prophet will be the subordinate ruler of it, not the Ten Kings.

Verse 12 states that the Ten Kings…

> "…did not yet receive a kingdom, but authority as kings for one hour they will receive together with the beast."

The angel is referring to the global empire that will be given to the Beast when he begins ascending from the abyss, also. Since the historical count of the seven evil empires is both literal and exact, I suspect that the count of the Ten

Kings, who are contemporaries of the Beast, will also be literal and exact. This does not mean the number "ten" is not symbolical here; it is a round or rough number connoting that the global empire will not be total, but nearly so.

Chapter 12 corroborates this view in verse 14,

> But the woman was given the two wings of/from the eagle the great one, so that she could fly unto the wilderness, to her place where she is nourished for a time and times and half a time.

It should be obvious to all, that the "wilderness," in her case, will not be the symbolical "wilderness" where John was taken "in spirit" to see the Great Harlot and the Beast; if it were, then, she would be jumping from the frying pan into the fire.

The Ten Kings are not to be confused with "the kings from the rising of the sun" in Chapter 16. The Romans, in John's day, were well aware of India and of China and the territories north of the Black Sea; caravans traveled trade routes to those places. Hence, "the kings from the rising of the sun" will come from kingdoms farther east than those kingdoms of the Ten in confederation. To demonstrate more clearly where the Ten Kings will set up their confederation, a digression to the book of Daniel will prove helpful.

The "ten horns" mentioned in Apocalypse 12, 13, & 17 are not the "ten horns" mentioned in Daniel 7. Confusion will not arise if one fact is kept before the mind: Daniel's vision begins the count of the evil empires from the Babylonian, whereas the Apocalypse begins the count from the Egyptian. Hence, the fourth beast in Daniel 7 represents the Roman Empire, which, by the Apocalyptic count from the Egyptian, is the sixth beast, i.e., the sixth of the seven historical heads on the "beast" in Apocalypse 17.

In Daniel 7:8, Daniel describes a "little horn" that appears suddenly from the midst of the fourth beast's "ten horns," and, then, someone in the vision explains this to the seer in verses 23-27,

> "I was considering the ten horns it [the fourth beast, i.e., the Roman Empire] had, when suddenly another, a little horn, sprang out of their midst, and three of the previous horns were torn away to make room for it. This horn had eyes like a man, and a mouth that spoke

> arrogantly…The fourth beast shall be a fourth kingdom on earth, different from all the others; it shall devour the whole earth, beat it down, and crush it. The ten horns shall be ten kings rising out of that kingdom [the fourth beast]; another shall rise up after them, different from those before him, who shall lay low three kings. He shall speak against the Most High and oppress the holy ones of the Most High, thinking to change the feast days and the law. They shall be handed over to him for a year, two years, and a half-year. But when the court is convened, and his power is taken away by final and absolute destruction, then the kingship and dominion and majesty of all the kingdoms under the heavens shall be given to the holy people of the Most High, whose kingdom shall be everlasting: all dominions shall serve and obey him."

Historical record shows that the Roman Empire broke up into more than ten kings/kingdoms, so the number of the "horns" is a round or rough one, not exact; but, it, nonetheless, represents the total territory that was once the Roman Empire. The "little horn" is the little Beast with "seven heads and ten horns" in the Apocalypse, as indicated by three things:

(1) Counting from the Babylonian Empire, he will be the fifth oppressor of God's people, counting from the Egyptian, he will be the seventh.
(2) His victorious reign will last 3½ years.
(3) After his defeat, the kingdom of God will be worldwide and everlasting.

So, the information about the "little horn" can be now applied to the little Beast, and thence to the Ten Kings.

The Beast will arise within that territory formerly of the Roman Empire, and he will seize about 30% of it by violence; but, no part of that 30% will include any part of the Confederation of the Ten Kings, because all of the Confederation will be given to him. In other words, the territory of the Confederation will lie outside the territory formerly Roman, which the Beast will seize by violence.

It has already been shown, however, that the Beast will rise from that formerly Roman territory designated as "the sea"; therefore, the Beast will initially seize about 60% of the "sea," not just 30% by violence, because the "sea" comprises North Africa and the Middle East, i.e., about half of all that was once the Roman Empire.

Of the "sea's" two main regions, the Asian is the larger and richer in oil: it includes Turkey and the small countries immediately south of the Caucasus Mountains—Syria, Iraq, Jordan, Lebanon, and Palestine. In order to seize that initial 60% of the "sea," the Beast or "little horn" must take possession of some part of the Asian region along with all of the African, or he will simply take all of the Asian, or he will take much of the Asian and part of the African, such as Egypt and Libya.

In Daniel's vision, "the little horn" appeared out of the midst of the fourth beast's "horns," and this suggests that the Beast will seize nations contiguous or adjacent to one another. In all three possible scenarios, one fact stands clear: it is impossible for all of the Confederation of Ten Kings, which requires a minimum of ten nations or kingdoms, to lie within the territory designated as the "sea," simply because the "sea" comprises a total of thirteen nations [including Israel, which the Beast will annex only at the start of his 42-month reign]. There is not room enough for both the Beast and the Confederation in the "sea."

I cannot cogently argue as to the exact region in which the Confederation of Ten will arise. However, the reader should bear in mind several things:

(1) The relationship between the Great Harlot and the Beast will be based on material wealth.
(2) The Beast will ascend from Islamic countries in "the sea."
(3) At present, oil is the great material wealth in Islam.
(4) All or almost all of the Confederation of Ten will be outside "the sea."
(5) If the second plague in 16:3 affects all of "the sea," then, it is absolutely certain that none of the Ten Kings will be within "the sea," for the Ten will be together with the Beast "until the words of the God shall be fulfilled" [17:17] at Armageddon.

(6) If the second plague affects all of "the sea," then, it is absolutely certain that the "throne of the beast" [fifth plague in 16:10] will be located outside "the sea," i.e., where the Beast's center or base of power is, namely, the Confederation of Ten.

The Roman Empire, at its greatest extent in 217 AD, included Mesopotamia in the east, where the Euphrates and the Tigris rivers flow, in the land now called Iraq. The Romans were unable to conquer farther eastward on account of the Parthians; the Parthians inhabited the territory now known as Iran. Also, the Romans never conquered the Saudi Arabian peninsula. It is, therefore, exceedingly probable that the Confederation of Ten will arise in the Middle East, constituted of such lands as Kazakhstan, Uzbekistan (the Uzbek people), Kurgyz (Kyrgyzstan), Tadzhikistan (formerly Tadzhik Soviet Socialist Republic), Turkmenistan (formerly Turkmen Soviet Socialist Republic), Pakistan, Afghanistan, Iran, Kuwait, and Saudi Arabia; for most of them are rich in oil, and all of them are predominantly Islamic.

Those lands, plus the Asian part of the "sea" contain 70% of the world's known oil reserves; and, if someday one man rules them, he will have great power, indeed. Even if the Beast could seize all of "the sea," he still would not have enough economic leverage to work his will upon "the earth"; in fact, he would be foolhardy to attempt it. But, when the Ten Kings give him their power and authority, he will, then, have the necessary leverage. Hence, it is that I suspect that the region between the Asian part of "the sea" and such countries as China and India, will be where the Confederation arises. However, I keep my mind open on the matter, because I cannot prove it from information in the text.

It should also be kept in mind that the number of the kings, which is ten, does not necessarily denote exactly ten nations; for a few of them may each rule over two nations or more, so that the number of nations in the Confederation may be as much as fifteen or twenty. I, therefore, consider it significant that the angel mentioned the number of the kings, not the number of the kingdoms that will constitute the Confederation. The number of the kings would be a useless item of information if the number is a round or rough one, because then too many possible scenarios would confuse the observer of events. For that reason, I strongly suspect the number TEN, in regard to the kings, is their exact number.

But, I reiterate: only Time will tell. It would be imprudent to lock reason in the "tunnel vision of an opinion." So, the reader should ponder the items of information in the text, and their relationships to each other, and, then, wait and see. I have brought some of those items to the reader's attention, but not all of them.

As best as I can judge, ye Friends, I have written enough about Chapter 17 to give you an adequate understanding of it. Now, I must do a more detailed explanation of Chapters 12 & 13. The long concatenation of arguments is probably a tiresome thing to you, at times, but I must be tedious, only to be tidy. Ultimately, the commentary will save you time, and, so, the arguments are worth the effort to understand them.

CHAPTER 13

—

APOCALYPSE CHAPTER 12

October 26, 1998

Dear Friends of the Lord,

Greetings. I assume all fares all fairly with all of you. Calculations from sister's comments yesterday come to the total conclusion that my littlest friend will soon draw <u>thrice</u> his original weight and is setting the trend toward subsequent substantiation of the prediction in my last letter. It shall come to pass that a dozen Boston Crèmes will not suffice—for him, not all of you. This statement does not in the least convey the intimation that I believe the other offspring have not been assiduously self-assistant for their appetites, or that it suggests my unwitting distraction from that fact. As the body wears apparel from shirts to shoes, so the soul wears genes.

I am pushing my pen at best pace. Even so, the concatenation of rational arguments for Chapters 12 and 13 have lengthened the commentary's third part considerably. Alas, some of John's verses were too difficult to leave unexplained; consequently, the third part is now a few pages short of one hundred [about 200 pages in a typical paperback]. I shall try to add not more than another 30. This problem of length is partially attributable to the material itself, in that a term or a verse often requires references to several other passages in order to construct a proof, or a collection of "indications" tantamount to one: for I abhor a work of mere assertions or opinions, which breed with the speed of bacteria and viruses into a pandemic disease. Nineteen hundred years have had too many of such plagues. Therefore, Friend, do not put too much effort toward the computer just yet; that will come perhaps by the middle of next year. I realize that too little was explained in the section on Daniel and the first and second parts on the Apocalypse, a lack I hope to change after a brief break in December. Hang on: such undertakings often go over the budget of our patience.

I will keep informing you during the next two months.

Your comical commentator,

Steve

Consider the first six verses of Chapter 12:

> 1 And a great sign was seen [ὤφθη = ophthe] in the heaven, a woman clothed with the sun, and the moon under her feet and upon her head a crown [στέφανος = stephanos] of twelve stars, 2 and holding in womb, and she cried out having birth pangs and being put to the test to bring forth. 3 and there was seen another sign in the heaven, and behold a great fire-colored dragon having seven heads and ten horns and upon its heads seven diadems, 4 and its tail dragged by force [σύρει = syrei] the third of the stars of the heaven and cast out them unto the earth, and the dragon took his stand in the presence of the woman the one about to bear, so that when she bore it might devour the thing born of her [τὸ τέκνον αὐτῆς = to teknon autës]. 5 and she bore a son virile [υἱόν ἄρσεν = yion arsen], who was about to shepherd all the nations with an iron rod. and snatched away was the thing born of her to the God and to his throne. 6 and the woman fled unto the wilderness, where she has therein a place prepared by the God, so that therein they may nourish her [τρέφωσιν αὐτὴν = trephosin auten] for days one thousand two hundred sixty.

A long time ago, in a mind far, far away, there sprang an opinion. Since then, many hundreds of millions of people have propagated that opinion and perpetuated it into an inveterate tradition throughout the Church, to wit, that the "woman clothed with the sun" is the Blessed Virgin Mary.

I would gladly agree with the many hundreds of millions who assert that 12:1 describes Mary, if I could with impunity take that verse out of its context. But, John warned rue not to add one word to the prophecy and not to subtract one word from it, as stated in 22:18-19; and, surely, what applies to one word in the prophecy must apply to a whole verse.

Let the reader please note the little comma after the noun "stars" at the end of verse 1; that comma is followed by the connective καὶ at the beginning of verse 2; and the "period," which ends the sentence composed of verses 1 & 2, comes after the infinitive "to bear" or "to bring forth" [τεκεῖν = tekein]. This all means that the contents of verse 2 are connected to and simultaneous with the contents of verse 1. Hence, according to the many hundreds of millions, the Blessed Virgin Mary, who has already died and been assumed, body and soul, into the glorified state and has been crowned Queen of Heaven, is again pregnant—in heaven above, no less!—where, according to Christ, there is no marriage.

Perhaps, the many millions are tacitly asserting that Mary became Queen of Heaven before Jesus was born, and that, therefore, either Mary or Saint Dominic confused the order of the glorious mysteries in the Rosary, so that the Coronation should precede the Assumption. Frankly, I find it a mystery that such an opinion about 12:1 has become the first reading in the Mass celebrated on the Feast of the Assumption. In Apocalypse 1:19, Christ told John,

> "Now write the things that you saw and the things that are and the things about to come into existence after these things."

In 4:1, John is told,

> "Come up hither, and I will show you the things that must come into existence after these things."

In 1:19, the term, "after these things" [μετὰ ταῦτα = meta tauta], refers to "the things that you saw and the things that are..." In 4:1; the term, "after these things," refers to the seven letters, i.e., "the things that are." Hence, the term, "the things that are about to come into existence," or, "the things that must come into existence," unmistakably refers to future things, things that would happen after the Apocalypse was copied and circulated by the year, say, 100 AD. Chapter 12 belongs to those future things, and, therefore, it has absolutely nothing to do with describing the birth and death and ascension of Jesus, the Holy Family's flight into Egypt, etc. So, the argument up to this point, alone, suffices to refute the opinion that the woman is Mary.

Now I will reason from the given information in the text to the woman's real identity, keeping alert to John's practice of using physical things as symbols of spiritual things, and paying attention to context, the context that does not extend merely to the whole Apocalypse, but to the whole Bible. After all, the Apocalypse is the culmination of Biblical prophecy.

John could have begun Chapter 12, typically, thus,

"And I saw a woman clothed with the sun,..."

Instead, he wrote,

"And a great sign was seen in the heaven,..."

With this introduction, John immediately gave the reader general instruction concerning the particulars that would follow. To call the reader's attention to this instruction, he repeated it in verse 3,

> "and another sign was seen in the heaven,..." [I trust the reader has learned that John did not employ idle repetition.]

Now, the prophetic term "sign" was mentioned often in the New Testament:

(1) The Apostles asked Jesus about the "sign" of his coming. [Mt. 24:3]
(2) The Pharisees demanded that Christ prove his divinity by a "sign from heaven." [Mt. 16:1]
(3) Saint Paul warned about "signs and false wonders" worked by evil powers. [2 Thes. 2:9]

(4) Saint John mentioned signs performed by the False Prophet. [Apoc. 13:13, 16:14]
(5) Simeon in the Temple prophesied of the infant Jesus: "This child is destined to be the downfall and the rise of many in Israel, a sign that will be opposed...so that the thoughts of many hearts may be laid bare." [Lk. 2:34-35]

From the aforegiven instances may be drawn the idea that "a sign is someone or something VISIBLE to the naked human eye." Therefore, according to John's instruction, the woman in Chapter 12 will be an entity that people CAN SEE; thus, the phrase, "in the heaven," must signify "in the Church as VISIBLE organization."

Many a "sign" is prophetic. In Chapter 12, the woman, as "sign," is also prophetic, for she is herself <u>and</u> <u>points</u> <u>to</u> <u>something</u> <u>else</u>: she is the "GREAT sign" that alludes forward to THE GREAT DAY OF ALMIGHTY GOD. But this "great sign" is not just the woman. Understand that this "sign" includes the son she will bring forth, and, thus, also the activity he will initiate in the Church.

The "sign" will culminate in casting the Dragon and his followers out of "the heaven," and this will point forward to the eventual expulsion of Satan and his kingdom from the whole world 3½ years later. For this reason, a loud voice in 12:10 prophetically proclaims,

> "Now have come the salvation and the POWER and the kingdom of our God and the AUTHORITY of his Messiah..."

Judgment will begin at the house of the God; so, when this "great sign" is seen, the informed faithful will know that the advent of the Antichrist is imminent, that the Beast is about to ascend from the abyss. The "great sign" belongs to that part of the Apocalypse that Christ designated as "the things that must come into existence," and, yet, John, in writing about the "great sign," used the past tense, starting with the verb "was seen." He wrote in the past tense for the primary purpose of connoting the divine omniscience. The infinite God knows even future things because, in one simple act, he creates all finite reality, which includes every moment of the everlasting existence of every rational creature; and, thus, future things, from God's point of view, are also history.

Hence, the phrase, "in the heaven," acts as a quick reminder concerning the divine omnipotence: that Jesus Christ is the One Living unto the ages of the ages,

> "who created the heaven and the things in it and the earth and the things in it and the sea and the things in it..." [Apoc. 10:6]

This means that the Dragon could not be "in the heaven" unless God permitted him to be there. Indeed, Satan, like every other finite entity, is a secondary agent that subserves the eternal fiat, "Thus saith the Lord," "Thus saith the Amen."

So, John's general instruction comprised two perspectives:

(1) Let the reader while reading, remember that God is the supreme power and authority in all things.
(2) Let the reader while reading, understand that the things described in Chapter 12 will happen here, in this world, not in the perfect paradise of the heaven above.

CHAPTER 14

THE HEAVENLY WOMAN

Consider this particle from verse 1:

"..., a woman clothed with the sun,..."

"Clothing" is the symbol for power, and the "sun" is the symbol for the divine. The divine power here is that of Jesus Christ, as indicated by John's description of him,

"...and his face [was] as the sun shines with its power." [Apoc. 1:16]

As one adds clothing to the body, so Christ has given his divine power to the woman; and the woman is only human, with all the frailty of human nature.

But, Christ cannot act in vain, and, therefore, his endowing her with divine power shall not be in vain; for, though she is being "put to the test/torture" by God's permission, by God's grace she shall not fail to prove her spiritual mettle, and shall bring forth that son whom her Lord has decreed "must come into existence."

As Christ has given her power, so he has given her authority,

"..., and the moon under her feet and upon her head a crown of twelve stars,..."

The phrase, "under her feet," signifies dominion, as Jesus himself indicated,

> "The Lord said to my Lord, 'Sit at my right, until I put your enemies under <u>your</u> feet'." [Mk. 12:36]

The term "moon" is the symbol for temporal or mutable things, as it is written,

> "The moon, too, that marks the changing times, governing the seasons, their lasting sign, by which we know the feast days and fixed dates." [Sir. 43:6-7]

Hence, the woman has the authority, for example, to allow or to forbid priests to get married, or to alter the laws on fasting and abstinence, or to declare that the Sabbath may be kept by attending Mass at 4:00 p.m. on a Saturday. More important is her authority in things eternal or immutable, namely, the truths about God and faith and morals taught by Christ; and, whereas the "circle" is the symbol for the eternal, she wears…

> "…upon her head a crown [στέφανος = <u>stephanos</u>] of twelve stars."

The noun <u>στέφανος</u> has sundry meanings:

> (1) that which surrounds, the wall around a city, a circle;
> (2) a crown, wreath, crown of victory; and
> (3) crown of glory, honor, especially, a crown as a badge of office.

All three basic meanings apply here. Since her crown with its symbolical number "twelve" is a component of the "great sign," it, too, in the second meaning, alludes forward to the universal victory that Christ and his Church will win on the Great Day of Almighty God [Chapter 16], and, in the first meaning, further alludes to the wall around the city called the New Jerusalem [Chapter 21].

In the third meaning, her <u>στέφανος</u> is the badge of her official authority in the Church. However, a <u>στέφανος</u> is the crown of a regent or subordinate ruler, and this means that, within the Church, there is official authority higher than hers. Note that her crown is twelve <u>stars</u> in a "circle" upon her head. It has already been shown that a "star" is the symbol for a member of the priesthood. For that reason did John use, throughout the Apocalypse, the masculine noun "ἀστήρ" [aster]; not once did he use the neuter noun "ἄστρον" [astron].

Since the woman's στέφανος is not made of gold, it is clear that she does not belong to that part of the clergy designated as the Twenty-four Elders in Chapter 4; therefore, she belongs to the Four Living Beings, i.e., the episcopate, for only the episcopate has authority to allow or to forbid priests to get married, to alter the laws on fasting and abstinence, etc. At this point, there arises the question of whether the woman symbolizes both the bishops and the cardinals in the episcopate, or the bishops only, or the cardinals only. Bear in mind that her crown is TWELVE "stars," that it is her badge of official authority, and that it alludes forward to the "wall" of the New Jerusalem, to that "wall"…

> "…having twelve foundations and upon them the twelve names of the twelve Apostles of the Little Lamb." [Apoc. 21:14]

It, therefore, stands to faith and reason that the "crown" upon the woman's head symbolizes APOSTOLIC AUTHORITY, and that the "woman" herself is actually the members of the Sacred College of Cardinals in assembly.

Only the pope has official authority higher than hers in the Church. When a pope does not occupy the chair of Peter, the "woman" rules as regent; but when a pope does occupy the chair of Peter, the members of the Sacred College are subordinate to him. Cardinals assemble chiefly for two reasons:

(1) to elect a pope, and
(2) to attend an ecumenical council.

I will now show that the forepart of Chapter 12 is a symbolical description of a papal election. But, first, a few terms should be explained.

The meanings of the verb "τεκεῖν" [tekein] are:

(1) to bring into the world; of the father, to beget; of the mother, to bring forth;
(2) of female animals, to bear young, to breed;

(3) of plants, to produce;
(4) metaphorically, to generate.

Derived from "τεκεῖν" [tekein] is the neuter noun "τέκνον" [teknon]:

(1) that which is born or brought forth, a child;
(2) of animals, the young;
(3) of plants, that which is produced.

The verb "ποιμαίνειν" [poimainein] means "to shepherd, rule"; it was derived from the noun "ποιμήν" [poimën], "shepherd."

The adjective "ἄρσεν" [arsen] is the older form of "ἄρρην" [arrën]; the Ionian variation is "ἄρσην" [arsën]. Aeschylus used it to denote the male of a species, and Thucydides used it in the plural to denote the male sex. Hence, the adjective was used for indicating the gender of a thing, such as a <u>masculine</u> <u>noun</u>. However, Euripides used it to signify "masculine," in the sense of "manly, virile, strong"; and Sophocles used it in the metaphorical sense of "mighty":

> "κτύπος ἄρσην πόντου" [ktypos arsën pontou], "the <u>mighty</u> din of the [open] sea."

So, yet once more I will leap into the middle of things, to verse 5; here it is, as John wrote it,

καὶ ἔτεκεν υἱόν ἄρσεν ὃς μέλλει ποιμαίνειν πάντα τὰ ἔθνη ἐν ῥάβδῳ σιδηρᾷ
Kai eteken yion arsen, os mellei poimainein panta ta ethnë en rabdö sidëra
And she bore a son virile, who is about to shepherd all the nations with a rod of iron.

Here are four translations of that first sentence in verse 5:

(1) And she gave birth to a son, <u>a</u> <u>male</u> <u>child</u>, who is to rule all the nations with a rod of iron. [NRSV]

(2) She gave birth to a son, <u>a</u> <u>male</u> <u>child</u>, who will rule all the nations with an iron scepter. [NIV]

(3) And she brought forth a male child, who is destined to rule all the nations with a rod of iron. [WV]

(4) She gave birth to a son- a boy destined to shepherd all the nations with an iron rod. [NAB]

In the NRSV and the NIV, the translators took yion arsen to be a case of apposition; and, so, because a son is a child [whether sixty seconds or sixty years old], they took arsen to mean "a male child" and indicated its apposition by adding a comma after "son" in both translations. The basically same thinking is evident in the WV and the NAB.

According to the translators, Protestant and Roman Catholic alike, the divinely inspired seer arrayed THREE masculine terms in a row to convey redundantly that the woman bore someone of the masculine gender: yion, arsen, os. Tacit in their thinking was the notion that the term "woman" is to be taken literally, and that she, therefore, brought forth in the physical sense, i.e., that the son really was a new-born infant.

Now, the text is pellucid of one point: not very long after being brought forth, this newborn "was taken/snatched/caught away to the God and to his throne," i.e., he was taken from the Church [the heaven below] to the God and to his throne [the heaven above], which simply means that HE DIED.

How is it, then, that this infant, who, but recently, had been dried off behind the ears, gained, by heroic works, such merit as to receive from God himself the honor of shepherding all the nations with a rod of iron? In the name of the God omniscient, in the name of reason, which is the very likeness of the Creator, and in the name of common sense, how can such a thing possibly be so?

The answer is that it cannot. Christ spoke on this matter,

> And the one conquering and doing even to [the] end my works, I will give him authority upon the nations, and he will shepherd them with a rod of iron as clay pots are shattered, as even I received from my Father…[Apoc. 2:26-28]

The phrase,

"even to [the] end" [ἄχρι τέλους = akhri telous],

is equivalent to the phrase,

"even unto death" [ἄχρι θανάτου = akhri thanatou]

as exemplified in Apocalypse 12:11, which reads,

"...and they did not love their life even unto death."

Christ's promise pertains to someone who has reached, at least, the age of reason, which, for most people, begins about the age of seven. Hence, the relative clause, "who is about to shepherd etc.," connotes two things:

(1) The son brought forth is, at least, seven years old and, therefore, most certainly, not an infant newly born.
(2) The son is about to die, but will die only after he has fulfilled Christ's purpose for him.

The translation, "is destined to," for the verb μέλλει = mellei, albeit correct, is less accurate than "is about to." Nowhere in the text did John explicitly state that the son is a boy; the translation, "boy," in the NAB, is an opinion imposed, one probably consequent upon the opinion that the woman is Mary. So, if John had intended to convey only the male gender of the one born, then, he would have sufficiently written,

"And she bore a son, who is about to shepherd etc."

The primary purpose of the adjective arsen, therefore, is NOT to inform the reader that the son was "male," or "a male," or "a male child," for the term "yion" confirms that much; but, RATHER, to inform the reader that the son was "manly/virile/strong/mighty" in the spiritual sense, in faith and character. The son "brought forth" by the "woman" is a full-grown man; thus, the "woman" must be a convenient symbol for an entity that is not a real woman at all.

In ancient Greek, the noun, "παιδός" [pais, paidos: nominative, genitive singular, respectively] signified a child seven years old or older; the masculine or feminine definite article could be used with it to indicate the sex of the child. The noun "παιδιόν" [paidion] signified a child six years old or younger; it was the diminutive of "παῖς" [pais] and neuter in gender. The noun signified a child, regardless of sex and age; a participle or relative pronoun, masculine or feminine, could be used with it to indicate the sex of the child.

So, John had a choice in signifying "child," yet, consider what he did. In 12:4 and then in 12:5, John used the term "τὸ τέκνον" [to teknon] to allude forward and then backward to the son in 12:5, thus bracketing or sandwiching the term, "a son virile, who etc." Hmmmmmmm. Obviously, if John had used "παιδιόν" [paidion], he would have contradicted "a son virile, who etc.." If he had used "παῖς" [pais], he would not have contradicted "a son virile, who etc.," but would have instantly informed the reader that the son was not a baby AND, therefore, that the "woman" was not a woman.

Bear in mind that the Seer indicated those two facts—albeit a little indirectly—by means of "a son virile, who etc." The noun "παῖς" [pais] would have expedited the reader's cognition of those two facts, but it would not have accomplished anything else. So, it logically follows that the noun, "τέκνον" [teknon: that which is born or brought forth], conveyed something that "παῖς" [pais] could not, something in addition to the meaning "child." As mentioned earlier, the noun "τέκνον" [teknon] was derived from the verb, "τεκεῖν" [tekein: of the mother, to bring forth]: To understand the noun, one must first understand the verb—according to the context, of course.

Now, in a physical "bringing forth," the activity of "bringing forth" does not cause or make the thing brought forth, i.e., the thing brought forth does not proceed from the activity of "bringing forth"; however, in a spiritual "bringing forth," the activity of "bringing forth" does cause or make the thing brought forth: in the former case, the activity of "bringing forth" and the thing brought forth are each extrinsic to the other; but, in the latter case, the activity of "bringing forth" contains within itself the thing brought forth as a potentiality, i.e., the thing brought forth is inherent in or intrinsic to the activity of "bringing forth."

To convey the meaning that "τέκνον" is inherent in "τεκεῖν," or, more precisely, in the woman herself, John wrote that she was "holding in womb" [ἐν γαστρὶ ἔχουσα = en gastri ekhousa]. The woman brought forth in the spiritual sense, not in the physical; therefore, she brought forth a spiritual entity.

However, the text unequivocally states that she bore "…a son virile, who…" The woman did not cause or make the man, as regards his body and soul, for God is the one who creates "the heaven" and the things in it. She did not make him mighty in faith and character during the time she was "holding in womb," for such strength in faith and morals comes from years of obedient love for God; indeed, the woman brought forth <u>him</u> precisely because he already was "a son virile."

Rather, the cardinals, IN ASSEMBLY, exercised their apostolic authority in order to bring forth spiritual authority. This is to say they brought forth a spiritual OFFICE. Thus, the "virile son" is depicted as both a <u>man</u> and a <u>thing</u>. John did not use a masculine participle or relative pronoun with "τέκνον" because he wanted the noun NEUTER.

"τέκνον" serves two purposes:

(1) It clearly alludes to the "virile son," for it does signify "child"; but,
(2) unmodified by any masculine participle or relative pronoun, it, by definition, renders no regard to the sex and age of the "child," and, thus it emphasizes the "virile son" as a thing, as "that which is brought forth," i.e., "the thing brought forth of/from her" [τὸ τέκνον αὐτῆς = to teknon autës].

The cardinals, in assembly, brought forth only one man, together with his spiritual authority, and that one man did not have that spiritual authority before they brought forth both him and it. Hence, the "bringing forth" described symbolically here cannot be other than a PAPAL ELECTION: for cardinals do not have to assemble in order to ordain a man to the office of an elder or to appoint a man to the office of bishop. To elect a pope, however, they must enter into formal assembly, and, at least, <u>the</u> two-thirds of <u>the</u> cardinals in the Church must vote the same to make a valid majority.

There is an old Chinese proverb that says: "A picture is worth a thousand words." So, too, the perception of it. The problem with symbolism is that it takes so long to explain it, for symbolism is a kind of picture-writing. To increase understanding of the symbolized series of events in the forepart of Chapter 12, consider what St. Paul wrote,

> 3 Let not someone deceive you regarding anything. That if the apostasy has not come first also the son of lawlessness is revealed, the son of annihilation, 4 the one opposed and exalted over all called God or worship, so that him unto the sanctuary of the God does he seat proclaiming himself that he is God. 5 Do you not remember that while I was still with you I told you these things? 6 And you know the thing restraining [τὸ κατέχον] at present until the revealing him in his own time. 7 For the mystery of lawlessness is operating already: only [there is] the one restraining, [ὁ κατέχων] right now until he is gotten out of [the] middle [ἐκ μέσου]. 8 And at this time [τότε] the lawless one will be revealed, whom the Lord Jesus will overcome with the breath of his mouth and annihilate with the manifestation of his presence,…[2 Thes. 2:3-8]

The "mystery of lawlessness" opposes the "mystery of the God," Jesus Christ and his Church. In the aforegiven excerpt, Saint Paul implied that the "mystery of lawlessness" would culminate in the "man of lawlessness." Saint John, too, implied the same in one of his own epistles,

> "Children, it is the last hour, and exactly as you heard that antichrist is coming, also at present many antichrists have come, thus do we know it is the last hour." [1 Jn. 2:18]

The "man of lawlessness," then, is the antichrist who is coming, i.e., the Antichrist. Relevant, therefore, to Chapter 12 is the order of events, as indicated by Paul:

(1) The apostasy comes;
(2) The "restrainer" of "the lawless one" is removed;
(3) The "man of lawlessness" is revealed; and
(4) Christ annihilates the Antichrist.

Note that Paul described the "restrainer" as both a man [verse 7] and a thing [verse 6], using a masculine nominalized participle and a neuter one, respectively; and this agrees with "a son virile" and "the thing born of her" in Chapter 12. Now, the "mystery of the God" opposes the "mystery of lawlessness," and, therefore, the "restrainer" of "the lawless one" is in the Church.

Like the other New Testament writers, Paul often used the noun "ναός" [naos], "sanctuary," as a symbol for the Church; hence, the phrase, "ἐκ μέσου" [ek mesou], is not just a Greek idiom here, but connotes the very middle of the sanctuary, the throne and the dais around it, where the Father and the Little Lamb and the Four Living Beings are.

The work of restraining the "mystery of lawlessness" properly belongs to the Vicar of Christ, as Jesus himself intimated,

> "And even I say to you that you are Peter [Πέτρος = Petros: the man], and upon this rock [πέτρᾳ = petra]: the thing] I will build my Church, and the gates of Hades shall not prevail against it."
> [Mt. 16:18]

Whereas men do not live long on this earth, and whereas the "restrainer" existed in Paul's day and will exist still when "the lawless one" is about to be revealed, it should have been obvious to all that τὸ κατέχον signified a spiritual office that is devolved from generation to generation, an office of great authority instituted and sustained by Christ himself. The term ὁ κατέχων indicated that only one man occupies the office at any particular time. The fact that only one man, because of his office, will be able to restrain the "mystery of lawlessness," the machinations of Satan himself to produce the Antichrist, should have induced in every Roman Catholic mind the conclusion that the office is the papacy. So often, the obstacle to the obvious is the ken of men themselves. Ach! I move on.

In Apocalypse 12:4, John wrote that the Dragon's tail...

> "dragged by force the third of the stars of the heaven and cast out them unto the earth..."

It has already been explained that the "stars" cast out unto the earth were those members of the clergy too tepid and too timid to resist the False Prophet, and so they apostatized. It is reasonable to assume that an equal or even greater percentage of the laity will also abandon Christ and the brethren.

The phrase, "of the heaven," signifies the Church, in general. However, the context in which a term appears should not be ignored. Observe that John did not use the definite article in the phrase, "a crown of twelve stars," but that he did use it in the phrase, "the third of the stars of the heaven," which, in its form, is the same as "the third of the men" [9:15]; to wit, the phrase means "THAT third of THOSE stars," thus making a special reference to the "stars" in the woman's crown. Taking into account the identity of the "woman" and the meaning of her "crown," the significance of "the third of the stars" becomes clear: Jesus will allow the crisis to reach the point that the third of the cardinals in the Church will betray, but not one cardinal more, because the two-thirds of the cardinals are necessary for a majority vote in electing a pope.

Bear in mind that before the "virile son" was brought forth, conflict was confined to the woman versus the dragon, and also that the dragon and his followers were still visible in "the heaven," i.e., "in the presence of [face to face with] the woman" [12:4]. But, after the "virile son" was brought forth, conflict was expanded to all the faithful versus the unfaithful, and the dragon and his followers were cast out, so that "not a place was found of them still in the heaven." [12:8].

Therefore, the term "stars" in the phrase, "the third of the stars," cannot represent all the clergy of the Church: rather, according to the context and the use of the definite article, it alludes to the woman and her crown, exclusively: for the defection of "the third of the stars" was a consequence only of the conflict between the woman and the dragon, not of the war described in 12:7-9.

Moreover, in the phrases of "Michael and his angels" and "the dragon and his angels" [12:7], the term "angels" signifies real angels as well as the episcopate, cardinals and bishops, with emphasis on the bishops who remained in their native countries. The term "angels" would have been too broad for 12:4; it was appropriate for 12:7-9.

Although John focused on the episcopate, it is safe to assume that unfaithful elders and laity will also be cast out during the war. Understand that, in 12:4, the third of the cardinals lose what little spiritual condition or state they have, but that Christ does not "vomit them out of his mouth," i.e., does not visibly rid his Church of them, until the war in "the heaven": for the False Prophet will bring the third of the cardinals into Satan's service, and they all will take their stand "face to face with" i.e., in opposition to, the woman, which means that they will still be in the Church, in the sense of visible organization.

Note well that the "virile son" is the central and pivotal figure in the evolvement of the "great sign." What Simeon said about the child Jesus, in regard to Israel, may be said about the "virile son," in regard to the Church,

> "This child is destined to be the downfall and the rise of many…a sign that will be opposed…so that the thoughts of many hearts may be laid bare." [Lk. 2:34-35]

Having supreme spiritual authority, the "virile son" will issue decrees of reform and will COMMAND their immediate implementation. Then, every member of the Church will have to choose either to remain with the "mystery of the God" or to join the "mystery of lawlessness."

Many will choose the latter, and this event will be the manifest apostasy, which Saint Paul mentioned to the Thessalonians.

Thus, the accounts of Paul and John accord:

PAUL	JOHN
(1) The apostasy comes first.	(1) The unfaithful are cast out of the Church formally and manifestly.
(2) The one restraining is gotten out of the middle.	(2) The "virile son" is snatched away to the God and to his throne.
(3) The "son of lawlessness" is revealed.	(3) The Beast becomes the Antichrist, Satan's champion of sin [Ch. 13].
(4) Christ annihilates the Antichrist.	(4) Christ annihilates the Beast and his empire during the third woe.

Verses 13-14 clarify the point that the war in "the heaven" will be fought and concluded BEFORE the woman flees. If the "great/loud voice" in 12:10 is that of the "virile son," then, he will be devoured or killed only after he has led the faithful through the war to victory over Satan and his followers. Having assassinated the "virile son," the Dragon will then realize that every faithful cardinal who survived the war is, potentially speaking, another "virile son"; and, for that reason, he will try to kill the woman, too.

Chapter 12 exhibits some looping, but its verses may now be arranged according to the order of events:

(1) verses 1-4, plus the first sentence in verse 5;
(2) then come verses 7-12;
(3) the second sentence in verse 5 [the "virile son" is snatched away] fits most plausibly, just after verse 12;
(4) and, finally, verse 6 is expanded into verses 13-18.

I say that the second sentence in verse 5 fits most plausibly after 12, i.e., before 13, simply because John placed it immediately before verse 6. In any case, the "they" in the verb τρέφωσιν = trephosin [verse 6] refers to the God and the "virile son," which connotes that the "virile son" will be "snatched away" before the woman reaches safety in the "wilderness." After the first sentence in verse 5, the "woman" symbolizes only the surviving faithful cardinals; the "seven thunders" in Chapter 10 are those same cardinals.

Consider now verses 13-18:

> 13 And when the dragon saw [aorist] that he was cast out [aorist] unto the earth, he pursued [aorist] the woman who brought forth [aorist] the virile one. 14 and to the woman were given [aorist] the two wings of the eagle the great one, so that she might fly unto the wilderness unto her place, where she is nourished therein for a time and times [dual noun] and a half time away from the face [mask] of the serpent. 15 and the serpent cast out [aorist] from his mouth after the woman water as a river, so that he might make her swept-away-by-flood. 16 and the earth came to the rescue for the woman and

> the earth opened [aorist] its mouth and swallowed [aorist] the river which the dragon cast out from its mouth. 17 and the dragon was enraged at the woman and went away [aorist] to do battle against the rest of her offspring the ones heeding the commandments of the God and holding the testimony of Jesus. 18 and he took his stand upon the sand of the sea.

To understand what John depicted symbolically in the above excerpt, a few terms must be explained first. However, let it be stated beforehand that the exact meaning of verse 16, even after explanation, will still be a matter that only Time will tell in full.

The term "eagle," like "head" and "horn," may be used as the symbol for either a ruler or the nations(s) he rules. For example, Moses wrote,

> "The Lord will raise up against you a nation from afar, from the end of the earth, that swoops down like an eagle,..." [Dt. 28:49]

And, God described Nebuchadnezzar, king of Babylon, and Hopha, pharaoh of Egypt, respectively, thus,

> "The Great Eagle, great of wing...came to Lebanon...But there was another eagle, great of wing, rich in plumage..." [Ez. 17:3 & 7]

Since a secular ruler derives his power from the nation(s) he rules, the greatness of the ruler connotes the greatness of the nation(s). John modified "eagle" with the definite article, even though he had not previously mentioned the term; and this tells the reader that this "eagle" will be easy to identify. The English equivalent would be "the eagle." But, John added the nominalized adjective "the great one." Thus, the whole expression signifies THE MIGHTIEST NATION ON EARTH. The reader has already met this emphatic form for designating the superlative, as in the title, "Babylon the Great" [Chapter 17], or "the tribulation the great one" [Chapter 7].

A Greek noun has a form called the "dual." Duals are used almost exclusively for things that naturally come in pairs or by twos, such as, eyes, hands, etc. It therefore, at first, seemed odd that John did not use just a dual and write "the wings of the eagle." His wording is saliently, because numerically, specific: "the TWO wings of the eagle."

The noun "πτέρυξ" [pteryx, wing] has several usages:

(1) the wing [of a bird];
(2) a winged creature, a bird;
(3) a thing like a wing, such as the flags or skirt of a coat of Greek armor; and
(4) anything that covers or protects like a wing.

In Greek, as in English, some nouns may be used in "synecdoche," a figure of speech in which a part is used for the whole or the whole for the part, the special for the general or the general for the special, as in "ten hands" for "ten sailors."

Bearing in mind, however, that the "eagle" symbolizes a nation, it should be clear to anyone that the two wings are not two parts of the "eagle," in itself, regarded as either territory or populace. Rather, the two wings are of the "eagle," in the sense that they are its possessions, just as someone may have two pets, two cars, etc.; and they are from the "eagle," in the sense that it is their origin, i.e., the "eagle" is the nation whence they came.

The reader has already met the genitive case, used for indicating both possession and origin, in the opening phrase of the prophecy, namely, "Ἀποκάλυψις Ἰησοῦ Χριστοῦ" [Apokalypsis Iësou Khristou]: for the revelation is of Christ, in that it is his prophecy that he will fulfill; and the revelation is from him, in that he is literally the origin or creator of it.

Understand one very important point here: the woman must flee from where she is to where she will be safe; therefore, God will not give her two parts of the "eagle's" territory or populace, but two objects, two things, which belong to the "eagle" and which the woman can use to escape to safety.

Like many other terms in the Apocalypse, the meaning of the word "wilderness" is found in the writings of the prophets.

Ezekiel wrote,

> "And I will bring you into the wilderness of people, and there I will plead with you face to face…" [Ez. 20:35]

This means that God led the nation of Israel into the seventy-year captivity among the pagan Babylonians, in order to cleanse the Jews of their inclination to idolatry, and to teach them the consequence of departing from the Ten Commandments.

Isaiah wrote,

> "And the wilderness shall rejoice, and shall flourish like the lily..." [Is. 35:1]

The prophet described the Gentiles as a "wilderness" because they did not yet have that spiritual life, which grows by faith in the true God.

Saint John the Baptist said,

> "I am the voice of one crying out in the wilderness, 'Make straight the way of the Lord'..." [Jn. 1:23, from Is. 40:3]

In this citation, the Jews, not the Gentiles, are the "wilderness" for two reasons:

(1) The religious leaders, even the seventy members of the Sanhedrin [who were appointed by the Romans], had become corrupt and taught many precepts merely human, to the result that the people, in general, did not worship God in spirit, as Jesus said of them,

> "...This adulterous and sinful generation..." [Mk. 8:38]

(2) The Jews did not have the "fullness of the truth by faith" in Jesus Christ, as Jesus himself defined someone who has this "fullness of the truth by faith,"

> "I tell you, among those born of women no one is greater than John [the Baptist]: but the least in the kingdom of the God is greater than he." [Lk. 7:28]

It has already been shown that the term, "the kingdom of the God," signifies the same as "the kingdom of the heaven," i.e., the Church, the visible organization established by Christ, not any other organization begun by a mere human being at a later time.

Hence, the term "wilderness" in 12:14 designates a region, which is not, and never has been, predominantly ROMAN CATHOLIC. If said "wilderness" had recently apostatized, then, John would have, at least, intimated harlotry or adultery.

Four items of interest may now be determined:

(1) the location of "the wilderness" [12:14];
(2) the general location of the "woman," when she will begin her flight;
(3) the location or identity of the Great Eagle; and
(4) the two objects or things by which the woman will make her escape.

First, juxtapose verses 6 & 14:

> 6 And the woman fled [aorist] unto <u>the</u> wilderness, where she has therein a place prepared by the God, so that they may nourish her [for] days a thousand two hundred sixty.
>
> 14 and to the woman were given [aorist] the two wings of <u>the</u> eagle the great one, so that she might <u>fly</u> unto the wilderness unto her place, where she is nourished therein [for] a time and times and a half time away from the face [mask] of the serpent.

It has already been shown that there will be only one period of 1260 days or 42 months, the "short time" or "little while" mentioned in 12:12 and 17:10; therefore, since 12:14's basic details and their order of mention are the same as 12:6's, it follows that both verses describe one and the same event. The aorist verb "fled," in verse 6, and the aorist verb "were given," in verse 14, tell that this event will happen only once.

In verse 6, John looped forward [to verse 14], perhaps, because he wanted to complete the account of the "virile son's" activities, i.e., that the God and he "may nourish her," and thus could John concentrate the narrative to the war in "the heaven."

The participial phrase, "prepared by the God" [verse 6], and the verb, "were given" [verse 14], indicate acts of Divine Providence. Hence, Divine Providence is the common denominator to the woman's place in the wilderness and to the two wings of the Great Eagle; thus, verse 14 initiates the idea that the Great Eagle, the mightiest nation on earth, is a part of that wilderness, the only region on earth where the woman will be safe for the 1260 days. Indeed, John introduced not only the Great Eagle with the definite article, but also the "wilderness," and this intimates that the "wilderness" can be easily identified too.

The woman will spend the 1260 days "away from the face of the serpent" [verse 14]. Note that John did not write simply, "away from the serpent." The noun "πρόσωπος" [prosöpos] means "face"; it also means "mask," the kind of mask that a Greek actor held up in front of his face to show what persona he was playing in the drama. John deliberately inserted the term to hint that the "Dragon," through most of the Chapter, symbolizes Satan in his political aspect or "mask."

Here, recall what was said earlier about the term "sign" in verses 1 and 3; also, bear in mind that, as the Dragon was in the presence of the woman [verse 4, like Latin preposition coram], so the woman was face to face with the Dragon. Yet, the phrase, "the face of the serpent," serves to remind the reader less about the visibility of the serpent's mask than about its description. The description is the more important because it involves not merely WHO the mask is, but also WHERE it is. The "face of the serpent" is the face of the DRAGON, and the salient features in the description of the Dragon are the SEVEN HEADS AND TEN HORNS [verse 3].

The phrase, "the face of the serpent," alludes forward to the description of the Beast, "while he was having SEVEN HEADS AND TEN HORNS" in Chapter 17, not of the Beast, "while he/it was having TEN HORNS AND SEVEN HEADS" in Chapter 13; and, whereas the events of Chapter 12 will happen in the politico-economic context of Chapter 17, Babylon the Great will also be part of Satan's mask at the time the Woman Clothed with the Sun begins her escape. Thus, the chief components of Satan's "face" or "mask" are Babylon and the Beast, and Satan is the mastermind behind them.

The Beast rules the "many waters/seven mountains," which are "the nations" of Asia and Africa; Babylon rules "the earth," which is Europe. The Beast is waging bloody persecution in his domain; Babylon is not yet doing so. Hence, the cardinals [the "woman," in verse 1] did not convene for the papal election in the Beast's domain, but in Babylon's—probably, in Vatican City in Rome, the traditional place. Thus, the surviving faithful cardinals [the "woman," after the first sentence in verse 5] must flee from a place in Europe to another place where she will be safe, "away from the face of the serpent."

For obvious reasons, she will not flee to Asia or Africa or Antarctica. She will not flee to any place in that territory that extends from Mexico down to the southern tip of South America, for two reasons:

(1) Said territory is, predominantly, Roman Catholic, and, therefore, cannot be called "wilderness."
(2) At least, two-thirds of the world's Roman Catholics reside in said territory, and the Beast cannot become a beast in the full sense of the term unless he persecutes the Catholics therein.

Thus, the woman will flee either to Australia or to that region of North America comprising Canada and the United States. Neither in present nor in prospect can Australia accommodate the description, "the mightiest nation on earth"; like South America, it will politically succumb to the Beast's economic coercion. Since the two wings given to the woman came from the Great Eagle, to the Great Eagle they will go: "the eagle the great one" is the United States of [North] America, which is not and never has been predominantly Roman Catholic.

The cardinals must travel fast and far, and the best possibility for succeeding in their escape is to go by air, not by land or by sea. The meaning of the term, "the two wings," is the synecdochical combination of usages #2 & #3 of pteryx, to wit, "the two winged objects" or "the two things with wings." In other words, the woman will, literally, "FLY unto the wilderness" by means of two aircraft. Since the two wings are possessions of the Great Eagle itself, they will probably be military transports.

Please note well this point: a beast, in the full sense of the prophetical term, is a king who uses his kingdom to afflict all or ALMOST all the members of

God's VISIBLE ORGANIZATION; therefore, the Beast can fulfill that definition ONLY IF he afflicts the Roman Catholics in the nations of Europe AND in the Hispanic nations of the Western Hemisphere, for they are five sixths of the total.

As long as said Hispanic nations remain, predominantly, Roman Catholic, and as long as Australia does not become the mightiest nation on earth, my statements about the "wilderness" and the Great Eagle in 12:14 will stand.

The prophetic term "earth," in its broadest sense, signifies temporal affairs or secular things. In 12:16, the term conveys the idea of "government agency," for note what John wrote,

"…and the earth <u>opened</u> <u>its</u> <u>mouth</u> and swallowed the river…"

"To open the mouth" is a Biblical expression indicating that someone speaks <u>with</u> <u>authority</u>. For example, when Jesus was about to deliver the Sermon on the Mount,

"…he opened his mouth and…" [Mt. 5:2]

After Christ finished his sermon,

> "…the crowds were astonished at his teaching, for he taught them as one having authority, and not as their scribes." [Mt. 7:28-29]

John used the same expression in regard to the Beast after God had allowed Satan to give the Beast "great authority,"

"And he opened his mouth…" [Apoc.13:6]

The noun "στόμα" [stoma] means "mouth"; like the English word, it can also signify "the outlet/entrance to a river or bay." But, the Greek noun has a usage that the English one does not: "the point [of a weapon]," "the edge of a sword." The mouth <u>devours</u>, the [edge of a] sword <u>kills</u>. In view of the verb "swallowed" in 12:16 above, the term "mouth" suggests synecdoche for "sword," the symbol for the military, and, therefore, the use of physical force in defense of the woman.

That John punned with the phrase, "opened its mouth," is corroborated by the context. The Old Testament prophets, sometimes, described a military force as a "river" or "flood." Isaiah wrote,

> "Therefore the Lord raises against them [the Jews] the waters of the river, great and mighty [the King of Assyria and all his power]…" [Is. 8:7]

And, again, Isaiah said,

> "Behold, the Lord has a strong one and a mighty [Assyria], who, like a downpour of hail, like a flood of water, great and overflowing…" [Is. 28:2]

Jeremiah wrote,

> "Egypt surges like the Nile, like rivers of billowing waters. ' I will surge forward,' he says, 'and cover the earth, destroying the city and its people'." [Jer. 46:7-8]

And, Jeremiah used the same idea in describing Nebuchadnezzar's campaign against the Philistines;

> 2 Thus saith the Lord: Behold there come up waters out of the north, and they shall be as an overflowing torrent, and they shall cover the land, and all that is therein, the city and the inhabitants thereof: then the men shall cry, and all the inhabitants of the land shall howl, [Jer. 47:2].

Thus, the meaning of 12:15-16 seems this, the serpent will send a military force after the woman to kill her, but the government of the Great Eagle will authorize its own military to destroy the force pursuing her.

Some people have asserted that the serpent's "river" in 12:15 symbolizes slanderous propaganda, and I have not even a velleity of doubt that they will be proved right; but, John used a Greek perfect participle that means "swept-away-by-flood," which tells me that the serpent intended to make the woman DEAD. So, the passage does not exclude the idea of false propaganda against the woman; it does include several terms that Old Testament prophets used in describing military force and destruction: considering the context of the passage, the very sequence of events leading up to it, I conclude that John meant to communicate the latter. I reiterate, however, that only Time will tell the meaning in full.

Here are four translations of 12:18, three of them being in current use:

(1) Then the dragon took his stand on the sand of the <u>seashore</u>. [NRSV]

(2) And the dragon stood on the <u>shore</u> of the sea. [NIV]

(3) And he took up his position by the <u>shore</u> of the sea. [NAB]

(4) And he stood upon the sand of the sea. [WV published 1915]

John actually wrote,

> καὶ ἐστάθη ἐπὶ τὴν ἄμμον τῆς θαλάσσης
> Kai estathë epi ten ammon tes thalassës
> And he took his stand upon the sand of the sea.

The meek Seer made verse 18 OXYMORONIC.

The adjective "oxymoronic" comes from the Greek "ὀξύς" [<u>oxys</u>, "sharp, keen, pointed"] + "μωρός" [möros, "foolish"], and, thus, means "pointedly foolish." However, one cannot see John's point of foolishness unless one knows grade school Greek here, specifically, the differentiation between "sand" and "sand."

The noun "ἄμμος" [<u>ammos</u>] signifies "sand," in the sense of "sandy ground or soil," whereas the noun "ψάμμος" [<u>psammos</u>] strictly denotes "sea-sand,"

and, in the plural, would signify "the links or dunes by the sea." In other words, the term "ἄμμος" [ammos] per se has absolutely nothing to do with a real sea or seashore; rather, it indicates the main characteristic of the terrain where the Dragon took his stand.

It has already been shown that John described the ancient Roman Empire as having two halves: the "earth" and the "sea." The "earth" is Europe, and the "sea" is North Africa and the Middle East. The main characteristic of the terrain in North Africa and the Middle East is, lo and behold, sandy ground or soil. John made verse 18 oxymoronic so that anyone who knows how to read will [hopefully] know how to read, and, thereby, get the point about "the sea." This "sea" is the one from which the Beast will initially ascend, and it is the one unto which the second plague of the third woe will be poured out.

The "loud voice" in 12:10 cried,

"Woe to the earth and the sea…" [12:12]

Yet, does anyone seriously hold the notion that the third woe's second plague will be inflicted on little wiggly fish? If one takes up translating the Apocalypse or commenting on it, surely, with the intention of getting down to its nitty-gritty, one ought, at least, to know the difference between "sand" and "sand."

When the woman reaches "her place" in the wilderness, the period of 1260 days or 42 months will commence; at that time, several events will happen:

(1) The Two Witnesses will appear.
(2) The Beast will occupy Jerusalem and the rest of Israel.
(3) The Beast will appoint the False Prophet as his regent over Europe.
(4) Saint Michael the Archangel will take his stand upon the "sea" and the "earth" [10:2 & 5].
(5) The Dragon [Satan himself, in person] will take his stand upon the "sand of the sea" [12:18].
(6) The "abomination of desolation" will take its stand in a holy place [Matthew 24:15, to be explained in comments on Chapter 13].
(7) The "seven thunders" will speak [10:3].

Although one cannot know beforehand exactly what the "seven thunders" will say, one can reasonably expect that they will do, at least, one or two of the following:

(1) They will counsel recent apostates to repent and return to the Church, and will urge "separated brethren" to rejoin it.
(2) They will issue severest warnings to those who are persecuting or intend to persecute God's holy ones.
(3) They will exhort the saints to persevere in the patient endurance of Christ unto death, and even to pray for their persecutors.
(4) They will remind the faithful that God is the supreme power and authority, and, so, they will instruct them that the Beast will go to annihilation after 3½ years, and, therefore, is not to be greatly feared.
(5) They will declare the principal teachings of Christ.
(6) They will ask God, the Blessed Virgin Mary, and Saint Michael to aid the faithful in spiritual battle and physical suffering.

Chapter 15

The Problem

John, under divine inspiration, deliberately wrote the Apocalypse rife with symbols and subtleties, so that the book would not be a breeze of a read for anybody. He understood that the symbols and subtleties constituted a major problem, one that would occasion many a pounding on pate and tearing of hair, and, perhaps, even splitting of wits and spitting of his name—none of which, may I point out, deterred him from his task; yet, it ought not to be thought that the Seer, a man whose mansuetude pervades every page of his epistles, had even one mean bone in his body. Aye, he intended the problem, but he also desired that the reader overcome it. John, therefore, designed the symbols and subtleties not merely as individual parts of the problem, but also as integral parts of the solution to it; and he evidenced this by making many of them mutually heuristic.

For example, the "seven heads and ten horns" of the dragon in Chapter 12 are the same chief features of the beast in Chapters 13 and 17. Each mention of the "heads" and "horns" points to the other two mentions of them; and the complete import of each, as well as the complete import of all three together, cannot be revealed unless each is cross-referred with the other two. Each depiction of the bizarre "heads" and "horns" should so impinge human imagination, that no one [hopefully] will praetermit what is so clearly a series of correlative clues.

Alas, the disadvantage of a heuristic device is told aptly by an old African proverb, "I pointed at the moon, and all you saw was my finger."

For another example, John used a four-part formula a total of four times, thus:

Formula #1…[all] nations and TRIBES and peoples and languages…[7:9]
Formula #2…[many] peoples and nations and languages and kings…[10:11]
Formula #3…[every] TRIBE and people and language and nation…[13:7]
Formula #4…[many] peoples and multitudes and nations and languages…[17:15]

John constituted the formula not merely by connecting four nouns with ands, but, mainly, by putting the same three nouns [peoples, nations, languages] in all four instances. Comparing the four formulas finds that the Seer randomized the order of mention for the four nouns in each instance, and this intimates that their order of mention is irrelevant to secerning the formula's import, individually or collectively speaking. Hence, attention narrows to the fourth noun, the odd object that does not appear in all four instances. Before proceeding, however, I reiterate that John did not have a mean bone in his body.

Formula #1 presents the symbolical number "four" regarding the totality of the Roman Empire; formula #3 presents it regarding the totality of the world. The time of Chapter 7 comes just before Christ opens the seventh seal for concluding the first major part of the Father's plan; the time of Chapter 13 comes just before the angel sounds the seventh trumpet for concluding the second major part of the Father's plan. In the time of Chapter 7, the conversion of the minority of the Jews is fulfilled; in the time of Chapter 13 [albeit, at the end of the second woe], the conversion of the vast majority of the Jews is fulfilled: John put the odd noun "tribe(s)" in formulas #1 and #3 to allude to the twelve tribes of Israel, and to clue the reader that the contexts of Chapters 7 and 13 are the same or very similar in certain respects.

Notwithstanding that formulas #2 and #4 relate to the same time, the odd noun in formula #2 is "kings," and the odd noun in formula #4 is "multitudes." It does initially seem that John should have put either "kings" or "multitudes" in both of those instances, even as he put "tribe(s)" in both formulas #1 and #3. However, formula #2 relates to the whole world where some heads of state or "kings" are subordinate to the Beast and some still independent of him; whereas, formula #4 relates only to the "many waters" where all the "heads" or kings are subordinate to the Beast.

As has already been shown, the "many waters" are the "seven mountains" [17:9], to wit, the Great Harlot is seated upon the "seven mountains," NOT UPON THE SEVEN KINGS; and for that reason John put "multitudes" instead of "kings" in formula #4.

A translation more accurate than "multitudes" for the odd noun [okhloi] is "disordered crowds" or "mobs." The Greek term refers to the bloody persecution in Asia and Africa, and, perhaps, to social turmoil in some places after the event of the 200 Million Horsemen earlier [9:15-19]. Thus, John appropriately restricted the term to formula #4.

Meanwhile, Babylon the Great in Europe has become the wealthiest city in the whole world, and the Eagle the great one in North America is still the mightiest nation on all the earth, because their societies have been stable and economies prosperous. Hence, John did not put [okhloi] as the odd noun in formula #2.

So, if formula #4 did not illuminate and corroborate 17:9, it would be utterly nugatory information, and it would not fit with any other piece of the jigsaw puzzle that Chapter 17 is. Formula #4 supports 17:9, but this cannot be perceived unless formula #4 [its odd noun, specifically] is compared with, at least, formula #2, which is what John intended the reader do in the first place.

Thus, each instance of the four-part formula, like each mention of the "heads" and "horns," was designed as a clue or lead to the others, as potentially, the beginning of a chain reaction of inquiry and discovery, as the start of seemingly mad loops forward and backward in the mind, as in the text itself. Sooner or later, indirection finds direction out. And, that is the advantage of a heuristic device, if only the reader takes it.

In 5:9, the Living Beings and Elders sing to the Little Lamb,

> "...You purchased for the God by your blood [men] from every tribe and language and people and nation..."

The formula, in this instance, concerns the totality of mankind, from the first to the last human being. The Little Lamb is the person both divine and human. It is eternally certain that he, as the Amen, purchased men from every tribe, etc.; and so it is absolutely certain that he, as the "mystery of the God," will progress from Jerusalem to the whole world, so that eventually he will offer the fullness of his purchase to the whole world, even to its last day.

Although the formula in 5:9 concerns mankind past and present and future, the other four formulas appear only in Chapters relating the future progress of the "mystery of the God" toward universality. Indeed, formula #1 and formula #3 may be regarded as progress reports or indicators. As soon as the "mystery of the God" achieves universality, the four-part formula is absented from the subsequent narrative, simply because it is absolutely certain that the "mystery of the God's" universality will continue to the world's last day; and, so, John appropriately never mentioned the formula again. By comparing only formulas #1–#4 in their contexts, one can understand them, completely, as has already been evinced; ergo, comparing them with the formula in 5:9 is not necessary. The point is that formulas #1–#4 pertain to only the future progress toward universality, starting soon after John's day, and that is why the Seer plied the reader with the formula for, exactly, a total of four times from Chapter 6 onward. Hence, I omitted the formula in 5:9 from the explanation of the other four.

CHAPTER 16

APOCALYPSE CHAPTER 13

Verse 1 reads,

> "And I saw from the sea a [little] beast ascending, having horns ten and heads seven and upon the horns of it ten diadems and upon the heads of it names of blasphemy."

The neuter noun "θηϱίον" [thërion] is, technically speaking, the diminutive of "θηϱ" [thër], but in usage was equivalent to it. "θηϱίον" [thërion] means:

(1) a wild animal, beast;
(2) an animal;
(3) a poisonous animal, a reptile, serpent, or a LITTLE ANIMAL.

By this term, John alluded to "the little horn" in Daniel 7. For this commentary, however, I will simply use the term "Beast." Bear in mind that next to the Beast ascending from the sea is the Dragon [Satan] standing upon the "sand of the sea." From this point on, Satan will not leave the side of the Beast.

Now, in Chapter 12, John described Satan thus;

> "a great flame-colored dragon having heads seven and horns ten and upon the heads of it seven diadems."

Cross-refer the description of the dragon in Chapter 12 with that of the beast in Chapter 13: behold! John reversed the order of mention regarding heads & horns; and the Beast that, in Chapter 17, wore NO DIADEMS, now in Chapter 13 is wearing ten of them.

The reason for this is stated in the latter part of verse 2,

> "And the dragon gave it [the Beast] his power and his throne and great authority."

A little chart shows this more easily:

	Dragon, Chapter 12		Beast, Chapter 13
Diadems (sovereignty):	7 diadems	from heads to horns	10 diadems
Order of mention:	Upon 7 heads and 10 horns	reversed	10 horns and 7 heads
	Beast in service of Satan	reversed role	Satan in service of beast

The present participle "ἀναβαῖνον" [anabainon], "ascending," agrees in number, gender, and case with "θηϱίον" [thërion], the direct object of "εἶδον" [eidon], "I saw"; the participle connotes continuous state or action.

The prepositional phase, "ἐκ τῆς θαλάσσης" [ek tës thalassës], "from the sea," signifies that he derives power and authority from "the nations," especially, from the Confederation of the Ten Kings; and this manner of phrasing is echoed in 17:11 so:

> "…καὶ αὐτὸς ὄγδοός ἐστιν καὶ ἐκ τῶν ἑπτά ἐστιν…"
> "…kai autos ogdoos estin kai ek tön epta estin…"

Hence, the Beast at the beginning of Chapter 13 is in the state or activity of "ascending from the sea," and he will continue in it until he suffers total defeat at Armageddon.

It is now clear that the "power and throne and great authority" the Beast receives from Satan himself are additional to those the Beast derives from the "sea"; and this explains the clause in 17:11, which says;

"...And himself is the eighth..."

This corresponds to what was said of "the little horn" in Daniel 7,

"...Different from those before him..."

The Beast will become an EIGHTH something because of Satan's decision to serve the Beast. Lucifer, who declared to God, "Non Serviam, I shall not serve!," will now serve a mere human being! Never once in the past has Satan done this; secular kings and their kingdoms had always served him.

If the reader doubts that what I have said accords with John's meaning, then, let the reader check the order in which John mentioned the Beast's features in Chapter 17, verse 3,

> "...and I saw a scarlet beast...having HEADS SEVEN and HORNS TEN."

This order of mention is the opposite of that in Chapter 13: HORNS TEN and HEADS SEVEN: But, it is the same as that in Chapter 12. Hence, the order of mention regarding heads and horns functions as a temporal indicator; it affords the reader another means of deducing the exact sequence of events, i.e., that the contents described in Chapter 13 follow immediately after Chapters 12/17.

It should now be evident to everyone that the Beast at the beginning of Chapter 13 assumes the additional state described as "ascending from the abyss," i.e., the Beast in Chapter 11 and Chapter 13 are one and the same entity. Similarly, the order of mention regarding heads and horns can be used to demonstrate that the 1260 days of the Two Witnesses and of the Woman Clothed with the Sun, and the 42 months of the Beast and of the nations trampling Jerusalem, are all one and the same tract of time.

The Beast, in the vision of Chapter 17, does not have diadems on its ten horns, but it does have them on its ten horns in Chapter 13. This fulfills what the angel in Chapter 17, verse 12, said,

> "And the ten that you saw are ten kings that have not yet received a kingdom, but they will be receiving authority as kings for one hour together with the Beast."

The angel was referring to the worldwide kingdom, the same kingdom which Satan offered to Christ atop a mountain. When the beast receives Satan's power wherewith to establish a global empire, the ten kings will become his regents in that empire.

Bear in mind that verses 1-4 describe the appearance and personal character of the Beast: the Beast regarded as a whore symbolizes the Antichrist. The Ten Kings serve the Beast. As a beast uses its horns for attack and defense, so the Antichrist will use the Ten Kings. Therefore, though the ten diadems are on the ten horns, one must remember that the ten horns are on the Beast; the Beast, not the ten kings, has sovereignty here.

Both the Dragon and the Beast have seven heads: As Satan is the maximum in evil among angels, so the Antichrist, after he receives from Satan the status of "ascending from the abyss," will become the maximum of evil among men. This does not mean the maximum possible, but the maximum permissible according to God's mysterious plan. God never acts in vain, and He will not allow evil greater than necessary to punish the rebellious and to perfect the faithful. Even so, verse 1 opens the chapter on a most ominous note, and subsequent verses resound it. The time has come: God has let loose the beast of hell.

It was the visible head of Christ's body, the Church that restrained the "mystery of lawlessness" from culminating in the appearance of the Beast. But, now the Dragon, having assassinated the Vicar of Christ, and having, at least, driven the "woman" into isolated refuge, is permitted to set a visible head on his own worldly body. Thus, it must be these two commanders, "τὸ θηρίον" [to thërion] and "τὸ ἀρνίον" [to arnion], the little Beast or horn, against the Little Lamb.

Satan desires a visible head for his global kingdom, because only by means of a visible supreme leader can he be most efficient in seducing souls and waging war against the Lamb and his brethren. However, it is one thing to induce ten kings to agree. It is another thing to coordinate the activities of a much greater number of agents and agencies on a global scale. Ever since the

Little Lamb and the brethren had dethroned paganism in the last beast, the sixth one called the Roman Empire, ever since they had beheaded it, Satan and his demons have had to use a cruder method of trying to achieve their ends; positing an agreeable "object" in the imagination of a human being, especially, in that of a habitually unreflective, impulsive individual, may be compared to dangling a carrot in front of a hungry donkey, except that the donkey seldom fails to pursue the one carrot.

But a leader whom people can see and hear, a man who can, by great natural talents, win admiration and vicarious approval—one who seemingly works signs and wonders—is the leader Satan desires and, therefore, is willing to serve in order to have. So great is Satan's hatred toward Christ and his Church. Imagine the pain, the horrible pain, from this abject contradiction in his intellect and in the warring rage of his will.

Most strictly speaking, the "ten horns" mentioned in Chapters 12, 13, and 17, regarded as a group, are not the "ten horns" on the fourth beast in Daniel 7. It is possible, albeit unlikely, that one or more of the apocalyptic horns will be among the fourth beast's seven horns, which the "little horn" in Daniel 7 will not tear away at the beginning of his ascendancy.

Historically, it has most often been the case that members of a confederation have been relevant to one another because near one another, such as the members of NATO or SEATO. Since the basis of the relationship between the Beast and Babylon the Great will be mainly wealth, and since most of the wealth of the "Burning Mountain" lies in the region just north, east, and south of the Caspian Sea, it seems exceedingly unlikely that the Confederation of Ten Kings, in entirety or part, will arise elsewhere, e.g., in Palestine or North Africa.

This does not absolutely rule out that John intended to remind the reader of the "ten horns" on the fourth beast in Daniel 7; for remember the "little horn" will spring up in their midst and lay low three of them; and those three will be in the territory quondamly of the ancient Roman Empire and will be Islamic.

Note well what was written about the Apocalyptic Beast in 13:2,

> "And the beast I saw was like a leopard and the feet of it as of a bear and the mouth of it as the mouth of a lion…"

As far as I know, the other place where the Bible mentions these symbolical beasts, the "leopard," the "bear," and the "lion," together in the same context, plus the fourth beast with "ten horns," is in Daniel 7:2-8,

> "In the vision I saw during the night, suddenly the four winds of heaven stirred up the great sea, from which emerged four immense beasts, each different from the others. The first was like a lion, but with wings of an eagle...the second was like a bear...after this I looked and saw another beast like a leopard; on its back were four wings like those of a bird. And it had four heads...After this...I saw the fourth beast, different from all the others, terrifying, horrible, and of extraordinary strength; it had great iron teeth with which it devoured and crushed, and what was left it trampled with its feet. I was considering the ten horns it had, when suddenly another, a little horn, sprang out of their midst, and three of the previous horns were torn away to make room for it."

As an incidental, but no less informative, note here, I direct your attention to the phrases, "each different from the others" and "different from all the others." The succession of beasts corresponds to the succession of metals in the "statue" of Daniel 2; likewise, the phrase, "different from the others," corresponds to the successive inferiority of the metals in that statue: each beast is different, in the sense that each metal was inferior to the one before it. I explained what this meant, as regards the metals: each succeeding empire will be more brutal than the one before it in attempting to impose idolatry on God's people.

A person present in the vision of Daniel 7 said that the "little horn" will be "different from those before him..." [7:24], and this means that the "little horn" [the Beast with seven heads and ten horns] will be the worst of all. He will also be the last.

Hippolytus, in his treatise on Christ and Antichrist (#49), wrote,

> "After the manner of the law of Augustus, by whom the empire of Rome was established, he [Antichrist] will also rule and govern, sanctioning everything by it, and taking greater glory to himself. For

> this is the fourth beast, whose head was wounded and healed again, in its being broken up or even dismembered, and partitioned into ten crowns; and he then [Antichrist] shall with knavish skill heal it, as it were and restore it."

In his commentary on Daniel 2, Hippolytus wrote,

> "As these things are destined to come to pass, and as the toes of the statue turn out to be democracies and the ten horns of the beast are distributed among ten kings, let us look at what is before us more carefully, and scan it, as it were, with open eye"…"The legs of iron are the 'terrifying and horrible beast' by which the Romans who now hold the empire are meant"…"the one other little horn springing up in the midst is the Antichrist."

The "lion," the "bear," and the "leopard" in Daniel 7 were the Babylonian, Medo-Persian, and Grecian Empires, respectively. The fourth beast was the Roman Empire, but, by counting from the Egyptian, as the Apocalypse does, it was the sixth beast. The beast in Chapter 13 and 17 has seven heads; it is the "little horn" in Daniel 7. Saint Iranaeus [d. 140 AD] held that the beast "ascending from the sea" in Apocalypse 13 is the Antichrist [Book 5: 28/2]. The "three horns," which the "little horn" will someday seize suddenly for himself, may or may not be the "lion," the "bear," and the "leopard."

Only Time will tell whether what I suggest about the territory of the Confederation of Ten Kings is correct. But, one thing is certain before hand: the "little horn" shall begin his ascendancy in what was once the territory of the Roman Empire, not the region that is now Christian, but the rest now Islamic.

The "ten horns" of the beast in Apoc. 13 wear diadems. The noun "διαδημα" [diadema] means, "a band or fillet, especially, the band around the "τιαρα" [tiara] of a Persian king." The Persians dwelled in the land now called Iran; and, Rome's eastern frontier never reached farther than the Tigris River. So, there are indications that the Confederation of Ten Kings will arise outside the territory once of Rome, yet they are too few to stand tantamount to a cogent argument. One must keep an open mind on the matter.

I strongly suspect that the Beast's symbolic components of a "leopard," "bear," and "lion" allude to the territory or general region of the same three beasts in Daniel 7; however, the point cannot be proved absolutely.

The chief traits or characteristics of the Beast are symbolized by the leopard, bear, and lion:

(1) The leopard is known for cunning, ability, and swift attack;
(2) The bear uses its clawed feet for battering and trampling; and
(3) The lion uses its powerful jaws and sharp teeth for "devouring" its prey.

Interestingly, most of the Beast is "like a leopard," but only its feet are "like a bear's," and only its mouth is "like a lion's." Note that John mentioned the term "mouth" TWICE.

To prevent confusion about the horns, keep before the mind one thing: the fourth beast in Daniel 7 was an EMPIRE, whereas the Beast in Apocalypse 13 is a PERSON who heads an empire. John surely suggests here that the apocalyptic Beast will be a synergism of all the other beasts' qualities, a synergism potentiated to the category of the demonic or diabolical by Satan's own PERSON.

The seer emphasized that the Antichrist's dominant characteristic will be extraordinary cunning, an intelligence so sharp and swift in practice and execution of plan, as will astonish many, so exemplified in Daniel 7,

> "...suddenly another, a little horn, sprang out of their midst, and three of the previous horns were torn away to make room for it."

Imagine the cunning and deception requisite for completing, as the text suggests, three coups d'état, simultaneously, under the very noses of those three rulers, a feat that will surely impress the Ten Kings.

The Beast's mouth [on the seventh head, obviously] was "as the mouth of a lion." In the Apocalypse, the "lion" is the symbol of the Papacy; and "thunder" aptly is the symbol for the voice of heaven, the Pope. Antichrist will be the Vicar of Satan, and he will roar forth his false teachings and propaganda throughout the world, and issue the decree of death to any and all who oppose him.

Christ said that Satan was a liar and a murderer from the beginning; so will the Antichrist be as a liar is to the soul, as a murderer is to the body; therefore, the symbol of the "lion's mouth" has a double significance: to devour or to kill the soul as well as the body.

Finally, the "feet" of the bear mean that the Beast will use whatever force necessary to batter his enemies into subjection, to trample down anyone or anything that does not promote his aims, and to demolish even the very foundations of civilization, so that humanity falls into the darkest barbarism, even to sacrificing millions of victims to the Beast, and drinking their blood. Those who do not have "the sign of God," those who do not have their names "in the scroll of the life of the lamb," will worship Antichrist.

God will permit Satan to give the Beast "his own power and throne and great authority"; and this tells us that the Beast, without Satan, could not do as much as he will do: The noun "δυναμις" [dynamis] here does not mean simply "power" or "might"; it refers to the very nature of the person who has that power, connoting all the natural faculties, skill, and knowledge of and in that person. St. Paul used the same word in regard to Christ's power, his innate or natural ability to subject all things to himself. Hence, John's meaning is unequivocal here: Satan will be allowed to use his angelic power in service to the Beast. Obviously, God will limit Satan; otherwise, in the blinking of an eye, a second belt of minute asteroids would orbit the sun where the earth once had.

The "ἐξουσία" [exousia], the authority or right, which Satan will give to the Beast, will be the opposite of Christ's authority or right. Here, John again indicates the inseparability of authority and power. The Father gave to Christ as Son of Man his divine task of redeeming mankind; similarly, Satan will give the Beast the task of destroying the mystical body of Christ, which continues the act of redemption. John wrote as clearly as language allows; the reader will, hopefully, discern that the prophet's words are serious and solemn.

CHAPTER 17

THE TWO SWORDS

Verses 3-4 of Chapter 13 read,

> "And one of its heads [was] like [one] slain unto death, and the plague of its death was healed. And the general earth wondered after the Beast. And they worshipped the Dragon, for it had given its authority to the Beast, and they worshipped the Beast saying, "Who [is] like the Beast, and who can fight against it?" [Apoc. 13:3, 4]

The noun "πληγὴ" [plëgë] means a "blow, stroke, impact, wound." The English word "plague" is derived from it, and, as a prophetic term, it means "divine punishment." Here, the noun alludes to the blow or stroke from a weapon, namely, the sword; this fact is eventually confirmed toward the end of verse 14,

> "...the Beast that has the plague [blow, wound] of the sword and lived."

The English word "sword" is a rather broad term: more specific are "rapier," "cutlass," "saber," and "broadsword." Greek also differentiates between "sword" and "sword." In verse 14, John used the noun "μάχαιρα" [makhaira], denoting a "standard short sword, for example, in the military." So, the blow or "plague" to one of the seven heads was inflicted by means of a sword, a "μάχαίρα" [makhaira] symbolically or prophetically speaking: that it was the sixth head, which was "like one slain unto death," can be easily deduced.

Historically, the beast, in the general sense, was continuous from the Egyptian to the Roman Empire. In the special sense, Satan was the animus, or soul, and mastermind of each beast. The second beast conquered and replaced the first, the third the second, etc. The sixth beast was the Roman Empire. When the throne of Caesar ceased to be occupied by a pagan, the head of the beast was lost, and Satan could not replace it. Hence, the continuity of the historical beast was ended.

This, in no way, means that paganism was completely eliminated from the Roman Empire, as the laments of the early Fathers of the Church so often attested. The head of the sixth beast received the blow of the sword, but not every other part of its body. Some paganistic elements or anti-theistic tendencies remained.

The two symbols, "beast" and "head," are now clearly understood: when the general population or society is anti-theistic in belief and practice, then, an incomplete "beast" exists; and, when an anti-theistic individual becomes the supreme ruler of that "beast," then, a "head" for the "beast" has come into existence, and, so, the "beast" is complete, it is a whole "beast."

The history books have recorded many "beasts," but John wrote only about those that come or would come into contact with all or almost all of God's people. This explains why the "Burning Mountain" in Chapter 8 was not depicted as a beast with a head, but it will become a considerable part of the seventh beast, as described in Chapter 17. Even now, the flame-colored dragon is at work, and the flames of Islam have been growing since World War II.

Notwithstanding these things, the significance of the makhaira has yet to be shown. The Apocalypse mentions only two kinds of sword: the "μάχαίρα" [makhaira] and the "ῥομφαίᾳ" [romphaia = rhomphaia]. Here, recall that the Greek noun "στόμα" [stoma] signifies "a mouth" as well as "the point or edge of a sword": a mouth devours, a sword kills. Hence, in turn, the two kinds of sword allude to the two kinds of death, namely, the first death and the second death.

Hereat, I can sense your puzzlement, ye Friends, and I must advise you that I am about to put your "σοφία" [sophia], your practical intelligence to the test, i.e., to the "βάσανος" [basanos = the rack or instrument of torture by which one is forced to divulge the truth]. For, though I will now provide the explanation, you will have to supply concentration and apply reason.

In case you have not caught John's hint, the part of which must be juxtaposed in order to catch it, then, I state here Christ's warning in Lk 12:4-5,

> "I tell you my friends, do not be frightened by one who is killing the body and after that is not having more that he will do. And I warn you of whom you should fear: you should fear those who after killing, are having authority to cast unto [the] Gehenna [εἰς τὴν γέενναν = eis tën geennan]."

The term "θάνατος" [thanatos] means "death"; capitalized "ὁ θάνατος" [o Thanatos], it denotes the personification of death, as the king or ruler of "Ἅδης" [Hades], the underworld or abode of the dead; and was regarded as the twin brother of sleep.

So, in the New Testament, those who die go to one of three "places":

> (1) "οὐρανός" [ouranos], heaven [in this case, the kingdom of heaven above, which shall not pass away];
> (2) "Ἅδης" [ades], Hades;
> (3) "ἡ λίμνη τοῦ πυρός" [ë/hë limnë tou pyros], the lake of fire.

Since "θάνατος" [thanatos] appertains only to:

> (1) "Ἅδης" [ades], Hades and
> (2) "ἡ λίμνη τοῦ πυρός" [ë/hë limnë tou pyros], the lake of fire,

only Hades and the lake of fire pertain to this present explanation.

John differentiates between Hades and the lake of fire, as 20:14-15 shows,

> καὶ ὁ θάνατος καὶ ὁ ᾅδης <u>ἐβλήθησαν εἰς τὴν λίμνην τοῦ πυρός</u>
> "And death and Hades <u>were cast out unto the lake of fire.</u>
>
> This is the second death, the lake of fire. And if anyone was not found written in the scroll of life, he was cast out unto the lake of fire."

In 20:10, John wrote that the lake of fire is everlasting,

> "And the Devil who deceived them [Gog and Magog] was cast out unto the lake of fire and sulfur where both the Beast and the False Prophet are; and they will be being put to the torture day and night unto the ages of the ages."
> [εἰς τοὺς αἰῶνας τῶν αἰώνων = eis tous aiönas tön aiönön].

In 19:20, he indicates that not only the soul, but also the body, will suffer therein,

> "The two [Beast and False Prophet] while living [ζῶντες = zöntes, present participle] were cast out unto the lake of fire [the one] burning with sulfur."

In view of Christ's statement in Lk. 12:4-5 above and in Mt. 10:28, Mt. 7:13, it is now clear that the second death is spiritual death, the death of the soul, and, therefore, the first death is physical death, the death of the body. When Lazarus died the first death, the physical one, Jesus, who is the Resurrection and the Life, told his apostles,

> "Our friend Lazarus has fallen asleep: but I am going there to wake him." [Jn. 11:11]

Those who die the first death go to Hades; their bodies are dead, but not their souls: from Christ's point of view, they are "asleep," in a temporary state.

The lake of fire is Gehenna, or hell proper; and those who die in a state of mortal sin die both the physical and spiritual, the first and second deaths: from Christ's point of view, they are "cast out" from his presence forever, as if they had never been, as if they had been cast into nothingness.

The rhomphaia was a long, double-edged sword used by Thracians; this is the kind of sword coming out of Christ's mouth in 1:16. It is double-edged [or double-mouthed: δίστομος = distomos] because Christ, who is the Word of God, has slain the first and second deaths for all those who believe in Him.

John mentioned the term "στόμα" [stoma], i.e., "mouth; point or edge of a sword," TWICE in his description of the Beast, because the Antichrist will have authority to kill both body and soul; and, next to Satan, to him will Christ's warning, in Lk. 12:4-5 above, appertain most of all.

The rhomphaia, when the time of judgment comes, will be used to inflict total destruction; indeed, the Greek term used in denoting this "plague" is "απωλεια" [apöleia], which carries the equivalence of annihilation, and which refers the reader's attention to the king of the locusts of the first woe: "Ἀπολλύων" [Apollyön] "Destroyer," the angel from the abyss— Satan.

In Chapter 17:8 & 11, John twice tells the destiny of the beast with seven heads and ten horns,

> "...καὶ εἰς ἀπώλειαν ὑπάγει,"
> "...kai eis apölen ypagei,"
> "...and unto destruction is going."

As soon as one finds a correspondence of this repeated phrase with 19:15, one can clearly ascertain the significance of the Thracian battle sword,

> "From his [Christ's] mouth comes a sharp rhomphaia, so that with it he may strike down the nations..."

Similarly, in the letter to Pergamum, Christ warns the Bishop there,

> "Repent then: and if not, I will come to you quickly and make war against them [the Nicolaitans and those like Balaam] with the rhomphaia of my mouth." [Apoc. 2:16]

The warning in the letter to Pergamum is a warning to all the Church for all time, especially, the time of the Beast: the wages of the sin of heresy is double death.

Since the rhomphaia, which is a long sword, symbolizes total destruction, it should not surprise that the makhaira is a short sword and symbolizes partial destruction; in most cases, the former relates to the second death and permanence, and the latter relates to the first death and temporariness.

In 13:3, John wrote,

Καὶ μίαν ἐκ τῶν κεφαλῶν αὐτοῦ ὡς ἐσφαγμένην εἰς θάνατον,
Kai mian ek tön kephalön autou ös esphagmenën eis thanaton,
And one of the heads of it as one slain unto death,

καὶ ἡ πληγὴ τοῦ θανάτου αὐτοῦ ἐθεραπεύθη.
kai ë plëgë tou thanatou autou etherapeuthë.
and the blow of the death of it was healed.

The first part of this verse is actually a continuation of the description in verses 1 and 2; and that is why the word "one" and the passive participle "slain" are in the accusative case: tacit is the idea that John saw one of the heads, etc.

In Chapter 17, John dealt with the term "head," mainly, as a "mountain," an empire; but, in Chapter 13, he dealt with it, chiefly, as a man, a king, or emperor. It has already been shown that the continuity of the historical beast, the beast in the general sense, was ended when the throne of Caesar ceased to be occupied by an anti-theistic emperor.

The first part of verse 3 refers to that special event that ended the beast's continuity, and, therefore, it is <u>the sixth head as king</u> that was "slain unto death." John clearly understood that the blow or wound to the sixth head was lethal, i.e., John knew that the head of the Roman beast <u>would</u> cease to be pagan at some point in the future. To say that the lethal wound was "healed" means not only that Satan has brought back the beast from the dead, so to speak, but also that he has put an anti-theistic individual man into supreme authority and power.

None of the seven heads on the beast in Chapter 17 was described as having received a lethal wound, because, at that time, the beast was still <u>regional</u>: It had not yet come into contact <u>with all or almost all of God's people</u>, and, therefore, like the "Burning Mountain" of Chapter 8, did not yet qualify as the seventh beast. For this reason, the empires of such men as Napoleon [generally, called the Beast in his own day] and Hitler do not qualify, and absolutely nothing was written of them in the Apocalypse.

As mentioned in 12:9, Satan has deceived <u>the whole world</u>; and, by the time of Chapter 13, all the nations, all save one, either belong, or soon will belong, to the seventh evil empire. When the great body of the beast received a head, then, and only then, could it be said that the lethal wound of the sixth head was healed. The healing of the sixth head is another indicator that Chapter 13, chronologically speaking, follows Chapter 17.

John chose the verb "θεραπεύειν" [therapeuein], deliberately, to convey irony, for it means "to attend, to treat medically, to heal or to cure." When Jesus was informed that Lazarus was ill, he replied,

"this sickness is not unto death…" [Jn. 11:4]

Christ knew Lazarus would die the first death, the physical one; but, since Christ is the one living unto the ages of the ages, he viewed physical death as a kind of sleep. Therefore, the "sickness unto death" is the state of serious sin, and the place that has <u>authority</u> over a soul in serious sin is the lake of fire. John expresses this, indirectly, in 20:6, which reads,

> "Blessed and holy are those who have a part in the first resurrection. Over these <u>the second death has no authority</u>."

Now, Satan is absolutely in the state of serious sin. It is, therefore, most ironical that the "physician" who cannot heal himself of the "sickness unto death," should resurrect, so to speak, the dead body of the historical beast, a beast that itself has the "sickness unto death" and "…goes unto destruction." Every thought and desire of Satan is an otiose motion. Hell is the place naturally right for him unto the ages of ages.

The weapon that inflicted the blow on the sixth head is mentioned in verse 14,

> "…it [the beast from the earth] deceives the inhabitants upon the earth…, telling them that dwell upon the earth to make an image for the Beast, one who has the blow of the <u>makhaira</u> and lived."

John used the term "makhaira," the short sword, because only a <u>part</u> of the sixth beast was dealt a deathblow, namely, the head, and because the head's death was only <u>temporary</u>. And, the rest of the body has now slept for almost 1700 years; only recently has it begun to stir.

The man who held that "makhaira" was Constantine, and he dealt the lethal blow to Emperor Diocletian when he defeated the emperor's army under the command of Maxentius in 310 AD. In 312 AD, Constantine was baptized, and, in 313 AD, he persuaded Licinius, then the co-emperor in the West, to join him in promulgating the Edict of Milan, which gave equal rights to all religions and restored confiscated property to the Christians. Finally, in 382 AD, the emperor Theodosius I proscribed paganism and proclaimed Christianity throughout the empire. Yea, the head of the beast was dead.

"Ah ha!," a clever pate may interpose, "Remembering that you said the fourth seal in Chapter 6 described the justice God decreed upon the Jews, I found the Greek text in the library and read what kind of sword was used: THE RHOMPHAIA! Yet, it is common knowledge that Israel was restored as a nation for the second time in 1948. Your mouth, sir, is full of fudge." Coincidentally, it is, right at this moment: I love chocolate fudge, umm-umh! Well, as to your problem, let us take the advice of Hippolytus and scan the text "with open eye." The pertinent passage is 6:8, thus:

καὶ εἶδον καὶ ἰδοὺ ἵππος χλωρός καὶ ὁ καθήμενος
Kai eidon, kai idou ippos khlöros, kai o kathëmenos
And I looked, and behold a horse greenish-yellow, and the one seated

ἐπάνω αὐτοῦ ὄνομα αὐτῷ ὁ θάνατος καὶ ὁ ᾅδης ἠκολούθει
epanö autou anoma autö o Thanatos, kai o adës ëkolouthei
upon it—the name for him [was] Death, and Hades follows

μετ' αὐτοῦ καὶ ἐδόθη αὐτοῖς ἐξουσία ἐπὶ
met autou kai edothë autois exousia epi
after him and there was given to them authority over

τὸ τέταρτον τῆς γῆς ἀποκτεῖναι ἐν ῥομφαίᾳ
to tetarton tës gës apokteinai en romphaia
the fourth of the earth to kill with the rhomphaia

καὶ ἐν λιμῷ καὶ ἐν θανάτῳ καὶ ὑπὸ τῶν θηρίων τῆς γῆς
kai en limö kai en thanatö kai upo tön thëriön tës gës.
and with famine and with pestilence and by the beasts of the earth.

The color of the horse, a pale-green or greenish-yellow is the color of a sickly or dead body. The rider on the horse is Death personified as the king of the underworld and all Hades [not Hell] follows behind him.

Thus, the verse opens with the idea of the first death, the physical one, and the intimation that it will be temporary. However, the personification of death by capitalizing the term [Greeks rarely used majuscules, except for proper names and for the beginning of a quotation or a new sentence] forebodes a very large number of deaths.

The verb "ἐδόθη" [edothë], i.e., "was given," indicates that it is God who has decreed the slaughter and has given Death and Hades authority to carry it out. The phrase, "over the fourth of the earth," in this case, means that the slaughter will happen within a minor part of the Roman Empire. Hence, a great slaughter in the Empire connotes <u>a general depopulation</u> of perhaps only one or two nations. The infinitive "ἀποκτεῖναι" [apokteinai], "to kill," is aorist; and so this mass killing will take place only once.

The four means of killing are stated in the formula of the Old Testament prophets: sword, famine, pestilence, and wild beasts. That Death and Hades will inflict <u>total destruction</u> is indicated in two ways:

(1) The sword to be used is the <u>rhomphaia</u>.
(2) The number of the means is the symbolic number FOUR.

The Old Testament prophecies, in most instances, mention only the first three: sword, famine, and pestilence, which three I have already briefly explained.

The fourth means, "the [wild] beasts of the earth," is quite informative, if even a modicum of common sense is exercised here, say, just a notch above that of a moronic ox. Among land animals, Man is rather large for his size; and, when he is large in number, then, he is virtually invincible to them. Among those species indigenous to those nations <u>within the Roman Empire</u>, only five could present a serious and frequent threat to man, in certain circumstances: the crocodile, the wolf, the bear, the leopard, and the lion.

Once one cross-refers this list with the historical record of Rome's domestic and foreign military actions during the second and third centuries AD, and once one bears in mind that John wrote only about those peoples and events that affected or connected with Christ and His Church, the list makes verse

8 point to only one place, one time, one event: the destruction of the nation of Israel by the emperor Hadrian in the second war to subjugate Palestine, 132–135 AD, and the further dispersion of the Jews carried out by Vespasian in the years that followed.

In the period 100–300 AD, Rome experienced many bloody rebellions and civil wars and famines, and the Church was sometimes involuntarily involved and had to suffer also, as the contents of the second and third seals imply; but, neither Europe, with its wolves and bears, nor North Africa, with its lions and leopards and Nile crocodiles, witnessed such devastation in that period as verse 8 describes.

When most of a society's able-bodied men have fallen by the sword, then, the weak of that society, the old and the lame, the women and children, grow weaker still on account of famine and disease, and, thus, become easier prey for the king of the wild beasts: the lion. In ancient times, whenever the human population in a tropical or subtropical area [like Palestine] decreased significantly, lions became quite numerous.

The phrase, "ὑπὸ τῶν θηρίων τῆς γῆς" [upo tön thëriön tës gës], "by the beasts of the earth," most certainly would include the lion; moreover, it intimates that the survivors would also be victimized by the lawless, namely, by robbers and brigands.

Thus, those who escape one form of violent death shall meet another, until all the wicked have been consumed. Violent death is a punishment for <u>apostasy</u>. Verse 8 describes a divine judgment, in the sense of condemnation; for, indeed, the infinitive "ἀποκτεῖναι" [apokteinai] does not merely mean, "to kill," but also "to condemn to death." The judge who pronounced the sentence of death was God, and the Roman legions under Hadrian were the secondary agents who carried out God's wrathful justice, as symbolized by the <u>rhomphaia</u>.

But, the "open eye," advised by Hippolytus, notes well that the rider on the horse is Thanatos of Hades. Therefore, though the destruction of the Jewish nation will be <u>total</u>, it will be <u>temporary</u>: though the apostasy of the Jews should be the "sickness" unto everlasting death, God, in his mysterious wisdom and mercy, has decreed that the Jewish people shall be merely "asleep" for a time, until the end of "this present age" [Galatians 1:3-4]. God always keeps his word, and among the last words God spoke to Israel through his servant Isaiah are these,

> "As the new heaven and the new earth which I will make shall endure before me, says the Lord, so shall your race and your name endure. From one new moon to another, and from one Sabbath to another, all mankind shall come to worship before me, says the Lord."
> [Is. 66:22-23].

So, the destruction of Israel as an entity called a nation was total, and the tract, thence, to the second restoration of Israel as a nation in 1948 was 1813 years long; and, for these two facts, the appropriate symbol was the rhomphaia—the double-edged sword, the long one.

Christ said to Nicodemus,

> "For God did not send his Son into the world so that he might condemn the world, but that he might save the world through him"
> [Jn. 3:17]

Therefore did Christ also say to his apostles,

> "Do not think that I have come to bring peace to the earth: I have not come to bring peace, but a sword…" [Mt. 10:34]

Which of the two swords did Jesus mention? The makhaira, of course, the short one. It is not in God's plan that all of mankind, for its sins, should perish from the earth. Concerning the end of this evil present age, Christ said,

> "For there will be at that time a great tribulation such as has not happened from the beginning of the world until now and never will happen again. And if those days were not CUT SHORT [μὴ ἐκολοβώθησαν = me ekoloböthnson (aorist)] all flesh would not be saved: but because of the Elect those days will be CUT SHORT"
> [κολοβωθήσονται = koloböthnsontai] [Mt. 24:21-22]

Hence, the rhomphaia for a man, the makhaira for mankind. As to the Bible's use of the term "sword," you now understand the long and the short of it.

In verses 5-7, John used the verb "ἐδόθη" [edothë = it was given, there was given] FOUR TIMES. One must discern sharply here: the concept of totality does not pertain to "...every tribe and people and language and nation," in the sense that the Beast will rule over every square inch of the earth, because Chapter 12 made it clear that he will not. Rather, the symbolical number "four" here signifies that the Beast, by God's permission, shall exercise total authority wherever he does in fact rule, that he will wage total war wherever he wages it, that he will decree total persecution against the brethren, especially the clergy, and that he will be totally invincible for 42 months.

The "general earth," i.e., the human race, in general, will worship him or his image [even in the land of "the Great Eagle" there will be some who follow the Beast].

John reminds the faithful four times that God himself will allow these things. The Antichrist's victory will be complete; he will be at the zenith of his worldly glory when he murders Enoch and Elijah in Jerusalem. He will shout loudest then,

> "Who is like the Beast, and who can fight against it?" [Apoc. 13:4]

Verses 9-10 may be translated thus,

> "If anyone has an ear, let him hear!
> If anyone [is] unto captivity,
> unto captivity he goes:
> If anyone [is] to be killed with the makhaira,
> with the makhaira he [is] to be killed.
> This is the patient endurance and faith of the saints."

Verse 9 is a solemn warning to all the brethren, like the warning that Christ uttered in the letter to Ephesus [2:7], to Smyrna [2:11], to Pergamum [2:17], to Thyatira [2:29], to Sardis [3:6], to Philadelphia [3:13], and to Laodicea [3:22]. The warning implies that anyone who does not heed it will incur the woe of the second death, for Christ has <u>commanded</u> that his followers practice patient endurance, as he indicated in the letter to Sardis,

"Because you kept the word of my patient endurance..." [Apoc. 3:10]

The reader must bear in mind the context in which the warning appears: it comes immediately after John reminded the reader FOUR TIMES that God has given the Beast authority and power over the saints for 3½ years. The meaning is plain and patent: that the Brethren suffer, it is the will of the Father. "Vengeance is mine," saith the Lord, "I shall repay." "There is a time for everything under the sun," and the Father has set the time when the hosts of heaven will, in obedience, take up the sword, the long one, double-edged and sharp, and fulfill God's word at the winepress of Armageddon.

But, the time is not yet: for a short while, they must endure the makhaira, and they must not fear the first death. Even during the greatest shedding of innocent blood, during the great tribulation decreed by the Beast immediately after he has murdered the Two Witnesses and declared himself God, the saints must persevere until Christ cries out again, "It is finished!"

What Jesus said to Pilate, the saints will say to their earthly judges,

> "You would have no authority over me unless it had been given you from above." [Jn. 19:11]

And, what the King of kings said to Peter who had used his makhaira on Malchus, the saints will remember,

> "Do you think I cannot appeal to my Father, and he will at once send me more than twelve legions of angels? But how then would the scriptures be fulfilled, which say it must happen this way?"
> [Mt. 26:53-54]

Understand, then, one of the reasons for so great suffering:

> Because of the Elect those days will be CUT SHORT...[Mt. 24:22],

lest all flesh should perish from the earth. Many a translation reads, "For the sake of the Elect..."; but, Matthew used the preposition "διὰ" [dia], which, with the accusative case, means, "because of, on account of, thanks to." The

Blessed Virgin Mary has her role in the revelation of the children of God, but the bride of Christ has her role, too, and she, "clothed with the sun" that is the power of Christ himself, together with Mary, shall crush the head of the serpent…in God's good time.

To some, the warning may seem a rigid mandate for fatalism. To those who pay attention to what they read, it is obvious the warning is conditional. TWICE, John used the word "if," the big "if." In view of what has been said here about the symbolical number "four," namely, that the Beast will exercise total authority wherever he does in fact rule, it follows that active resistance is permissible wherever the Beast has not yet assumed total authority. At the beginning of the 42-month tract, some nations, including Christian ones, will not be under the Beast. Verse 7 implies this,

> "And it was given to him to make war against the saints and to conquer them."

Now, according to my own experience and understanding, there are two opposing sides in a war. Just so it will be when the Beast commences the War of the Ten Kings. John put the warning after he had mentioned four examples of "ἐδόθη" [edothë = it was given, there was given], in order to indicate that the warning would apply only after the Beast had assumed total authority. Notice the stipulation of the warning,

> "IF anyone [is] unto captivity,…IF anyone [is] to be killed with the makhaira…"

Passive resistance pertains when active resistance would be futile; yet, "passive" here must be acknowledged as the greater name of action. Christ's words from the cross were those of the most heroic soul,

> "Father, forgive them, for they know not what they do." [Lk. 23:34]

Verses 11-17 are straightforward, for the most part. I have already demonstrated to you, that "the beast ascending from the earth" and the False Prophet in 16:13, 19:20, and 20:10, are one and the same individual, the chief henchman to the Beast.

In verse 1, John wrote,

> καὶ εἶδον ἐκ τῆς θαλάσσης θηρίον ἀναβαῖνον...
> And eidon ek tës thalassës thërion anabainon...

In verse 11, he wrote,

> καὶ εἶδον ἄλλο θηρίον ἀναβαῖνον ἐκ τῆς γῆς
> And eidon allo thërion anabainon ek tës gës...

You can see for yourself that John presented a parallelism of two participial phrases, which tell the respective origins of the two beasts: the former "ascending out of the sea," and the latter "ascending out of the earth" [ἀνα = ana: up + βαῖνειν = bainein: to come, to go, to walk or step]. This fact, when added to the fact that John described both, at length, in the same chapter, indicates that their ascendencies will be synchronous. Note the order of mention: the beast from the "sea" is described first, and the beast from the "earth," second.

John used the same device in Chapters 12/17 over to 13 for the heads and horns, in order to show that the one mentioned second serves the one mentioned first. It is implied, therefore, that, when the Beast begins his ascendancy from the abyss, at that time or shortly afterwards, he will give regency over the "earth" to the False Prophet.

Note what John wrote next about the Beast's most fanatical follower in the rest of verse 11:

> ...καὶ εἶχεν κέρατα δύο ὅμοια ἀρνίῳ καὶ ἐλάλει ὡς δράκων.
> ...kai eikhen kerata dyo omoia arniö kai elalei ös drakön.
> ...and it had horns two like a little lamb and spoke as a dragon.

A "horn" ordinarily symbolizes a king/kingdom; sometimes, it symbolizes simply authority, or power, or both.

Verses 12-17 make it clear that the False Prophet will have authority and power in secular and religious affairs, i.e., in all buying and selling as well as in worshipping the Beast or its image, but that his power to perform "great signs" will come from the Beast—from Satan, actually—and only when the Beast is present, as 19:20 evidences,

> "And the beast was captured, and with it the False Prophet [ὁ ψευδοπροφήτης = o pseudoprophëtës = "pseudoprophet"] who had performed in the presence of it the signs by which he deceived the ones receiving the mark of the beast and worshipping the image of it."

Again, when the False Prophet is face to face with the Beast, he will exercise ALL the authority of the Beast [v.12],

> καὶ τὴν ἐξουσίαν τοῦ πρώτου θηρίου πᾶσαν ποιεῖ ἐνώπιον αὐτοῦ...
> Kai tën exousian tou prötou thëriou pasan poiei enöpion autou...
> And the authority of the first beast all it did in the presence of it...

The syntax in verse 12 was designed to emphasize the word "all" [πᾶσαν = pasan].

So, the False Prophet's "two horns" allude to his twofold authority/power in material and spiritual things. The "two horns" are modified by the phrase, "ὅμοια ἀρνίῳ" [omoia arniö], "similar to/like [to] a little lamb." In the Apocalypse, the term "ἀρνίον" [arnion = little lamb] signifies Jesus Christ; however, after Christ rose from the dead [Hades], he referred to his followers as "little lambs" when he told Peter, the first three times, to "feed" them,

> "βόσκε τὰ ἀρνία μου..."
> "Boske ta arnia mou..."
> "Feed the little lambs of me."
> [Jn. 21:15]

Since John did not use the definite article in regard to the False Prophet, the term "ἀρνίον" [arnion = little lamb], in this case, signifies a follower of Christ; to wit, the False Prophet looked like a follower of Christ, but he spoke as a dragon.

Now, I have shown that the "reed like a rod," in 11:1, and the "tail" of the dragon, in 12:4, both symbolize the "false prophet".

Bearing in mind that the Dragon:

> "…took a stand in the presence of the woman" [and where the Dragon was, there was his "tail" also], [Apoc. 12:4]
>
> and that the False Prophet looked like a Christian [i.e.. was in the outside court] and spoke as a "dragon,"
>
> and that, chronologically speaking, Chapter 13 follows immediately after 12,

I cannot eschew the strongest suspicion that the "reed like a rod," the "tail" of the Dragon, and the "beast ascending out of the earth" are all one and the same individual: the False Prophet. Hence, it is also quite reasonable to suspect that he will be an apostate Cardinal or bishop, one who will be given to act as the vicar of the Beast.

Recalling what was said about Babylon the Great, one can also reasonably suspect that the False Prophet will make that very city his capital. In which case, the "two horns" may also allude to his having regency over the "earth" and the "many waters" mentioned in Chapter 17:1 & 15. In brief, the False Prophet will second the Beast. He will be of that most abject ilk the modern world now breeds prolifically: the sycophantic fanatic. You know: that political animal washing a ton of shoes with his tongue, the critter as happy as a hog in warm mud, wherein never yet has a hog been known to become— disgruntled.

The False Prophet will tell the inhabitants upon the earth to make an image to the Beast. Then, John added verse 15,

καὶ ἐδόθη αὐτῷ δοῦναι πνεῦμα τῇ εἰκόνι τοῦ θηρίου ἵνα καὶ λαλήσῃ
kai edothë autö dounai pneuma të eikoni tou thëriou, ina kai lalësë
And it was given to it to give a spirit to the icon of the beast, so that might even talk

ἡ εἰκὼν τοῦ θηρίου καὶ ποιήσῃ ἵνα ὅσοι ἐὰν μὴ προσκυνήσωσιν
e eikön tou thëriou kai poiësë ina osoi ean më proskynësösin
the icon of the beast and do so that as many as will not worship

τῇ εἰκόνι τοῦ θηρίου ἀποκτανθῶσιν.
te eikoni tou thëriou apoktanthösin.
the icon of the beast are condemned [to death].

The key to understanding this passage is the phrase,

> "δοῦναι πνεῦμα τῇ εἰκόνι"
> "dounai pneuma të eikoni"
> "to give a spirit to the icon"

The infinitive, "δοῦναι" [dounai] is aorist, and, so, it means, "to give only once." Aye, there's the rub whereat many a translator has stubbed toe and taken tumble, for they interpreted that little infinitive as meaning merely "to give." Consequently, both the NIV and NRSV read,

"to give breath to the image…"

The WV reads,

"to put life into the image…".

The NAB reads,

"to give life to the image…"

To understand why the translations of "breath" and "life" are erroneous, it is necessary to understand, first, why the False Prophet gave what he gave,

"…so that the icon of the beast might even talk and do…"

The verb "λαλεῖν" [lalein] means "to talk, chat, prattle"; the verb, "ποιήσῃ" [poiësë] [subjunctive] here alludes to the Beast's "ἐξουσία ποιῆσαι" [ezousia poiësai], his "authority to do..."[v. 5]. In other words, the icon will be able to carry on casual conversations as well as pronounce, like a judge, the official death sentence on as many as will not worship it; and there will be many brave thousands or tens of thousands, at the least, who will refuse to worship the icon.

If the noun "πνεῦμα" [pneuma] is translated as "breath," then, the False Prophet, since he will give only once, will have to give the icon a supply of breath sufficient to last a duration of perhaps 3–3½ years. Truly, that would make the icon the most long-winded talker of all time. Indeed, it is tacit that the icon will "talk and do" even when the Beast is not present; and the fact that it will be able to carry on a conversation connotes that it will do so with intelligence, with rational intelligence.

But, this does not and simply cannot mean that the Top Toady in the empire will be able to give LIFE to the icon. The last time I heard, only God could give life. For goodness sake! In the whole Bible, let alone the Apocalypse, there cannot be found a single instance in which life is attributed to anyone other than the Creator Himself. What John meant is found in 16:13-14,

> "And I saw out of the mouth of the dragon and out of the mouth of the Beast and out of the mouth of the False Prophet three foul spirits [πνεύματα = pneumata] as frogs: for they are the spirits of demons doing signs...
> [πνεύματα δαιμονίων ποιοῦντα σημεῖα]..."
> [pneumata daimoniön poiounta sëmeia]..."

In the New Testament, the noun "πνεῦμα" [pneuma] is used commonly to denote a "spirit," i.e., a being with the powers of reason and volition. In the case of 13:15, John meant an evil spirit, a demon. Now, notwithstanding that John neither named the material of which the icon or image will be made, nor specified whether the icon will be a statue or a portrait of some kind, it is not unreasonable to suspect that the icon will be a statue—probably, made of gold—and that the statue will move.

Note that the term "εἰκών" [eikön] is in the singular number, indicating that there will be only one statue. That Satan or his fellow demons, with God's permission, can occupy and render flexible the molecular structure of an inanimate object, and, thus, make it <u>seem</u> alive, has been recorded in <u>Exodus</u> 7:12, wherein the two Egyptian priests threw down their two staffs, and the two staffs changed into two snakes.

> 12 And they every one cast down their rods, and they were turned into serpents: but Aaron's rod devoured their rods. [Ex. 7:12]

As for occupying the icon, it is dubious that any demon will volunteer for such lugubrious duty.

Chapter 18

The Beast's Name

The last three verses of this Chapter run thus,

> 16 And it makes all, the small and the great, both the rich and the
> poor, and the free and the slave, so that they give to themselves a
> mark upon the hand of them the right one or upon the forehead of
> them 17 even so that not anyone is able to buy or to sell if he is not
> one having the mark: the name of the beast or the number of the
> name of it. 18 Wisdom is thus: Let the one having the mind calculate
> the number of the beast, for the number is of a man, and the number
> of him [is] 666.

The Apocalypse was addressed to the seven Churches, and, thus, to the Church in all places and times; this implies that it was, is, and will be intended for the brethren, FIRST AND FOREMOST. Verse 18's clue will be helpful in ascertaining the Beast's identity before he ascends from the abyss; it will be redundant thereafter. Pertinent here is the public name by which the Beast will be generally and formally called; and that name is not a problem in translation, but in transliteration: for, if the faithful cannot cognize it in the news, especially, in print, then, verse 18's clue is an otiose codicil to the Chapter. In Christ's eyes, his "little lambs" come first; and, in light of this fact, the problem of transliteration is to be pondered.

The brethren, because they reside in many nations, read and write many languages. The vast majority of them have, for many centuries, used only one set of symbols for reading and writing: THE ROMAN ALPHABET. However, it seems thrice most doubtful that the Beast's name will be originally spelled with Roman letters, not because the usage of Roman letters to denote specific numerical values is obsolete, as a look at my living room clock confirms, but because the usage proffers a paucity of possibility, with the possibilities themselves contradicting plausibility.

The fact is that the Roman system has only six letters relevant here; and, since the usage of V for U is obsolete, the system comes with only one vowel:

I = 1,
V = 5,
X = 10,
L = 50,
C = 100,
D = 500.

There are only two rules in spelling the name:

(1) Individual letters may be put in any order.
(2) The value of only one letter may be subtracted only from the value of the next letter.

For example, the value "16" may be written thus:

XVI, XIV, VXI, VIX, IXV, or IVX,

but the value "14" must be written thus:

XIV, IVX, VIX, or IXV

Adhering to these letters and rules results in such possibilities as:

DIVILCIX, DICLIVIX or VIXILDIC

If the D is substituted with C's or L's, a typical result is this:

LICCILLICCICIXI

Even if the letter V is allowed for U, the case for the Roman system does not improve. Let us hence.

Three requisites must be met:

(1) The system of symbols used for writing the Beast's name, as it will be originally spelled, must be extant.
(2) The symbols of that system must be used, or must have "been used," to denote specific and numerical values.
(3) The many languages of the faithful must be able to duplicate, with very close consistency, the pronunciation of the Beast's name.

Clearly, the first requisite eliminates such systems as the hieroglyphics of the ancient Egyptians, Aztecs, Mayans, etc. In fact, by 1200 AD, the use of Arabic numerals had become ubiquitous in the modern world. In the modern world, their use has become virtually universal.

The use of letters to denote specific numerical values is now obsolete, except for a few instances of the Roman and Greek. However, in the territory that was once the Roman Empire and whence the Beast will arise, there are yet three other extant alphabets that once used every symbol or letter to denote specific numerical values: the Hebrew, Arabic, and Greek.

Both Hebrew and Arabic are north-Semitic languages, and both present a two-fold problem:

(1) Most of the faithful do not read or write either of them.
(2) Transliterations of them into Roman letters, in the attempt to duplicate their respective pronunciations, have been inconsistent.

For example, the transliterations "Elias" and "Elijah" denote the same man, who was an ancient Hebrew prophet, and more inconsistent are "Jehovah" and "Yahweh," which denote God. Many people do not know that "Qur'an" signifies the Holy Book of Islam: the Koran.

This is only the English version of the problem, not the French, German, Spanish, Italian, etc. The problem arises from the fact that both Hebrew and Arabic are written with consonants only. Therefore, the usefulness of verse 18's clue would depend on two things: the brethren must learn basic Hebrew and Arabic well, and transliterations must become conventional—at least, in each nation. That either of these will come to pass "stands not within the prospect of belief."

The faithful must be able to cognize the Beast's name in print: This requisite has emerged as the most important. Verse 18 begins with a terse, interesting statement:

"ὧδε ἡ σοφία ἐστίν" [Öde ë sophia estin],

whose literal translation is,

"In this manner, [the] wisdom is."

The term "ὧδε" [öde = in this manner] is a demonstrative adverb; it points forward to whatever follows. The noun "σοφία" [sophia = wisdom] here does not signify the wisdom of God; rather, it means:

(1) skill, knowledge of, acquaintance with.
(2) sound judgment, intelligence, practical wisdom.

John then added the command:

> "Let the one having the mind [νοῦν = nonn] calculate the number of the beast…"

In other words, anyone who has common sense and knowledge of basic mathematics is mentally qualified to solve the problem. The problem itself defines the level of difficulty, and to total the numerical values of a few letters is not very difficult at all…IF one can perceive the problem, in the first place. That is the crux of the matter. The reader must be acquainted with the letters and their numerical values, which will be in the Beast's name.

Indeed, it may be that the faithful are already acquainted with all or some of those letters, and they need only to become familiar with their numerical values. Subtly, very subtly, John has hinted that the knowledge in the reader is in the problem that follows; to wit, at least some, perhaps all, of the letters, which will be in the Beast's name, are in the Roman alphabet.

Of the four possible alphabets extant, namely, the Hebrew, Arabic, Greek, and Roman, the inquiry has narrowed down to the Greek: the name of the Antichrist will be originally spelled in Greek. [Author's note: I thank you, Father, for the little word, "ὧδε" [öde = in this manner], whose significance you have hidden from those who do not love your Word.]

I have appended a copy of the Greek letters, with their Roman equivalents, at the end of this commentary [Appendix A]. A swift survey of only the majuscules [capitals], those which are possibilities for the Beast's name, discovers that 50% of them are immediately recognizable by the faithful. Note bene that the digamma [#6] is used only for mathematics, never for words. Mark also that the koppa [#90] and Psi down to san [700-900] may not be used.

As I proceeded with this commentary, I presented excerpts from the Greek text, both to facilitate your own judgment of my explanations relative to John's own words, and to begin your acquaintance with printed Greek. An excellent method of learning the letters and their numerical values is to juxtapose or to collate them first in print, and, then, cognize them in imagination. In this way will they become indelible in your memory. Practice makes perfect: a saying quite trite, but, nonetheless, true.

As to the name of the Antichrist, do not opine. Wait. Then, if the four angels bound at the great river Euphrates are loosed during your lifetime, begin watching the regions of the near East and Middle East: for it is not coincidence that most of the body of the Beast was "like a leopard" [13:2] and the "leopard," as you may remember from Daniel 7, was the third "beast" from the "sea," the "beast" called the Greek empire. Sorry: the name Alexander is not a possibility. You can count on that.

There's more to be said about this Chapter. John made three points perfectly clear:

(1) The Beast will be a man, a mere man, an individual male of the human species.
(2) The number [numerical value] of his name will be 666; i.e., the total of the numerical values of the letters in his name will be 666.
(3) The mark of the Beast will optionally be either his name or the number of his name.

The noun "ὄνομα" [onoma = name] was written in the singular, and this fact presents a compound problem that the icon of the Beast did not: the term "name" can denote a person's praenomen [first name], cognomen [last name], or both.

The Beast's name will be the "χάραγμα" [kharagma], which has generally been translated as "mark." The Greek noun conveys the idea of "any mark made by engraving, imprinting, biting, carving, impressing, inscribing, etc." The English words "character" and "characteristic" are derived from it; and John's intimation here should be clear to everyone.

The mark of the Beast will be on the forehead or on [the back of] the right hand. To carve or cut letters into flesh, especially, on the bony back of a hand, would forfeit uniformity and, thus, result in a thing unaesthetical, in a mutilation of the beautiful Greek alphabet, but an act of blasphemy against the one the people will worship.

I, therefore, strongly suspect that the mark of the Beast will be branded on forehead or hand, just as it was the ancient Roman practice to brand the foreheads of slaves. The branding iron would have to be somewhat concave to conform to the convex surface of the forehead or hand, and the number of letters in the Beast's name will probably be eight or fewer, but not fewer than four. I say this, because the letters will have to measure about 3/8" in height in order to be legible at a distance of 15 to 20 feet. I have big hands, yet it would be difficult to fit 7 or 8 letters of that size in a row across the back of one, without touching the very sides of it. Human skin is not as thick and tough as cowhide; hence, it would also be difficult to brand two names onto areas as small as the forehead and the hand, without inflicting disfigurement of the mark itself.

All these things suggest that the Beast will be known by only one name. Here is an example of the height and length of seven letters:

ΑΝΤΙΡΕΣ

In the movie called "The Omen," the boy, who will become Antichrist, the man, has a name with six letters in it. This idea is not as far-fetched a possibility as it first seems. The rest of the movie was moronic, except for one other point I will mention later. Here, the dimensions of the mark are limited mostly by the size of the average adult forehead and hand: and, so, the letters must be neither very small nor very large, relatively speaking.

John indirectly gives the reader an interesting item of information: the phrase, "the number of his name," implies that someone will retrieve the ancient use of letters for numbers and apply it to the Beast's name, the public name by which he will be originally called. Either the Beast himself will do this, or he will approve someone's suggestion of it.

I am inclined toward the former, because John stated why the world, in general, will, with amazement, follow the Beast: He will heal the blow of the makhaira on the sixth head of the historical beast; that is to say, he will revive imperial paganism and "the glory that was Greece, the grandeur that was Rome."

The False Prophet will be the Pontifex Maximus, supreme spiritual and temporal authority and power of the Roman Empire restored through the power of the Beast (the new Roman Empire will not be as extensive as the ancient one because the "kingdom of the Beast" [see: 16:10] will occupy some of the territory formerly of ancient Rome).

The Beast will bring back the ancient pagan practices; for, as Daniel wrote of...

> "...the little horn, he shall think himself able to change times and laws..." [Dn. 7:25]

One of the customs of ancient Greece, in the days of Simonides, Sophocles, Socrates, Democritus, Aristophanes, Aristotle, and Alexander, was to be generally known by ONE NAME. Hence, the available evidence favors the suspicion that the Beast will use only one name. The use of the number 666, instead of the Beast's name, implies something yet more appalling: either the general Christian population, especially, Europe, shall have become ignorant of the number's significance or, if not ignorant, completely complicitous with the Beast and False Prophet, out of cowardice or malice. John's words probably impute both motives,

> "And it [the Beast from the Earth] makes all...so that they give [to] themselves a mark..." [Apoc. 13:16]

No, I have not erred in translation, for here are John's exact words,

> "καὶ ποιεῖ πάντας...ἵνα δῶσιν αὐτοῖς χάραγμα..."
> "kai poiei pantas...ina dösin autois kharagma..."

As for the mark of the number, there are two possibilities: either it will be the Arabic numerals "666", or the Greek letters for numbers, "ΧΞΣ" [majuscules], but, most likely, "χζσ" [miniscules]. To keep aesthetical consistency, the anti-Christians will most likely choose the latter in miniscules.

To understand God's purpose regarding the Beast, I quote, at length, St. Paul's second letter to the Thessalonians, Chapter 2, verses 3-11:

> 3 Let no one deceive you in any way. For only if the apostasy comes
> first will he be revealed, the man of lawlessness, the son of destruc-
> tion [ὁ υἱὸς τῆς ἀπωλείας = o uios tës apöleias], 4 the one opposed
> and exalted over all things called god or worship, so that he seats
> himself in the presence of the temple of God, proclaiming himself
> to be God. 5 Do you not remember I still spoke to you in reference
> to these things? 6 And now you know the restraint toward his being
> revealed in his own right time.[1] 7 For the mystery of lawlessness
> already is operating: only until the one [masculine genitive] restrain-
> ing is gotten out of [the] middle [ἐκ μέσου γένηται = ek mesou
> genëtai].[2] 8 And at that time will be revealed the lawless one, whom
> the Lord Jesus will annihilate with the breath of his mouth and will
> destroy with the manifestation of his presence, 9 whose coming [the
> Beast's] is according to the working of Satan with all power and
> signs and false wonders 10 and with every fraud of wrongdoing for
> those who are perishing, because they did not show [demonstrate]

the love of the truth unto saving them. And on account of this God sends [to] them the working of deception unto trusting themselves to the lie, 11 so that they may be judged [condemned], all who did not believe the truth but delighted in wrongdoing."

[1] His own "καιρός" [kairos], which means "right time, season, critical time"; the same word John used for Satan's time in 12:12; and for the woman's 1260 days in 12:14.

[2] The person and thing that restrains must be a power in the Church; the phrase, "ἐκ μέσου" [ek mesou], implies the restrainer at present is "ἐν μέσο" [en meso], i.e., in the middle of heaven: the throne area.

Church tradition holds that Antichrist shall come from the tribe of Dan; some early Fathers of the Church cited three passages from the Old Testament:

"Let Dan be a serpent by the roadside, a horned viper by the path, that bites the horse's heel, so that the rider tumbles backward." [Gn. 9:17]

"Of Dan he [Moses] said: 'Dan is a lion's whelp, that springs forth from Bashan!'" [Dt. 33:22]

"From Dan is heard the snorting of his steeds; the neighing of his stallions shakes the whole land. They come devouring the land and all it contains, the city and those who dwell in it." [Jer. 8:16]

The tribe of Dan apostatized completely during the Babylonian Captivity and gradually spread out into the lands now known as Turkey, Syria, and Iraq. After the Captivity, it was never enumerated again among the Tribes. After Hadrian's destruction of the Jewish nation in 135 AD, the other twelve tribes also lost their identities.

John 5:43 is often cited as a reference to Antichrist; Jesus said to the Jews,

"ἐγὼ ἐλήλυθα ἐν τῷ ὀνόματι τοῦ πατρός μου καὶ
"egö elëlytha en tö onomati tou patros mou, kai
"I came in the name of the father of me, and

οὐ λαμβάνετέ με ἐὰν ἄλλος ἔλθῃ ἐν τῷ ὀνόματι
ou lambanete me . ean allos elthë en tö onomati
you do not receive me: if another comes in the name

τῷ ἰδίῳ ἐκεῖνον λήμψεσθε."
tö idiö, ekeinon lëmpsesthe."
the [his] own one, that [person] you will receive."

Most translations read,

"...if another comes in his own name, him you will receive."

Christ used syntactical emphasis for the idea of "ἴδιος" [idios], an adjective that means, "own, personal, private, distinct, separate." The phrase, "in the name of," is equivalent to saying, "authorized or empowered by," which alludes to the term "Messiah," "the anointed one." The term "ἄλλος" [allos] may be translated here as "the other [one]," meaning the other one who will come as the Messiah, the false Messiah.

Jesus referred to himself as the Son of the Father and as the Son of Man; he never referred to himself by his personal name, i.e., Jesus. It, therefore, may be rationally deduced that the Antichrist will refer to himself by his personal name, and that he will claim he is the Messiah foretold by the prophets. He will come to the Jews, and they will receive him.

In view of these things, it is understandable that exegetes, such as Iranaeus, Hippolytus, and Victorinus, among many, regarded the aforecited passage about the tribe of Dan as indicative of Antichrist's ancestry. Frankly, I find those said passages are connected to the Antichrist by a blond hair. What Jacob and Moses said of Dan came to pass, even by Jeremiah's day; and, since no man could prove so remote an ancestry, the traditional tenet that Antichrist will be descended of Dan is too loose in the loop.

On the other hand, Christ's statement, albeit subtly, is informative to human reason; and, when cross-referred with many other statements in the Old and the New Testaments, it helps edify the reader's understanding, feed and build it into as complete a construction of concrete evidence as Scripture permits.

The "θηρίον" [thërion], the [little] Beast, will refer to himself by his personal name, and this, in turn, suggests that he will use only one name: either his praenomen [first name] or one that he himself will invent, i.e., a name that he will give to himself.

As a Biblical idiom, "to give a name to an entity" means "to have dominion over that entity." Man has dominion over the birds of the air, the beasts on the earth, and the creatures in the sea; but, he does not have dominion over himself: God alone is Lord over man; there is no other. As the Beast will think himself a self made man, I suggest that he will give himself his own new name.

Christ promised he would give a "white stone" to everyone who conquers, and on the "stone" would be written a new name that no one will know except the one who receives it [2:17]. That name is the indelible "χάραγμα" [kharagma = mark] on the Christian's soul, on one who has become the new creation.

As for the Beast, bear in mind that he is Antichrist: his "χάραγμα" [kharagma] will be his name, and his name will be his "χάραγμα" [kharagma] inspired by Satan. His name will not be a Christian one, but pagan; and it will, in some sense, relate his character or the chief characteristic of the man.

"What's in a name?" the Poet wrote. Jesus was sent to save the world, not to condemn it; and, so, Joseph was commanded to name him Jesus [Mt. 1:21], which means, "He who saves," for, as the angel said, "he will save his people from their sins." What's in a name? God will send Antichrist to those who are perishing,

> "...because they did not demonstrate the love of the truth unto saving them. And on account of this God sends them the working of deception unto trusting themselves to the lie so that they may be judged [condemned], all who did not believe the truth but delighted in wrongdoing." [2 Thes. 10. 11]

So, then, by his name, you will know him, even before he begins "ascending from the abyss." He will be "the little horn" in Daniel 7. A "horn" symbolizes a king or a kingdom, and a "little horn" indicates a little kingdom—such as, Greece. Only time will tell the exact place, and the informed faithful will cognize or recognize him before Satan takes his stand upon the "sand of the sea."

Now, ye Friends, I cannot go beyond this point: I have brought you as near to the brute's actual name as the information in Scripture permits, and to say more would be to envelop my brain in the sphere of speculation, a bubble that, sooner or later, so exalts itself, that it simply goes "POP!" Jesus has advised us, "Be as wise as serpents, but innocent as doves." With faith in the wisdom of God's Word that always illumines the discursive wisdom of Man's Reason, you will understand, you will know...in God's good time.

So, let's go pick some more bones with those translators.

CHAPTER 19

—

PREPARATION FOR CHAPTER 14 ONWARD

April 1, 1999

Dear Friends of the Lord,

I send you the first of four or, maybe, five sections of part three in the commentary. The others will follow one by one as soon as each is tidied up a little. Besides, I don't think, Friend, you will input each section quickly.

As you will yourself discover, some passages are tedious, and others not. I have focused on rational proofs drawn from Biblical material, almost exclusively, so that there is NOT just another set or bag of opinions, which is what makes current confusion of the Apocalypse, BUT a presentation of letting God speak for himself and define his own terms.

The commentary is, principally, an appeal to reason, not an apologia pro fide,—though it is unmistakable that the author believes every word of it. I also concentrated on the sequence of events, i.e., where each Chapter or part of a Chapter fits into the sequence.

Do not expect to grasp all after one reading. You will have to become familiar with it, gradually. The Apocalypse can be understood, in entirety, only by seeing the relationships among the integral parts. The worst thing you could do would be to isolate with "tunnel vision" one part from the rest.

It is like learning a park, a very big park: after a while, you know exactly the paths and trees and everything, each in relation to all the others.

Indeed, as you will find out for yourself, the whole Bible is one resounding theme: "that one, far-off divine event toward which the whole creation moves." [Tennyson: In Memoriam]

Happy Easter! From me to y'all.

Yours in Christ,

Steve

To reckon each Chapter from 14 onward, in regard to its placement in the order of visions, in the actual order of events, it is necessary to understand, first, the term customarily translated as "witness" or "testimony."

The Greek noun "μάρτυρ" [martyr] means a "witness" or "one who testifies." Since so many of Christ's witnesses were beheaded, or killed in other ways, during "the great tribulation" of the imperial persecutions, the term came to signify "one who suffered death for the faith, one who became a martyr or suffered martyrdom." Originally, however, it meant simply "witness." From this noun are derived the verb "μαρτυρειν" [martyrein], "to witness or to testify," and the noun "μαρτυρία" [martyria], "witness or testimony."

Here are a few examples that show these words in concrete use; the first is about John [Apoc. 1:2],

> ὂς ἐμαρτύρησεν τὸν λόγον τοῦ θεοῦ καὶ τὴν μαρτυρίαν
> os emartyrësen ton logon tou theou kai tën martyrian
> who witnessed the word of [the] God and the testimony
>
> Ἰησοῦ Χριστοῦ ὅσα εἶδεν.
> Iësou Khristou osa eiden.
> of Jesus Christ such [things] as he saw.

John "witnessed," in the sense of "showed and demonstrated," by speaking and doing, by word and deed, the good news of salvation, which is the same witness or testimony that Jesus gave in word and deed. This meaning should be remembered in regard to Chapter 13: the icon of the Beast will witness for the Beast [and Satan]; it will "talk and do" in the name of its master [the implication being that the word of God is not idle chatter]. Therefore, the terms that refer to the speaking and doing of Christ and his followers are different from those that refer to the Beast and his every follower [who will "speak like a dragon"].

An inadvertent use of language cannot be found in the Apocalypse or anywhere in the Scriptures. In 6:9, John wrote,

> "...I saw under the altar the souls of the ones who were slaughtered on account of the word of God and on account of the testimony which they held." [διὰ τὴν μαρτυρίαν ἣν εἶχον = dia tën martyrian ën eikhon]

In 11:7, John wrote about the Two Witnesses,

> "And when they will finish the testimony of them..."
> [τὴν μαρτυρίαν = tën martyrian].

In 12:17, John described that...

> "...the Dragon went off to make war on the rest of the woman's offspring, those who are keeping the commandments of God and holding the testimony of Jesus," [ἐχόντων τὴν μαρτυρίαν Ἰησοῦ = exontön tën martyrian Iësou]

In addition, in 19:10, John wrote,

> "ἡ γὰρ μαρτυρία Ἰησοῦ ἐστιν τὸ πνεῦμα τῆς προφητείας"
> "ë gar martyria Iësou estin to pneuma tës prophëteias"
> "For the testimony of Jesus is the spirit of prophecy"

This last example refers to the Holy Spirit, who reminds about all the things Christ said and did, and teaches about those things that are and things that will take place. Whoever is willing to receive will hear what the Spirit is saying, even about the Apocalypse: the Spirit knows all the deep things of the Father and the Son, for he proceeds from both of them.

The term "μαρτυρία" [martyria] would present no problem, if it were not for Matthew 24:14, in which Christ said,

> καὶ κηρυχθήσεται τοῦτο τὸ εὐαγγέλιον τῆς βασιλείας
> kai kërykhthësetai touto to euaggelion tës basileias
> And will be proclaimed this [the] good news of the kingdom
>
> ἐν ὅλῃ τῇ οἰκουμένῃ εἰς μαρτύριον πᾶσιν τοῖς ἔθνεσιν,
> en olë të oikoumenë eis martyrion pasin tois ethnesin,
> in whole the world up to the witness to all the nations,
>
> καὶ τότε ἥξει τὸ τέλος.
> kai tote ëxei to telos.
> and at that time will come the end.

Other translations will read "throughout the world" for "in the whole world," or they will have "gospel" instead of "good news"; but, these variations do not differ in essential meaning. What should catch the reader's attention is that Matthew used the neuter noun "μαρτύριον" [martyrion = witness, testimony (neuter)] rather than the feminine noun "μαρτυρία" [martyria = witness, testimony (feminine)], and, yet, the correct English translation of the neuter noun is also either "witness" or "testimony."

It would be easy to ascribe the use of "μαρτύριον" [martyrion (neuter)] to the aesthetical maxim that variety is the spice of life, no less in vocabulary than in many other things, if Matthew had been an aesthetical author writing a work according to aesthetical standards. The fact is that Matthew, as a man, lived divinely revealed faith in Christ, and, as an author, he wrote divinely-inspired words: This should cause a pause in any cautious mind.

Nota bene that the two terms have the same root, but different genders. The significance of this cannot be understood by standing here.

Rapid references to the gospels of Mark and Luke make an interesting discovery:

...καὶ ἐπὶ ἡγεμόνων καὶ βασιλέων σταθήσεσθε ἕνεκεν ἐμοῦ
...kai epi ëgemonön kai basileön stathësesthe eneken emou
...And before leaders and kings you will be stood on account of me

εἰς μαρτύριον αὐτοῖς.
eis martyrion autois.
<u>up</u> <u>to</u> <u>the</u> <u>witness</u> <u>to</u> <u>them</u>. [Mk. 13:9]

...ἀπαγομένους ἐπὶ βασιλεῖς καὶ ἡγεμόνας ἕνεκεν τοῦ ὀνόματός
...apagomenous epi basileis kai ëgemonas eneken tou onomatos
...[you] brought before kings and leaders on account of the name

μου. ἀποβήσεται ὑμῖν εἰς μαρτύριον.
mou apobësetai umin eis martyrion.
of me : it will be issued to you <u>up to the witness</u>. [Lk. 21:12-13]

It is obvious the word "αὐτοῖς" [autois = to them] at the end of the excerpt from Mark may be added to the end of the excerpt from Luke, without altering the meaning thereof. It has already been explained that the term "king" connotes "kingdom," and vice versa; hence, the ending of the excerpt from Matthew may substitute "αὐτοῖς" [autois = to them] at the end of the excerpt from Mark. In other words, the excerpt from Matthew is the most detailed and explicit of the three.

However, all three excerpts have one thing <u>in common</u>: the special use of the noun "μαρτύριον" [martyrion = witness, testimony (neuter)], not "μαρτυρία" [martyria = witness, testimony (feminine)], as denoting a relationship of <u>cause and effect</u> between the "<u>μαρτύριον</u>" <u>and</u> <u>the</u> "<u>τέλος</u>" [telos = end], at the "end," i.e., the end of the age, this present evil age of Satan's kingdom. And there's the rub: for, throughout the New Testament, the witnessing of the faithful, either as word, or deed, or both, is constantly denoted by the noun "μαρτύριον."

Christ himself, before his Resurrection, referred to his words and deeds as "μαρτυρία" [Jn. 8:14]. Surely, then, the act of proclaiming the gospel throughout the world fits this term. Even so, the possibility that "μαρτυρία" and "μαρτύριον" are synonymous has not been eliminated, and that is why all translations read either "for a witness to the nations" or "as a testimony to the nations."

The problem here is that the preposition "εἰς" [eis] does not signify "for" or "as"; indeed, it denotes change or motion in regard to condition, state, place, or time, by such translations as "into, unto, onto, into the presence of, toward, up to, until."

If the preposition indicates a change of state or condition, the sentence will mean that proclaiming the gospel IN the whole world becomes or changes INTO a testimony to the nations, i.e., "witnessing" changes into "witnessing." This would be an absurdity, at best a redundancy, if the two terms are synonymous. To get a clearer idea of how the preposition is used, here is Christ's reply to Pilate [Jn. 18:37],

> ...ἐγὼ εἰς τοῦτο γεγέννημαι καὶ εἰς τοῦτο ἐλήλυθα εἰς τὸν κόσμον...
> ...egö eis touto gegennëmai kai eis touto elëlytha eis ton kosmon...
> ...I unto this was born and unto this I came [aorist] into the world...

Suppose the preposition "εἰς" [eis] indicates <u>temporal motion</u>; then, the sentence has a completely different meaning,

> "And this good news of the kingdom will be proclaimed in the whole world unto/up to/until the testimony to the nations, and <u>at that time</u> will come the end."

In other words, there will be "μαρτυρία" in the whole world UNTIL or UP TO the "μαρτύριον" to the nations. The prepositional phrase, "to the nations," now clearly modifies "μαρτύριον," in the sense that the "μαρτύριον" will relate strictly <u>to them</u>. The term "τέλος" applies to "the nations," and "μαρτύριον" is the cause of this effect to them.

In the last line of the quote from Matthew 24:14 a page or so back, note that the word "τότε" [tote = at that time], like "ὧδε" [öde = in this manner], is a <u>demonstrative adverb</u>. Just as "ὧδε" [öde] <u>points forward to whatever follows</u>, "τότε" [tote] <u>points backward</u> to the "μαρτύριον" itself. This "μαρτύριον," like "μαρτυρία," must originate <u>in the Church</u>; and its authority and power will effect the "end" upon the nations, so that the duration of the former determines the duration of the latter.

Since the act of proclaiming the good news is a spiritual work of mercy, it is clear that the time of the "μαρτυρία" is the time of mercy, but the time of the "μαρτύριον" will be the time of JUDGMENT. Moreover, as the excerpt from Luke 24:14 indicates, the time of large-scale persecution against Christ's followers will come to an end at that point, when the "μαρτύριον" begins.

Now, all these things relate to the time of the Beast and "the nations"; therefore, the words from St. Paul's Second Epistle to the Thessalonians apply here,

> "And at that time will be revealed the lawless one, whom the Lord Jesus will annihilate with the breath of his mouth and will destroy with the manifestation of his presence..."

The "μαρτύριον," then, will be an undoubtable demonstration of the presence and the power of the Lord Jesus Christ in His Church; and, when that demonstration comes, that witness, or evidence, or proof will not be the work of mercy to the nations, but the work of the "ῥομφαίᾳ" [rhomphaia], the long sword, double-edged and sharp.

It, perhaps, has been asked among you why John did not write a passage about the "μαρτύριον" in his gospel, like those of Matthew, Mark, and Luke. The answer is that, as neither the Father nor the Son is a dunce for redundancy, so neither is the Holy Spirit: After all, John was to write the Apocalypse. Hence, attention shifts back to the little book.

It should be patent, to everyone, that Matthew's term "the end" means "The Seven Last Plagues," or third woe. Those plagues are described sequentially in Chapter 16; therefore, mention of the "μαρτύριον" would have its logical placement in Chapter 15. And, in 15:5-6 is it found,

> καὶ μετὰ ταῦτα εἶδον καὶ ἠνοίγη ὁ ναὸς τῆς σκηνῆς
> kai meta tauta eidon, kai ënoigë o naos tës skënë
> And after these things I looked, and there opened the sanctuary of the tent

τοῦ μαρτυρίου ἐν τῷ οὐρανῷ καὶ ἐξῆλθον οἱ ἑπτὰ
tou martyriou en tö ouranö, kai exëlthon oi epta
of the witness in [the] heaven, and there came out the seven

ἄγγελοι [οἱ] ἔχοντες τὰς ἑπτὰ πληγὰς ἐκ τοῦ ναοῦ…
aggeloi [oi] exontes tas epta plëgas ek tou naou…
angels [the ones] holding the seven plagues from the sanctuary…

John concludes with verses 7-8,

> "And one of the Four Living Beings gave to the seven angels seven golden bowls full of the wrath of God the one living unto the ages of the ages. And the sanctuary was filled with smoke from the glory of God and from his power, and no one was able to enter into the sanctuary until the seven plagues of the seven angels could be ended."

Hereat, I will repeat a passage I wrote in part two of the commentary, concerning Chapter 5: In verse 5, an Elder calls Christ "the Lion of Judah, the root of David." This refers to Isaiah 11:10,

> "On that day the root of Jesse…the Gentiles shall seek out, for his Dwelling shall be glorious."

The Dwelling was the Holy of Holies in the Old Testament. In Exodus 40:35, it reads,

> "Moses could not enter the meeting tent, because the cloud settled down on it and the glory of the Lord filled the Dwelling."

Moses could not enter because God was present, and no man could see God face to face and live. The scene of Chapter 15 is the inner court, the sanctuary, of the Church. In Chapter 5, the laity was described as a "sea of glass, like crystal"; but, here in Chapter 15, the "sea of glass" is "mixed with fire." The people standing there are those who have demonstrated their love of the Truth by conquering to the extreme, by winning…

ἐκ τοῦ θηρίου καὶ ἐκ τῆς εἰκόνος αὐτοῦ καὶ ἐκ τοῦ ἀριθμοῦ τοῦ ὀνόματος αὐτοῦ...,
ek tou thërion kai ek tës eikonos auton kai ek tou apithmou tou onomatos auto...
"beyond the Beast and beyond its icon and beyond the number of its name..."

So great has been their "μαρτυρία," individually and collectively, that they have won or conquered <u>for far more than themselves</u>: they are the little lambs who have won salvation and abundance of graces for many generations yet unborn. Now they can sing the song of Moses and the song of the Little Lamb in anticipation of the true and just judgment about to begin; for they <u>know</u> their "μαρτυρία" has won the "μαρτύριον," so that all flesh should not perish from the earth.

John tells, in plain speech, which of the three Divine Persons will send the judgment: the Living One, the one living unto the ages of the ages, which is a title Christ said of himself in 1:17-18,

"I am the first and the last and the living one."

Clearly and precisely, John informs the reader that the plagues will be "the wrath of God," his unmitigated justice: The Beast and his followers have inflicted terrible suffering and death upon Christ's little lambs, continuously, for 3½ years. They did so with Christ's permission, and that permission was an <u>act of mercy</u>: for the patient endurance of the saints was a gift to move the hearts of the persecutors to conversion or repentance. But, the anti-Christians, having rejected the extreme "μαρτυρία" of the saints, have also rejected the extreme "μαρτυρία" of the Spirit: they have passed the point of no return by committing, in extreme, the sin against the Holy Spirit, the sin that Jesus warned would not be forgiven; and so, they have incurred upon themselves the extreme penalty of the second death.

In Chapter 15, it is made perfectly clear that the time of mercy has passed,

> "No one was able to enter the sanctuary until the <u>seven</u> plagues of the seven angels would be ended."

The <u>seventh</u> angel from 8:2 will blow his trumpet <u>not long after</u> the Two Witnesses have been resurrected and ascended into heaven everlasting [11:14, ταχύ = takhu: quickly, soon]. It seems most improbable that God will give more than another 3½ days for the conversion of those Jews who will convert, simply because they will already have had 3½ years, and because it should not take more than a few days for the news about the Two Witnesses to spread throughout the small country of Israel, especially, with modern telecommunications.

When the number of Jews has reached completion, the <u>seventh</u> trumpet will be sounded, and the <u>seven</u> "angels" with the <u>seven last</u> plagues will appear in the Church. Those "angels" will be the "sign" that is "great and amazing" [15:1], the one that will signal to the faithful that the Divine Power of the Church is about to act. It is "the sign of the Son of Man" mentioned in Matthew 24:30,

> "And at that time the sign of the Son of Man will be <u>manifested</u> in heaven…"

The sign itself is not the "μαρτύριον," but points to it and ominously indicates the imminent activity that will be the "μαρτύριον." For this reason, Matthew wrote concerning this manifestation of the sign,

> "And at that time all the tribes <u>of the earth</u> will mourn…" [Mt. 24:30]

The "μαρτύριον" will be the actual infliction of the seven last plagues only upon the anti-Christians, and, thus, it will be a witness or testimony, a demonstration or proof, not only of the fact that Christ is present in his Church, but also that He is present with great power and glory. For this reason, Matthew wrote,

> "…and they [all the tribes of the earth] will see 'the Son of man coming on the clouds of heaven' with much power and glory."
> [Mt. 24:30]

This corresponds with Apoc. 15:8, where John wrote,

> "and the sanctuary became full of smoke from the glory of God and his power…"

At the time that the sign is manifested, God will send out his angels to gather the harvest of those slaughtered during the several days after the Two Witnesses were killed. This implies an exceedingly short delay between the manifestation of the sign and the beginning of the "μαρτύριον," probably, as an eleventh-hour opportunity for any faithful members still in Babylon the Great to escape the fast-approaching judgment upon that city. When all who can be saved have been saved, the "μαρτύριον" will begin.

The plagues, while in progress, will greatly impede persecution against the Church but will not terminate it, totally, until Armageddon is over. Christ warned many times about persevering to the end, and he meant the very end of the end. Some of the faithful will fail in the very last days of general persecution, as Matthew 24:29 indicates,

> "Immediately after the tribulation of those days [the 1,260 days] the sun will be darkened, and the moon will not give its light and the stars will fall from [the] heaven, and the powers of the heavens will be shaken."

The Beast will be everywhere triumphant [except in the land of the Great Eagle]: his followers will be putting to death so many of the faithful, so quickly, and so many of the faithful will be apostatizing, that it will seem the Church is finished, that the light of the world will surely be extinguished; and this reign of terror and lawlessness will be the darkest time in the history of the Church and of the earth. God alone will be able to stop it,

> "As the lightning comes out of the east and becomes manifest [φαίνεταν = phainetan: to appear, become] even unto the west, so will the presence [παρουσία = parousia] of the Son of Man" [Mt. 24:27]

Remember St. Paul's words to the Thessalonians,

> "The lawless one will be revealed, whom the Lord Jesus will annihilate with the breath [πνεύματι = pneumati] of his mouth and

> destroy with the manifestation of his presence..." [ἐπιφανείᾳ τῆς παρουσίας αὐτοῦ...= epiphaneia tës parousias autou...].
> [2 Thes. 2:8]

In all other versions, the term "παρουσία" [parousia] above has been translated as "coming." There are two reasons for this:

(1) Christ himself said in the Apocalypse, "Yes, I am coming soon."
(2) The virtually universal opinion is that the "parousia" here pertains to Christ's Second Coming at the end of human history.

First of all, I would like to point out that, when Christ comes for the second time, he will return at the Mount of Olives at the end of human history, not at the end of this present evil age. Secondly, Christ used the verb "ἔρχομαι" [epkhomai], which means "I am coming" [Apoc. 22:20]; but, the term "παρουσία" [parousia] is derived from the verb "πάρεῖναι" [pareinai], "to be present," and the noun means "a being present, presence." If a thing is not, and, then it is, it can be said that the thing "came," in the sense of "came to be"; and, thus, its "being present" is a "coming." Christ does not have to come to his Church nor does he have to come to be in his Church; for he has been present in his Church from the beginning, is present now, and ever will be present, even to the consummation of the world.

The "smoke" in the sanctuary symbolizes the Real Presence, and the whole point of Paul's words is that Christ will manifest his presence in the Church: "the manifestation of his presence," i.e., also the genitive case of ORIGIN, in the sense that the manifestation will proceed from Jesus Christ himself. This syntax recalls the very first words of the little book, "The revelation OF Jesus Christ." It is the "μαρτύριον" that will "come [to be]," not Christ's real presence in the Church.

Christ was a "sign" that would be opposed, and his apostles became "signs" of him. Whoever received them received him; similarly, whoever sees the sign of the seven "angels" with the seven last plagues sees the "sign" of him, i.e., indirectly sees him, Jesus Christ. Whoever persecutes his followers persecutes him, as Christ made clear to St. Paul on the road to Damascus,

"Saul, Saul, why do you persecute me?" [Acts 9:4]

Therefore, when John says in Apoc. 1:7,

> "Look! He is coming with the clouds, and every eye will see him, even those who pierced him, and on account of him all the tribes of the earth will mourn,"

this does not necessarily mean that people will see Jesus, directly; rather, it means they will see "the sign of the Son of man" [Mt. 24:30].

It has already been mentioned that the "sign" of the Son of Man will not be the "μαρτύριον"; and, though St. Paul used the noun "ἐπιφανεία," this term must be viewed according to the meaning of "μαρτύριον," and not according to the epiphany of the Child Jesus, in person, before the Three Magi.

The Greek word, "ἐπιφανείᾳ," denotes an appearance or apparition, it is true; but, St. Paul distinguished between a manifestation, in the sense of the actual visible person, Jesus Christ, as at the Epiphany, and manifestation in the sense of something visible that will indicate that Christ is really present in his Church. It is the latter sense of the term "ἐπιφανεία" that St. Paul meant.

If he had meant that Christ would manifest himself in the flesh and that his glorified body would be visible to the naked eye, then Paul would have simply stated that Christ will appear in person, in the sense that Christ himself will become visible. "Lightning" symbolizes a visible demonstration of God's power, an effect such as, a miracle; it does not symbolize God himself. The "lightning" comes from the throne in heaven, the throne where God has seated himself. Hence, in Matthew 24:27, Christ said,

> "As the lightning comes out of the east and appears [becomes manifest] unto the west, so will be the presence of the "Son of Man."

This means the whole world will know that the "μαρτύριον" comes from the Living One, Jesus Christ. As it is written,

> "…A sword, a sword is drawn for slaughter, burnished to consume and to flash lightning…" [Ez. 21:33]

It is the "ῥομφαία" rhomphaia], double-edged and sharp.

So, now you have an important point of reference, the "μαρτύριον," with which to get your bearings from Chapter 14 onward. But, John loops very often, and some rough reckonings are still to come. Remember the "βάσανοσ" [basanos = the rack or instrument by which one is forced to divulge the truth]: the Apocalypse is that, and it is also a stumbling block for those who would impose their own opinions on the words of God. The greatest obstacle to understanding the Apocalypse is a hardened heart.

Two more terms you should know are these: "θλῖψις" [thlipsis] "tribulation" and "τὸ βδέλυγμα τῆς ἐρημώσεως" [to bdelygma tës erëmöseös], and the "abomination of desolation." Christ himself has commanded you to understand these things. It would not be an act of wisdom to ignore him.

The noun "θλῖψις" signifies "ordeal, suffering, distress, tribulation." Modern translators prefer the first three, perhaps, because "tribulation" sounds old-fashioned, almost archaic. I, on the other, am getting old and have become becomingly fit, though fat, in my fashion; and, so, I prefer the translation "tribulation."

Here are three examples of "θλῖψις" from the Apocalypse:

(1) I, John, your brother and one sharing in the tribulation and kingdom and patient endurance in Jesus…[1:9]
(2) Beware, I am throwing her [Jezebel, a false prophetess] on a bed, and those who commit adultery with her I am throwing into great tribulation, unless they repent from her works. [2:22]
(3) These are they who have come out of the tribulation the great one…[7:14]

The "tribulation," in the first sentence, was the persecution under the emperor Domitian; in the second instance, it was the coming persecution under the emperor Trajan; and, in the third instance, it was the persecution, the last one, under the emperor Diocletian. Note that each succeeding tribulation was worse than the one before it. Judging by these examples, I conclude that the term, "θλῖψις," denotes bloody persecution on a relatively large scale. Considering the size of the Church, today, in its extent and in the number of its members, it may reasonably be inferred that the next persecution will be the biggest and bloodiest of all.

According to Christ's statement in Matthew 24:21, it will be that...

> "For there will be <u>at that time</u> [τότε = tote] a great tribulation such as has not happened from the beginning of the world until now and never will happen again."

The demonstrative adverb "τότε" [tote = at that time] points <u>backward</u> to what Christ mentioned in Mt. 24:16-20, and, therefore, the event he mentioned in Mt. 24:15 marks the time when the "θλῖψις" will become "μεγάλην" [megalë], "great." Before that event, there will be "θλῖψις" [Mt. 24:9, compare with Apoc. 1:9], but it will be only in some part or parts of the world, not in the whole world.

The event, at which the "tribulation" will escalate to "great," concerns the "abomination of desolation." Here are Christ's words from Mt. 24:15,

> ὅταν οὖν ἴδητε τὸ βδέλυγμα τῆς ἐρημώσεως τὸ ῥηθὲν διὰ
> Otan oun idëte to bdelygma tës erëmöseös to rëthen dia
> When so you see the abomination of [the] desolation, the one mentioned by
>
> Δανιὴλ τοῦ προφήτου ἑστὸς ἐν τόπῳ ἁγίῳ ὁ ἀναγινώσκων νοείτω,...
> Daniël tou prophëtou estos en topö agiö, o anaginöskön noeitö,...
> Daniel the prophet having taken its stand in a place holy [let the one reading understand!]...

Whereas Christ referred the reader to the book of Daniel, regarding the "abomination of desolation," I will here put three excerpts from it:

> "Half the week he [Antiochus IV] shall abolish sacrifice and oblation; on the temple wing shall be the horrible abomination until the ruin that is decreed is poured out upon the horror." [Dn 9:27]

> "Armed forces shall move at his command and defile the sanctuary stronghold, abolishing the daily sacrifice and setting up the horrible abomination." [Dn. 11:31]

> "From the time that the daily sacrifice is abolished and the horrible abomination is set up, there shall be one thousand two hundred and ninety days." [Dn. 12:11]

From these three excerpts may be drawn four very important items of information:

(1) The "horrible abomination" was a thing, i.e., an idol or icon.
(2) The idol had to be "set up."
(3) The idol was to remain in the sanctuary of the temple for "half the week" or "1290 days," which would be about 3½ years.
(4) The tract of 3½ years would be a time of religious persecution.

In the New Testament, the term "βδέλυγμα" [bdelygma] denotes a loathsome thing, most especially, an idol. The idol mentioned in Daniel had to be set up, but the idol to which Christ referred will take its own stand in a holy place, i.e., in the sanctuary of a Roman Catholic church.

The word "ἑστὸς" [estos], in Mt. 24:15, modifies "βδέλυγμα"; it is the perfect participle [in the neuter singular accusative] of the verb "εστάναι" [estanai], which is intransitive in the second aorist and perfect tenses, conveying the idea "to take a stand, to take up a position, to stand firm."

Note that Christ used the definite article, even though he had not mentioned the "abomination," previously. This means the idol will be the one and only during the tribulation, easily recognized by the informed faithful, as the idol mentioned by Jesus in Mt. 24:15. The "abomination of desolation" will be the image of the Beast described in Apocalypse 13.

Christ's use of the perfect participle "ἑστὸς" indicates that the icon of the Beast will be able to move; and it alludes to the similar fact that Satan will take his stand upon the "sand of the sea," thus intimating that the image of the Beast will become operative in the earliest days after Satan takes his stand. The idol in Daniel was a prefigurement of the icon in Apocalypse 13; and, as the former lasted about 3½ years, so will the latter.

As to the specific church wherein the icon of the Beast will take its stand, the New Testament does not tell; for the same reason, John did not tattle about the name of the Beast or Babylon the Great. I do not know which one it will be. I absolutely refuse to opine; and I loathe idle speculation.

You are now ready to reckon your bearings from Chapter 14 onward. I shall move swiftly, because much of the material you can understand by yourself, and I do not see why you would need elaboration from me. Henceforth, my primary goal is to show you the sequence of events.

Chapter 20

—

Apocalypse Chapter 14

This Chapter resumes the narrative from 11:8. The reader must bear in mind that the Beast has just killed the Two Witnesses, Enoch and Elijah, whom no one else for 1260 days had been able to kill. Consequently, their deaths were perceived by the anti-Christians, as testimony or proof of the Beast's superior power, and of his claim to divinity. The people had feared the two prophets who had tormented them with terrible plagues for so long; but the Beast has relieved them of whatever restraint their fear had compelled. Understanding this, the Beast and the False Prophet have seized the opportunity to incite pent passions; and so, now, the followers of the Beast are about to release their hatred and revenge upon the followers of the Little Lamb.

The vision of Chapter 14 begins with the Little Lamb standing on Mount Zion surrounded by 144,000 who have His name and His Father's name written on their foreheads. This description contrasts with the Beast and his followers who wear the name of the Beast or the number of his name. In view of the situation I just described in the above paragraphs, it should be evident to all that Christ and the 144,000 are not actually standing on Mount Zion. "Mt. Zion" here symbolizes the Church, and verse 3 corroborates this fact,

> "…and they [the 144,000] sing a new song before the throne and before the four living beings and before the elders."

This scene is like those in Chapters 4 and 5, 7 and 15. Verse 3 informs the reader that the 144,000 are members of the laity. The number "144,000" signifies a minority, a small minority out of the entire laity, just as this number in Chapter 7 indicated that only a small minority of the Jews had converted to Christ by the fourth century AD. However, the number "144,000" in this chapter, does not represent all who have remained faithful, but a special minority of them.

In verse 4, John explains who they are,

> "They have been redeemed from mankind as <u>first fruits</u> for God and for the Little Lamb."

This means they are the choicest ones, the best, of the harvest about to begin. They are the Elite of the Elect; there stand the men and women of the Imperial Guard of the Lamb. No stain of mortal sin is in their hearts, no lie is in their mouths, and nothing of the earth can attract them: they follow only the Little Lamb.

Only they can sing the new song. Other saints hear it, but they themselves cannot sing it, because their hearts are not as large. The song is not new, in the sense that it is completely different from the song of old; rather, it is new in the sense that never before was the old song sung with such ardor and perfection. The Church has experienced other times of trial but the reign of Antichrist will put to the greatest test the virtues of faith, hope and love. The "144,000" have overcome the world, the flesh, and <u>Satan himself</u>, and their "μαρτυρία" surpasses human imagination and speech.

There stand the Imperial Guard of the Lamb, ready, <u>knowing</u> that Christ is about to command them to do one thing more. Those who live for this world will think the command not just foolishness, but insanity. It always is that God's thoughts are not men's thoughts: so is His love.

In verses 6-7, an angel [cardinal or bishop] proclaims…

> "everlasting good news upon the inhabitants upon the <u>earth</u> and upon every nation and tribe and language and people."

This is the first of the last three warnings, which will be given to the anti-Christians. Anyone living in the early centuries of the Church, or even up to the beginning of the nineteenth century, would have been inclined to assume that this verse implied a miracle, in order for the proclamation to reach so many, so quickly, over such great distances. The advent of the telegraph should have elicited alertness among the faithful; alas, it did not, except for people like John Henry Cardinal Newman. When Zionism began in the 1880's, followed quickly by Marconi's wireless, anyone familiar with the Apocalypse should have easily perceived that the shadows were gathering fast. Today, it is perfectly clear that the fulfillment of verse 6 will not require a miracle; modern communications already suffice.

In verse 8, a second angel warns,

> "Fallen, fallen is Babylon the Great! She has made all nations drink of the wine of the wrath of her fornication."

This statement is a combination of the foreparts of verses 1 and 3 in Chapter 18; it is only anticipatory at this point in time, not factual. In prophetic works, future events are often stated in the past tense, because, from God's point of view, these events are as good as done. Hence, the angel in verse 8 speaks in the same manner as the angel in verse 6, to wit, respectively, "Fallen, fallen is Babylon the Great!" and "the hour of his judgment has come." The reason for the appearance of the second angel is, probably, that the first was silenced, as will probably be the case for the second and third, as well.

Verse 9-11 corroborate what was said about verses 6-8, as being anticipatory, because the warning in 9-11 is stated in the future tense,

> "If anyone is worshipping the Beast and its image and is accepting the mark upon his forehead or his hand, the same also will drink of the wine of the wrath of God, poured unmixed in the cup of his wrath, and will be tormented with fire and sulfur in the presence of holy angels and the Little Lamb."

This is the third and last warning to the anti-Christians, but it also applies to the Brethren, encouraging them to hold fast till the end. Verses 12 and 13 were written to remind the faithful that they must practice patient endurance. In verse 12, John used the demonstrative adverb "ὧδε" [öde = in this manner], which points forward to the contents of verse 13,

> "Blessed from now on are the dead who are dying in the Lord." 'Yes,' says the Spirit, 'in that they will rest from their labors, for their works follow with them.'"

Again, I remind you that the time here is just after the Beast has killed the two prophets, Enoch and Elijah. The anti-Christians are rejoicing and exchanging gifts: and, doubtless, they are killing some of the faithful for sport. Many Catholics will be very tempted to comply externally with the commands of the False Prophet, thinking to refuse internally to worship the Beast. The warnings from the three "angels" will partially negate the Beast's and the False Prophet's efforts to force the faithful into submission.

Persecution up to this time may have been somewhat more of a political and economic one than bloody; but now the patient endurance of the saints will present only one course of action to the Beast: to decree total persecution to death for any and all who will not worship him. It is at this point that the "tribulation" will escalate to such extent and degree as no one now living can imagine even near its half.

The term "ὧδε" [öde = in this manner] makes the term "patient endurance of the saints" apply, most especially, to verse 13, wherein the voice from heaven commands John to write,

> "Blessed from now on are the dead who are dying in the Lord" [literally, ἀπ' ἄρτι = ap arti: from right now, i.e., from this moment on]

This clearly explains what is meant here by the term "patient endurance": martyrdom. I suspect that the Beast will issue his decree of total extermination within half a day after he kills the Two Witnesses, and verse 13 pertains to that moment and predicts what is to follow: the great harvest in verses 14-16. The Imperial Guard of the Lamb is ready. They are singing the new song, the song of the new "heaven" and new earth, which their terrible sufferings and martyrdoms shall win for the generations to come after them, the song foreordained in 5:9.

This is what the Spirit means in the words,

"...for their works follow with them."

They will not only have the reward of their works with them in heaven, but they will also have their reward in what follows: the destruction of the Beast and his empire, and, then, the new "heaven" and new earth. They have the names of the Father and of the Son written on their foreheads, and the Holy Spirit is written in their hearts. They desire only what God wants, and, therefore, the destruction of the Beast and the coming of the new "heaven" and earth will be their reward also. The works, which bring them a reward in heaven, will be the same works, which bring them a reward on earth. Thus, it can be said that "their works follow with them": they will lose nothing, neither in heaven above nor on earth below, because all they want is what God wants. They are the Imperial Guard of the Lamb.

Mount Zion stands in the city of Jerusalem, and on Mount Zion once stood the Temple built by Solomon, from which, in Old Testament times, God thundered forth his decrees. It was from Mount Zion that Christ's apostles, clothed with power from on high, went boldly forth to convert a world hostile to its Creator.

"Mount Zion" itself symbolizes the culmination of virtue, perfection, and power. In the Old Testament, it symbolized the theocracy of Israel; in the New Testament, it signifies the Church: here, it specifically indicates that the Imperial Guard of the Lamb will prove the decisive factor.

Thus, the vision, up to verse 13, anticipates the terrible potentiation of the persecution tersely mentioned in verses 14-16, but it also signals the certain outcome mentioned in verses 17-20.

Of this phase in the persecution, Christ warned that...

> "the sun will be darkened, and the moon will not give its light, and the stars will fall from heaven, and the powers of the heavens will be shaken." [Mt. 24:29]

"The moon will not give its light" means that this brief period will be one of total lawlessness, the darkest barbarism; but, the Little Lamb and his followers will win, for this has already been written,

"the law shall come forth from Zion" [Is. 2:3]

At or shortly after the time when Enoch and Elijah are resurrected and assumed into heaven, the sign of the Son of Man will become manifest in heaven. The Beast and the False Prophet, furious that the Jews, in large numbers, are converting to the Little Lamb, will strain every agent and agency, civilian and military, to implement the decree of total extermination of the Church.

This is where verse 14 applies. Recalling what was said about the "sign of the Son of Man," it is not surprising John saw "one <u>like</u> the Son of Man" seated on a white cloud. This corresponds to what Matthew in 24:30 wrote,

> "...they will see the Son of Man coming on the clouds of heaven."
> [Mt. 24:30]

The one seated on the cloud is a <u>real</u> angel, not Jesus Christ, as indicated by the phrase, "like the Son of Man," and by the "golden crown" [στέφανος = stephanos] on his head. This corresponds to Matthew 24:31,

> "...and he [Son of Man] will send out his angels with a loud trumpet call, and they will gather his elect from the four winds, from one end of the heavens to the other."

In Chapter 14, the angel and the "cloud" are <u>representative</u> of the plural "angels" and "clouds" mentioned in Matthew's verses, just as the "sickle" in the "angel's" hand represents all the evil agents and agencies instrumental in carrying out the Beast's decree. The "loud trumpet call" in Matthew becomes the angel who "calls with a loud voice" to the angel on the "cloud," sending him out with the command, "Use your sickle and reap..."

The angel <u>from the sanctuary</u> belongs to the Four Living Beings; his calling in a loud voice indicates that he has authority superior to that of a real angel. Indeed, he commands in the name of Christ; and therefore, ultimately speaking, it is Christ who sends the real angel out to reap the harvest. Since God lives in his obedient servants, it can be said that where the servant is, God is, and what the servant does, God does. Unless this point is discerned, it will seem that Matthew's passage and John's do not agree.

Now, the "angel from the sanctuary" will probably be the pope [elected by the Sacred College during the 1260 days in the "wilderness"], and he will be divinely inspired to know exactly when the hour to reap the faithful has come. Much of the harvest will be gathered during the 3½ days that the Two Witnesses lie dead in a street of Jerusalem, and during the few days immediately after they are assumed into heaven. Strictly speaking, the harvesting will not be completed until the Beast and all his followers have been destroyed.

Verses 17-20 are a succinct description of the Battle of Armageddon. This final section of the Chapter is obviously a loop or leap forward in the order of events, because the great battle will be the penultimate event of the seventh plague; not the event immediately subsequent to the harvest described in verses 14-16.

The purpose of this passage is not to present an offset to the rest of the foregoing Chapter, but to show the exactitude of God in the ways of men; for it is written,

> "As you sow, so shall you reap." [Gal. 6:8]

The exactitude of the translations, however, suggests that the translators alternated between translating the verses and playing poker, as Chapters 11 and 12 also suggested, since the mistakes made here are the same as those made there; and as luck often has it, their game did not work out well: sooner or later, someone was bound to call their bluff.

What John wrote in verses 17-20 was this [see Joel 3:4-5; 4:1-2, 11-16],

> 17 And another angel came out from the sanctuary the one in heaven, himself holding also a sharp [ὀξύ = oxu] sickle. 18 And another angel came out from the altar, the one who holds authority over the fire, and he called out in a loud voice to the one holding the sickle the sharp one saying, "Take your sickle the sharp one, and gather the

clusters of the vine of the earth, because its grapes [have] ripened."
19 And the angel cast out [ἔβαλεν = ebalen] its sickle unto the earth
and gathered the vine of the earth and cast [it] out [ἔβαλεν = ebalen]
into the winepress of the wrath of God, the great one. 20 And the
winepress was trampled outside [ἔξωθεν = exöthen] the city and
blood came out from the winepress even up to the bridles of the
horses from stadia one thousand six hundred.

Three times—twice, by syntactical emphasis—John alludes to the "ῥομφαίᾳ" [rhomphaia], the sharp one, in verses 17-18: The "ῥομφαίᾳ," dear reader, was not a straight blade, but a curved one called a "scimitar," and the shape of the sickle is similar to it. In verses 19-20, John thrice alludes to 11:1-4, that is, the GREAT SIGN in Chapter 12, and, thus, the SIGN GREAT AND AMAZING in 15:1. The adjective "great," in these instances, alludes to the GREAT DAY OF ALMIGHTY GOD, the great and terrible day.

As Satan and his followers were cast out from the Church, so here they are cast out from the whole world, because the "city" mentioned in verse 20 is not only Jerusalem, in the literal sense, but also the New Jerusalem, in the symbolical sense—the New Jerusalem, which is the city of God, the kingdom of heaven, about to be realized over the whole earth.

The works, the "μαρτυρία," of the faithful, especially, of those who are the first fruits for the Father and the Little Lamb, have brought about the "μαρτύριον," whose final phase shall include the grapes of wrath. The warnings and promises in verses 6-13, and the sign in Chapter 12, and the words about the "mystery of God", as announced to his servants the prophets, are here being fulfilled.

But, bear in mind that verses 17-20 are a flash forward. Verses 14-16 fit immediately after verse 1 in Chapter 15, and then comes 15:2-8. Chapter 14:17-20 will come near the end of the seventh plague, just after Babylon the Great is destroyed, as proved by cross-referring Chapters 16 and 19. But, I am getting ahead of myself.

The Hebrew word "Armageddon" means "the hill of robbers." Megiddo was an ancient city on the Plain of Esdraelon, about forty miles north of Jerusalem. When Napoleon saw this plain, he unwittingly prophesied, "All the armies of the world could maneuver here." The Plain of Esdraelon stretches from Mt.

Carmel, at the edge of the Mediterranean Sea, to the Jordan River, a total distance of about forty miles.

But there's the rub: John mentioned 1600 stadia. A stadium measured about 607 feet; therefore, 1600 stadia would be about 184 miles. This suggests that the approximate center of the Christian battle line will be on the Plain of Esdraelon. Since the Christian forces can expect to be attacked from the north, east, and south, they will dispose themselves according to natural features of terrain. So, a battle line extending from the edge of the Mediterranean Sea, about 35-40 miles north of Haifa, over to the Sea of Galilee, and thence southward along the west bank of the Jordan River to the north edge of the Dead Sea; and then from the western middle edge of the Dead Sea to the edge of the Mediterranean at Gaza, would have a length of about 184 miles [not 150 or 200]; and, perhaps, it is merely coincidental that it also would have the shape of a giant sickle.

The specific detail that "blood flowed out from the winepress even up to the bridles of the horses from stadia one thousand six hundred," is to be understood as literal. Now, the bridle on a horse is part of the tack or harness, consisting usually of a headstall, bit, and reins. Since John did not mention the species or breed of horse, I assume he meant the typical "beastie" of his day used in the military, which was somewhat smaller than a modern one.

Hence, the depth or height, in question here, will probably be about 3 to 4 feet, maximum. Moreover, this depth of blood will not be reached along every yard of the 1,600 stadia, but, certainly, in large pools or ponds here and there along said length.

This amount of blood connotes two things:

(1) Many millions of combatants will be engaged.
(2) The latter part of the battle, after munitions have been depleted, will be fought hand-to-hand with pointed and edged weapons, such as, bayonets, swords, knives, axes, etc.

The phrase, "even to the bridles of horses" [ἄχρι τῶν χαλινῶν τῶν ἵππων = arkhi tön khalinön tön xppön], is peculiar for two reasons:

(1) the use of the definite article.
(2) the plurality of the nouns.

The definite article is used with a person or thing previously mentioned, or with one whose identity is unmistakable or easily ascertained; and the plurality of nouns is unnecessary, if only an approximate measurement is intended. I suspect that John was referring mainly to the remnant number of the 200 Million Horsemen from the opening phase of the second woe. If anyone has a more plausible explanation, I would like to hear it.

John did not indicate when the great Battle of Armageddon would be fought. However, bear in mind that the three Divine Persons in one nature, though they are not dunces for redundancy, have, in the past, evidenced a penchant, if you will, for repetition.

Now, the festival of Passover commemorates the exodus of the Jews from Egypt; it begins on the eve of the 14th day of the month of Nisan, the first month of the Jewish calendar, and is celebrated for seven days by Reform Jews and Jews in Israel.

The festival of Easter commemorates the resurrection of Jesus Christ; it is observed on the first Sunday after the first full moon after the vernal equinox [as calculated on the Gregorian calendar, not the Julian, which the Orthodox churches use].

Well, the way it works out, Passover and Easter come about the same time in the spring, the time of renewal. In Matthew 24:32-33, Christ said,

> "And from the fig tree learn the lesson: when already its branch is becoming tender and it is sprouting its leaves, you know that summer is near: so also you, when you see all these things [πάντα ταῦτα = panta tauta], know that he is near, at the doors."

In Apocalypse 3:20 [the seventh letter, Laodicea], Christ used the expression "ἐπὶ τὴν θύραν" [epi ten thyran], "at the door," which is similar to "ἐπὶ θύραις" [epi thyrais], "at the doors," in Matthew 24:33. Jesus punned on the noun "θέρος" [theros], "summer," and "θύρα" [rypa], "door, gate," to make the point memorable.

Now, the critical time for crops in Israel [if this old brain remembers faithfully] comes between Passover and the festival of Shavuoth, that is, during the Omer, the period of 49 days [7 weeks] from the 2nd day of Passover to the 1st of Shavuoth [the 6th day of the month of Sivan]; for, if the hot winds blow from the desert, too early, there will be little or nothing to harvest.

The festival of Pentecost comes 49 days [7 weeks] after Easter. The first Pentecost was the descent of the Holy Spirit upon the Apostles; and that Pentecost is regarded as the birthday of the Church.

So, first comes Easter/Passover, then 7 weeks later comes Pentecost/Shavuoth. To these facts, relate three more:

(1) The "fig tree" is the symbol for the nation of Israel.
(2) The "birth pangs" mentioned by Christ in Matthew 24:8 will end when the seventh plague [in the Apocalypse] ends.
(3) The period of the seven Apocalyptic plagues will be, at least, several weeks long, especially, because it will take a few just for the armies under the kings from the East to travel westward, cross the dried-up Euphrates, and move into Palestine—even if the armies are totally mechanized.

All these things together, plus the fact that...

(1) the noun for "harvest" is "θερισμὸς" [therismos],
(2) and the verb for "reap" is "θέρειν" [therein], both relevant to the "θηνίον" [thërion] or "θήρ" [thër], the Beast to which the nouns "θέρος" [theros] and "θύρα" [thyra] bear similitude,...

give me the impression of being a big hint.

Aye, whereas Apocalypse 4:1 reads,

> "After these things I looked, and behold, an opened door [θύρα = thyra] in heaven!";

and whereas 15:5 reads,

> "And after these things I looked, and the sanctuary of the tent of the witness [μαρτύριον] in heaven opened, and out came the seven angels having the seven plagues from the sanctuary…";

and whereas 19:11 reads,

> "And I saw heaven opened, and behold, a white horse and the one seated on it called faithful and true…";

I am compelled to assert that Christ's phrase, "at the door," or "at the doors," refers to the door(s) of the sanctuary, and that it means he is about to issue judgment.

Hence, I strongly, very strongly, suspect that:

(1) The Two Witnesses will be in Jerusalem for Easter/Passover at the end of their 1260 days.
(2) The conversion of the Jews will be when the "fig tree sprouts its leaves."
(3) During the 7 weeks until Pentecost/Shavuoth will come the 7 last plagues [μαρτύριον] to the nations.
(4) On or about Pentecost/Shavuoth, there will come, to Armageddon, the Great Day of Almighty God.

Oh, incidentally, the word "Allelujia" is sung by the Church on all occaissions, not of mourning or penitence, but it is sung most especially on Easter up to TRINITY SUNDAY, a week after Pentecost. I just thought you might like to know that, if you didn't already. Yet, this scenario cannot tell the exact day and hour, and only Tme will tell how well I have read the subtle message.

Chapter 21

—

Apocalypse Chapters 16 And 19

The "loud voice" in 16:1 is that of the Living Being in 15:7, who gave the seven plagues to the seven "angels"; it is the voice of the Lion, the supreme authority in the Church. This verse continues the scene of the sanctuary, as mentioned in 14:1-5 and 15:1-8.

The plagues are <u>seven</u> in number, which hold the symbolical number "four" within it; and so, the number "seven" here indicates that the plagues shall affect the <u>totality</u> of the earth, simply because the Beast's kingdom is universal. This does not mean every plague will affect the whole earth equally in every part; rather, all of the plagues <u>combined</u> will inflict a universal effect: the annihilation of the Beast and his followers. <u>Not even one</u> anti-Christian shall survive this judgment.

The Church will overtly inflict the plagues; and everyone, whether learned or unlearned, great or small, shall <u>know</u> that the plagues come directly from Almighty God, Jesus Christ. In the past, even those who profoundly pondered the Apocalypse sometimes did not know exactly which seal had already been opened, was being opened, or would be opened next; and the rest of the people, especially those "outside" the Church, simply regarded the evolvement of history, as a series of natural phenomena. The destruction of Jerusalem and the temple, and, later, the destruction of Israel as a nation, were, manifestly, judgments of God in the eyes of Christians; but Jews and pagans did not perceive them as such.

The seven last plagues will make ignorance or doubt an impossibility: All, all without exception, shall see the power and the glory of the Lord. As it is written,

> "All nations shall come and shall adore in his sight." [Apoc. 15:4]

As God has said it, so it must take place.

In verse 2, the first angel…

> "poured his bowl unto the earth, and there came an ulcer bad and festering upon the people the ones having the mark of the Beast and worshipping its icon."

The cardinal or bishop will probably pour blest water or oil, as Moses sprinkled ashes upon the air. The ulcer will be inflicted only upon the anti-Christians. Deuteronomy 28:35 reads,

> "The Lord will strike you with malignant boils of which you cannot be cured, on your knees and legs, and from the soles of your feet to the crown of your head."

This is, perhaps, what God did to the Israelites for adoring the golden calf in Exodus 33:35, which reads,

> "thus the Lord struck the people for having had Aaron make the calf for them."

Antichrist will not be able to cure his followers of their painful ulcer. This first plague is similar to the sixth plague in Egypt.

Verse 3 states,

> καὶ ὁ δεύτερος ἐξέχεεν τὴν φιάλην αὐτοῦ εἰς τὴν θάλασσαν καὶ
> Kai o deuteros exekheen tën phialën autou eis tën thalassan, kai
> And the second poured out the bowl of him unto the sea, and

ἐγένετο αἷμα ὡς νεκροῦ καὶ πᾶσα ψυχὴ ζωῆς ἀπέθανεν
egeneto aima ös nekrou, kai pasa psykhë zöës apethanen
became blood as of one dead, and every breath of life ceased

τὰ ἐν τῇ θαλάσσῃ.
ta en të thalassë.
the one in the sea.

Keeping in mind the <u>vocabulary</u> and <u>syntax</u> of this verse, look at 8:8-9 which states,

καὶ ὁ δεύτερος ἄγγελος ἐσάλπισεν καὶ ὡς ὄρος μέγα πυρὶ
Kai o deuteros aggelos esalpisen . kai ös oros mega pyri
And the second angel blew the trumpet: even as a mountain great with fire

καιόμενον ἐβλήθη εἰς τὴν θάλασσαν καὶ ἐγένετο τὸ τρίτον
kaiomenon eblëthë eis tën thalassan, kai egeneto to triton
burning was cast out unto the sea, and became the third

τῆς θαλάσσης αἷμα 9 καὶ ἀπέθανεν τὸ τρίτον τῶν κτισμάτων
tës thalassës aima kai apethanen to triton tön ktismatön
of the sea blood and died [ceased] the third of the creatures

τῶν ἐν τῇ θαλάσσῃ τὰ ἔχοντα ψυχάς καὶ τὸ τρίτον
tön en të thalassë ta ekhonta psykhas kai to triton
the ones in the sea the ones having breath and the third
[psykhë = breath, spirit, soul, mind]

τῶν πλοίων διεφθάρησαν.
tön ploiön diephtharësan.
of the ships were destroyed.

Excerpt 8:8-9 was a preparation for understanding 12:18,

"And he took his stand upon the sand of the sea,"

and for 16:3; and, for this reason is 8:8-9 more explicit. Even a cursory comparison of 8:8-9 and 16:3 by any attentive reader will perceive the fundamental similitude of the latter to the former, in both vocabulary and syntax. Recall the exactitude of God shown in 14:17-20; such is the case here in 16:3, which, albeit abbreviated, is recognizable of 8:8-9 by containing key terms: "unto the sea," "blood," and "breath."

In other words, 16:3 continues the theme, "As you sow, so shall you reap." Indeed, as there were seven seals, so there were seven trumpets, and, so, there were seven plagues:

(1) It is the <u>second</u> [real] angel whose trumpet blast announced the "sea" event described in 8:8-9.
(2) It was the <u>second</u> [angel] who poured out the second plague "unto the sea" in 16:3.
(3) Just as the <u>sixth</u> [real] angel's trumpet blast announced the release of the four angels bound at the Euphrates River, so it will be the <u>sixth</u> angel who pours out the <u>sixth</u> plague upon the same river to dry it up.

Also, the last clause of 16:3, which begins with "*καὶ πᾶσα*..." [kai pasa...], was so worded in order to remind the reader of what the angel said in 10:6,

"...τὴν θάλασσαν καὶ τὰ ἐν αὐτῇ..."
"...tën thalassa kai ta en autë..."
"...the sea and the things in it..."

<u>Nota bene</u> the syntactical emphasis in 8:9, namely,

"...and the third of the creatures died THE ONES IN THE SEA THE ONES HAVING BREATH..."

The literal meaning of the noun "ψυχή" [psykhë, or psyche] is "breath"; hence, like "πνεῦμα" [pneuma], it can also mean "spirit, soul, mind."

Obviously, an entity that can die a physical death must have a soul in the first place: vegetative, sensitive, or intellectual, within which selection are translators found, though under which rubric I cannot say, except that many of them do not slurp soup, as I have long observed.

John could not have been more explicit here; in fact, I cannot recall any passage in the Apocalypse as saliently emphatic as this one: the clause, dear folk, is OXYMORONIC. The verb "ψύχειν" [psykhein] means "to breathe, to respire," and that is what John, literally, means in 8:9. Creatures in the sea do not have breath; they do not use lungs for respiration. Therefore, the term "sea" is symbolic of some region of the earth whose chief characteristic, as 12:18 later informs, is "sand, sandy soil." There is cause for doubting that translators and commentators, at least, slurp their morning coffee before they direct their eyes upon the Sacred Scriptures.

Notice this: in 8:8-9, it was the Burning Mountain that made the third of the "sea" become blood; so, in 16:3, because the "sea" became the Burning Mountain, i.e., because the Burning Mountain became the "sea," it is the Church that is making the blood of the "sea"/Burning Mountain become "as of one dead," i.e., coagulated, so that breathing, the "breath of life," becomes futile—and ceases.

Just as it is said that an engine "dies" or stops running, so the breath of life, the breathing of the anti-Christians, will cease. They will simply die from lack of oxygen. After many centuries, justice will be done: the BURNING Mountain will be made a BURNT Mountain.

The first plague was poured out on all, but the second will affect only those regions designated as "the sea," because the second plague, like the fifth and the sixth, will be special preparation for the climactic clash—on the Plain of Esdraelon.

Even as this second plague is being poured out, the armada, built during the 1260 days by the mightiest individual nation on the earth, will be approaching the Capes of Spartel and Trafalgar. Yet, once more, and for the final time, the armies of the Eagle, the great one, will fight for freedom on the earth. And Israel? Israel will be waiting, at long last, to receive those who come in the name of the Lord.

In verse 4,

> "the third 'angel' poured out his bowl unto the rivers and the springs of the waters, and blood was coming to be."

This plague affects the <u>specific</u> region mentioned in 8:10-11, which states,

> "The <u>third</u> angel blew his trumpet: and there fell from heaven a great star burning as a torch and it fell upon the third of the rivers and upon the springs of the waters, and the name of the star is called "Wormwood."

Again, an example of the Divine exactitude. This third plague is different from the second, in that the waters became blood. The third trumpet in Chapter 8 announced the next major event after Islam shed the blood of the saints in North Africa and destroyed their "ships," the symbol for "churches"; and that next major event took place in a region well watered by springs and streams.

Since the first trumpet announced the barbarian invasions in the western and northern regions of the Roman Empire, and since the second announced the spread of Islam in North Africa, there are only two large regions left: the Middle East and the Balkans. The Middle East does not fit the description. Besides, as will be shown, the fifth plague will affect the Middle East; and God does not indulge in redundancy. So, the Balkans it is, and the event was the Greek Schism.

The "great star" indicates that a Patriarch, an archbishop, defected from the Church. The "waters" symbolize the life or graces of Christ's Church, as given through the sacraments. The Patriarch was <u>given the name</u> "Wormwood" on account of his defection; thus, the waters became "wormwood"; and many of the people died [spiritually] because the water "was made bitter." Wormwood is bitter but it is <u>not</u> poisonous. Therefore, since the metaphor contradicts nature, it means that something contradictory to God's order happened.

Note that the "great star" continued burning brightly, <u>as it fell</u>; this means the Patriarch continued to teach all the truths Christ taught, <u>except one</u>: to remain in the Catholic Church. That Patriarch led one third of the Church's territory into schism.

Jeremiah, in 9:12-14, gives an explanation,

> The Lord answered: Because they have abandoned my law, which I set before them, and have not followed it or listened to my voice, but followed rather the <u>hardness</u> of their hearts and the Baals, as

> their fathers had taught them; therefore, thus says the Lord of hosts, the God of Israel: See, now I will give them wormwood to eat and poison to drink."

The spiritual and temporal graces or blessings for the Jews' obedience to God were "milk and honey"; disobedience resulted in their being fed wormwood. The people are culpable, but God knows who the principal culprits are:

(1) pseudo-prophets who make false claims about receiving revelations, apparitions, locutions, etc., even though they knew that God had not appointed them to the office.
(2) perverse priests who give scandal, by example of injustice and fornication, to the people, thus inciting imitation of their evil activities, until general death eventuates.

Jeremiah, in 23:11-15, spoke as God commanded him,

> 11 Both prophet and priest are godless! In my very house I find their wickedness, says the Lord. 12 Hence their way shall become for them slippery ground. In the darkness they shall lose their footing, and fall headlong; evil I will bring upon them: the year of their punishment, says the Lord. 13 Among Samaria's prophets I saw unseemly deeds: they prophesied by Baal and led my people astray. 14 But among Jerusalem's prophets I saw deeds still more shocking: adultery, living in lies, siding with the wicked, so that no one turns from evil; to me they are all like Sodom, its citizens like Gomorrah. 15 Therefore, thus says the Lord of hosts against the prophets: Behold, I will give them wormwood to eat, and poison to drink…

So far, the worst consequence of the Greek Schism has been Communist Russia; after a brief respite, far worse will come, for the schism will still be unhealed "unto the testimony to the nations." Schism does not per se pollute the sacraments; but, those who receive them from schismatics, knowing they are schismatics, will commit sacrilege, will "drink poison."

It was the layman Photius, a crafty courtier, who got himself consecrated as patriarch, contrary to the laws of the Church, and, soon thereafter in 876 AD, broke away from Rome. Photius remained in power until 886 AD, at which time the schism was healed.

In 1054 AD, Patriarch Michael Caerularius resumed the schism, and from that year, the Greek Schism, in finality, has been dated. The whole Eastern Church of the Greek Rite eventually sided with Caerularius; a short time later, Russia was converted and, then was quickly drawn into the schism. The "great star" in 8:10 was Caerularius.

Communist Russia persecuted the Church horribly, becoming responsible for the murders of 55 bishops, 12,800 priests and monks, and 2,500,000 of the Brethren; and it imprisoned or deported 199 bishops, 32,000 priests, and 10,000,000 believers. All this was done just by 1959; I leave to your imagination what the communists have done in the 40 years thereafter.

It may be that the <u>conversion</u> of Russia, as promised by the Blessed Virgin Mary, will not come until the "μαρτύριον" has exacted penalties due. Only time will tell. The term "conversion" cannot make sense as a Catholic term, unless it denotes a return to the Catholic Church.

The <u>fourth</u> plague will be intense heat from the sun. The text in no way suggests this plague will be applied only to a specific region, such as the second or third were. To the contrary, the symbolical number "four" indicates that the plague of heat will be applied universally, as was the first plague.

John reminds the reader that the time of mercy has passed, and the grace for repentance or conversion will not be given. Despite great suffering, the people...

"did not repent and give him [God] glory." [Apoc. 16:9]

Obviously, the heat, which will literally scorch the anti-Christians, will not be applied to other living things on the earth; and that will be an undeniable demonstration of divine power in finest, minutest exactitude.

The fifth plague will be poured out on the throne, i.e., capital, of the Beast and <u>his kingdom</u> will become darkened. Verse 10 clearly indicates that the region, wherein the Confederation of Ten Kings will exist, cannot be the same region wherein Babylon the Great will have dominion: the "sea" and the "earth" as used in Chapter 13, for example, are different areas. John repeats what was said about the people when the fourth plague was inflicted,

> "...they did not repent of their deeds." [Apoc. 16:11]

The capital of Antichrist, at this point, will not be Jerusalem, because the conversion of the Jews will have compelled him to choose another city. I do not wish to speculate about the name of that city. Of importance here is the darkness, like the plague of darkness on the Egyptians. This darkness will be utterly impenetrable and will not allow light whatsoever; it will last until the anti-Christians gnaw their own tongues in agony, even on account of hunger pangs. The darkness will render all electronics equipment useless; indeed, it will immobilize the beast's entire kingdom.

While this plague is in effect, the armada of the Great Eagle will move through the Mediterranean Sea to the coast of Israel, where about 10,000,000 of foot will disembark from 4,000 transports. These figures are rough estimates and do not include supply ships, aircraft carriers, etc.; they represent the minimum necessary to form the sickle-shaped line of defense previously described, in a line of defense in depth of ten lines, in anticipation of attack(s) by some 150 to 300 million ground troops, most of them from Europe and Asia.

When the Catholic armies are in disposition, the plague of darkness throughout the Middle East beyond Israel will be lifted. Then, the armies of heaven will wait, and they will know their orders: no surrender, no retreat, no prisoners.

As soon as the darkness is lifted, Antichrist will learn of the Catholic invasion in Palestine. The sixth angel will pour out his bowl and dry up the Euphrates River...

> "so that the way might be prepared for the kings from the rising of the sun" [16:12]

Isaiah, writing a prophecy about messianic times and not about the ancient city of Babylon, in 11:15 stated,

> "the Lord shall dry up the tongue of the Sea of Egypt, and wave his hand over the Euphrates in his fierce anger and shatter it into seven streamlets, so that it can be crossed in sandals."

In what seems the chronological order of events, Isaiah wrote in 11:12 that…

> "He shall raise a signal to the nations and gather outcasts of Israel; the dispersed of Judah he shall assemble from the four corners of the earth."

In other words, the second restoration of Israel as a nation will occur first; and at a later time, when God applies unmitigated justice [fierce anger = wrath], the Euphrates will be reduced to the point where "it can be crossed in sandals."

The term, "tongue of the Sea of Egypt," refers to the body of water between Egypt and Palestine, i.e., where the Israelites crossed the Red Sea during their exodus from Egypt. This item of information may be added to what was said about Easter/Passover and Pentecost/Shavuoth.

As for Antichrist, he, the Dragon, and the False Prophet will send three demons to the kings of the whole world; and those demons will work signs…

> "…to assemble them unto the battle of the day the great one of God the almighty" [Apoc. 16:13-14]

Note that Antichrist does not send just a verbal summons; rather, the Dragon himself and the Beast and the False Prophet send demons performing signs, which implies that extraordinary measures will be required to convince or to persuade those kings all is not yet lost.

Antichrist has not been able to prevent or nullify the plagues; thus, his followers have become doubtful and reluctant, and some of them have become imperiled by revolts and riots. In spite of these things, the leaders in the nations of Europe and Asia will be able to raise armies and move toward Palestine. As for those nations south of the United States, from Mexico to Argentina and Chile, I doubt that they will be able to send any auxiliaries thither.

The situation will become so serious that Antichrist will then take a drastic measure to terrorize his followers into obedience; and that measure will be the first event of the seventh plague, whose sequence of events I will now unscramble.

Chapter 22

—

The Seventh Plague: The Sequence of Its Events

As the anti-Christian armies begin to converge on Palestine, Christ's warning in 16:15 must be heeded,

> "Behold, I am coming like a thief! Blessed is the one who stays awake and is clothed, not going about naked and exposed to shame."

This verse makes it perfectly clear that persecution or the threat of it will continue until the total defeat of the Beast. When Christ said that the one who perseveres to the end would be saved, he meant the end, the very end. Christians free of persecution must remain faithful to that standard of conduct set by Christ; and the warning applies, especially, to the soldiers in Palestine, because the vast majority of them will not survive the coming battle.

In 16:17,

> "the seventh [angel] poured out his bowl upon the air, and a loud voice came out of the sanctuary from the throne, saying, 'It is done!'" [Literally, it came to be, or it came into being; aorist tense: Γέγονεν = Gegonen]

Since it was Christ who began the "μαρτύριον," it will be he who utters that it is finished. Again, the statement is prophetic, in the sense that the end is certain, it is as good as done from Christ's eternal point of view. This brief statement alludes to the "birth pangs," as well, for the new "heaven" and new earth are about to be born, and the pain and suffering will be over, the former things have passed away.

The events of the seventh plague are listed in 16:18-21. The order in which these events are listed or mentioned is not the order in which these events will actually happen. To demonstrate the actual order of events, each event must be understood for what it is, and, then, its occurrence in the sequence can be accurately ascertained.

In verse 18, the "lightnings" or "flashes of lightning," the "voices," and the "peals of thunder," are the same as those "flashes of lightning and voices, and peals of thunder" mentioned in 4:5. They come <u>from the throne</u>. The "lightnings" symbolize miracles wrought by the Church to counteract the false signs and wonders of the Dragon, Beast, False Prophet, and the demons they sent out to the kings of the world. The "voices" are those of the Four Living Beings who are preaching, exhorting, and instructing the faithful.

The "thunders" are direst warnings from the headquarters of the Church, warnings about the imminent defeat of the Beast and his hordes, as well as about the great earthquake soon to strike the world; and the "thunders" are anathemas against all false teachings, false miracles, and false prophets.

The "earthquake" in verse 18 is in a <u>separate clause</u> modified by adjective clauses to impress upon the reader the intensity of that earthquake,

> "...and a great earthquake happened, such as did not happen since man came to be upon the earth, the violent earthquake was so great."

Verse 19 continues:

> "And the city, the great one became unto three parts <u>and</u> the cities of the nations fell down."

In view of the fact that this event happens during the <u>seventh</u> plague, the phrase, "the cities of the nations," must be understood as relating to the cities of the whole world, including those of the Great Eagle, and not as relating only to those in the nations designated "the sea."

The "city, the great one" is not Babylon the Great, but Jerusalem. John makes this point clear by stating the Great Harlot's fate in the next sentence of verse 19,

> "And Babylon the Great was remembered in the presence of God to give to her the cup of the wine of the fury of his wrath."

Verse 20 mentions that...

> "every island fled away and mountains were not found."

The symbols here are the same as those in 6:14; however, in this case, the "islands" and "mountains" are not merely moved out of their places, but vanish altogether. "Islands" are prophetic symbols for provinces and dependencies, and "mountains" represent kingdoms. This verse indicates that there will be absolutely nothing left of the political structure of the Beast's global empire, and with that structure will also go the neo-paganism of Antichrist.

Verse 21 states,

> "And hail great as a talent fell from heaven upon the people, and the people from the plague of hail cursed God, because great is the terrible plague of it."

This verse describes an aspect of the battle of Armageddon itself. Note two things here:

(1) The "hail" is "from heaven," which means it is from the Catholic armies.
(2) Each "hail" weighs a talent, a Greek unit of measurement equivalent to almost 50 pounds.

The "hail's" uniformity of weight indicates that the "hail" is man-made. Extant in the ordinance of the U.S. military, besides artillery rounds, are two weapons that fit the description of this "hail": cluster bombs and anti-personnel missiles. A cluster bomb can break up into a wide spread of smaller bombs, like grenades, either in the air or upon impact with the ground. An anti-personnel missile flies about a hundred yards above the battlefield, ejecting numerous small bombs left and right to various distances as far as 100 yards, thus cutting a swathe 200 yards wide through a large mass of assaulting infantry. Note again that impenitence is implied in this last verse, notwithstanding that the slaughter, as described in 14:20, will be appalling.

The sixth plague will dry up the Euphrates River, so that the vast hordes of anti-Christians from the east [China, India, etc.] can arrive at Armageddon within a specific tract of time to fight the battle. This means before the great earthquake.

The reason Antichrist will order the destruction of Babylon the Great is to occasion fear in his followers, fear that will override any feelings of reluctance to obey his summons. Babylon's destruction will send a clear message: if the Beast will destroy his most valuable city that did not defect, it can only be imagined what he will do to those who, in fact, defect. The psychological value of destroying Babylon would become irrelevant as soon as the battle began.

Chapter 19 contains a song of jubilation and thanksgiving to God for the Great Harlot's destruction, followed by a description of Christ as the commander of the armies of "heaven" going into battle, followed, in turn, by a brief description of the capture of the Beast and False Prophet; and this sequence corresponds to that implied by 14:8-11.

Furthermore, since the great earthquake will fell the cities of the world, it must be assumed that bridges and roads will be severely damaged, and that mountain passes will have avalanches. Consequently, the armies from the east could not possibly traverse the Zagios Mountains, for example, at the western side of the plateau of Oran, or the Siahan, Kirthan, and Sulaiman Ranges to the east.

Also, the Beast would not be able to destroy Babylon during the fifth plague of darkness; therefore, if he destroyed it earlier, the inhabitants of the city would not be punished by the fourth plague that falls upon all.

For the same reasons, the great earthquake cannot occur earlier than the battle; and, if it occurred during the battle, it would become not only difficult or impossible to fight the battle, but also it would negate an important sign to the world: that the armies of "heaven," though vastly outnumbered, defeated the anti-Christians led by the Beast and the False Prophet themselves.

Hence, the given information indicates that the seventh plague's sequence of events will run thus:

(1) "Lightnings," "voices," and "thunders," from the beginning of the seventh plague until its end.
(2) Destruction of Babylon the Great.
(3) The plague of "hail" during the battle of Armageddon.
(4) The capture of the Beast and the False Prophet at the end of the battle will signal the time for the great earthquake: Jerusalem will be split into three parts, the cities of the world will fall to the ground, and, thus, the Beast's "islands" and "mountains" will exist no longer.

I leave to the reader's imagination what destruction the worldwide earthquake will cause, even after it has ended: burning cities and towns, no usable roads or bridges, tsunami hundreds of feet high from oceans and great lakes, vast forest fires, etc. It is reasonable to assume, however, that Enoch and Elijah shall have prepared the Church for what it must do in the aftermath.

I do not see that much explanation for Chapter 19 is necessary, for its contents are easily understood. One important point is that the "bride" mentioned in 19:7-8 is the whole Church, and the "armies of heaven" mentioned in 19:14 are a part of the Church; hence, both are described as wearing "fine linen, bright and pure." In the Old Testament, there was only one nation that worshipped and served God: Israel. Thus, there was only one "army of heaven," a term that becomes plural at Armageddon because the members of the Church are from many nations. The United States of America is the "melting pot"; its citizens or their ancestors have come from all over the world. The "armies of heaven," however, seems to imply that the Catholic force at Armageddon will not be American only.

At this point, speculation rears its pin-head, for only time will tell what the United States will do in regard to the Catholic nations south of it, especially those down to the isthmus of Panama, when the Beast begins "ascending from the abyss."

Two things more: it is obvious that 14:17-20 corresponds to 19:11-19; and it is possible the sword, the <u>rhomphaia</u> [19:15], alludes to the "armies of heaven" in sickle-shaped battle line.

Chapter 17 has already been explained, and enough has already been said about Chapter 18. As to the items John mentions in 18:12-13, it is obvious he uses those of his day to denote the future luxuries enjoyed by the wealthy, because there were no words yet for television, computers, VCR's, automobiles, airplanes, etc.

Note also that the captains and crews <u>can see the smoke</u> rising from the burning city [18:9]; John did not write that they could see the city itself. This connotes that Babylon the Great could be as far as 120 miles inland from the coast, and the great column of smoke rising from it would be clearly visible to men on ships in the harbors or just off the coast.

Remember: this city will be destroyed in one hour [18:10]. All information points to a Catholic country <u>in Europe,</u> as the place wherein the city that will be called Babylon the Great stands, even now; and it is reasonable to assume the city's population numbers in the millions. Again, one must keep an open mind about this matter.

Chapter 23

—

Apocalypse Chapter 20

In verse 1, John wrote he…

> "saw an angel coming down from heaven, holding the key of the abyss and a great chain."

The angel here is not the "mighty angel" in 10:1, but, probably, a cardinal or bishop. I say this, because John used the definite article with the noun "key," referring to that "key" given to the "fallen star," Martin Luther, in 9:1, "the key of the shaft of the abyss." The "key" symbolizes the authority to open or close the shaft of the abyss; and, since it was an apostate member of the clergy who opened the shaft, it is fitting a member of the clergy should close it again.

In verses 2-3, the angel seized the Dragon, Satan, and "bound him a thousand years," i.e., bound him in such manner as would hold Satan for a "thousand years"; and, then, the angel…

> "cast him out into the abyss, and locked it and sealed it after him, that he might not still deceive the nations until the thousand years could be ended. After these things it is necessary he be loosed for a short time."

Note that the duration of Satan's internment in the abyss is set before he is cast into the abyss, which simply connotes that God is omniscient.

The key symbolizes the Church's authority over the abyss, and the chain symbolizes her power to hold Satan and his demons. The Church alone can bring peace and plenty and security to mankind. If men are left to the authority and power of the Church, and do her teachings, then, they will make a society, a civilization that will approach as close to perfect as possible for the offspring of God. If not, then not. So, the first time Christ bound Satan; the next time His Church will chain him.

Verse 4 depicts a scene,

> "…thrones and they sat upon them [the thrones] and judgment [decision] was given to them [the ones that sat down]…"

John did not identify the ones who sat on the thrones, but it is reasonable to assume they were the Four Living Beings and the twenty-four Elders. The court in session here is the one predicted in 11:18.

John also saw…

> "the souls of those beheaded on account of the testimony of Jesus and the word of God and whoever did not worship the Beast and his icon and did not receive the mark upon the forehead and on the hand."

The term "beheaded" is a metonymy for any kind of violent death. So, these are the souls of martyrs as well as those who, though they did not suffer martyrdom, remained faithful, even to death from disease, famine, drought, battle, earthquake, etc., during the reign of Antichrist.

The important point here is that they were confronted with the choice of accepting or rejecting the Beast or his icon, i.e., none of them was someone hiding in the depths of the Amazonian rainforests [where people like me would be, with hair dyed green and bodies painted to look exactly like the local vegetation—leaves, twigs, bark, and all]. They deserve the highest recognition from the Church, and the Church now gives it.

Note well, in verse 6, the only thing said about their reward,

"...they will be priests of God and of Christ and they will rule with him [Christ] for the thousand years."

This verse indicates, beyond all misunderstanding, that the highest honor on earth or in heaven everlasting is the office of priest. These souls will reign with Christ until the end of human history, and they shall have great power and authority in both religious and secular affairs, for weal to the good and woe to the wicked [2:27]; for, even in the new "heaven" and new earth, men will still be permitted to choose evil, and some will go that way.

The last sentence in verse 4 has long been controversial; this is what John wrote,

...καὶ ἔζησαν καὶ ἐβασίλευσαν μετὰ τοῦ Χριστοῦ χίλια ἔτη
...kai exësan kai ebasileusan meta tou Khristou khilia etë
...and they came to life and reigned with Christ a thousand years.

The two verbs are in the aorist tense, and this means the actions of the verbs are performed only once: there will be only once this tract of a "thousand" years. All translations of the verb "ἔζησαν" [exësan] read "they came to life," in order to convey the meaning of the verb, the same verb used in the aorist tense in verse 5,

"...the rest of the dead did not live [did not come to life] until the thousand years were ended."

Clearly, John meant that they had suffered the first death, the death of the body, for he used the explicit term "οἱ λοιποὶ τῶν νεκρῶν" [oi loipoi tön nekpön], "the rest of the DEAD." They were in [union with] Christ when they died; therefore, they were not dead in the spiritual sense. It follows, then, that they were dead in the physical sense.

Hence, the verb "ἔζησαν" [exësan] must denote that they lived in the physical sense, i.e., they lived again in the corporal sense. In other words, they received glorified, imperishable bodies. The last sentence in verse 5 corroborates this, completely,

"This [is] the resurrection the first one."

The term, "the resurrection the first one," cannot signify simply "the resurrection from the dead" or "the resurrection of the body"; rather, it denotes THE First, as differentiated from the second, the second resurrection connoted in the first sentence of verse 5 [usually put in parentheses],

> "...the rest of the dead did not live [did not come to life] until the thousand years were ended,"

i.e., at the Last Judgment or at the General Judgment. The first resurrection, then, is a special honor in reward for extraordinary heroism in the face of the enemy; and this is fitting and accordant with their receiving the office of priest.

Enoch and Elijah, for their extraordinary service, will also be given glorified bodies, for 11:11-12 is perfectly clear on this point,

> "...the breath of life from God entered them, and they stood up on their feet...then...a loud voice from heaven, saying to them 'Come up here!' And they went up to heaven in a cloud while their enemies watched them."

So, there will be the special resurrection for those mentioned in 20:4, and this will be the first resurrection; and, then, at the end of the "thousand" years, at the Last Judgment, there will be the second resurrection, the general one. I can find no fault in my logic, which followed only the text; and, if error be upon me proved, then, let it be presented.

The title "Christ" is used in verse 4; and, except for 1:1, it is used in only three other places in the Apocalypse: see 11:15, 12:10, and 20:6. In each case, it alludes to Psalms 2:2, which reads,

"I myself have set up my king on Zion, my holy mountain";

and the text of Chapter 20 makes it absolutely clear that the "thousand" years of Christ's reign from Zion will come AFTER the defeat of Antichrist. Once the visions began in 1:10, the title "Christ" was presented exactly FOUR TIMES, and always in regard to the defeat of Satan and the Beast, and thus the beginning and duration of the "millennium."

This fact should stand out most conspicuously to the reader, as if John had written in bold face. As it has been written, so it shall be done,

> "...I saw one like a Son of Man coming on the clouds of heaven; when he reached the Ancient One and was presented before him, He received dominion, glory, and kingship; nations and peoples of every language serve him. His dominion is an everlasting dominion that shall not be taken away, his kingship shall not be destroyed." [Dn. 7:13-14]

> "But when the court is convened, and his [little horn's] power is taken away by final and absolute destruction, then the kingship and dominion and majesty of all the kingdoms under the heavens shall be given to the holy people of the Most High, whose kingdom shall be everlasting: all dominions shall serve and obey him." [Dn. 7:26-27]

I do not see how the Bible could speak more simply and more plainly on this matter. If anyone in possession of faculties does not understand, he or she does not understand because of a will hardened and, so, an intellect darkened against the Holy Spirit. Such a person has a "hidden agendum": to give names to all, even to God. Oh, Christ will not comply, for on his head...

> "he has a name inscribed that no one knows but himself." [19:12]

This is only proper for the King of kings and Lord of lords. Six times within seven verses, John stated the "one thousand years" as a <u>round number</u>, to denote not the exact length of time, but the continuous <u>proximation</u> to a state of total perfection. The "millennium" will be a period of peace for the Catholic Church, the Church that will be factually universal; and this peace will endure until the rise of Gog and Magog. It is impossible to determine whether this round number symbolizes two thousand or ten thousand or fifty thousand years; however, it is certain that it does not mean one thousand actual years, because then men would know when the end of the world would come. That knowledge is held by God alone.

The Greek verb "δεί" [dei] means "it is necessary." The release of Satan near the very end of the "millennium" is a necessity, because God wills it to work out his plan; and his plan comes of his omniscient wisdom. Then, Satan, after the destruction of Gog and Magog will be "cast out unto the lake of fire" [20:10]. This is a mystery insoluble; and there does not exist a finite mind that can "justify the ways of God to men," except ultimately by faith.

John wrote very little about Gog and Magog in 20:8-9: one would have to be very stupid, indeed, not to get his hint that one should read the prophecies at least, in Ezekiel 38 and 39. Clear to you now will be the meaning of such passages as these:

> "...At the end of years thou [Gog and Magog] shall come to the land that is returned from the sword, and is gathered out of many nations, to the mountains of Israel which have been continually waste, but it hath been brought forth out of the nations, and they shall all of them dwell securely in it." [Ez. 38:8]
>
> "In the last days I will bring thee upon my land, that the nations may know me, when I shall prove my holiness through thee. O Gog, before their eyes." [Ez. 38:16]

The Apocalypse and the book of Ezekiel agree about the time of Gog and Magog: most proximate to the end of mankind's history. The descriptions of the armies of Gog and Magog are very detailed, very specific, which argues against their being symbolical; and, so, they indicate that men will never again reach the technological civilization that now exists; for the great earthquake mentioned in 16:18 will totally destroy the "works of their hands" [9:20]. The earthquake will so change the face of the earth that forests will grow again in Israel, as Ezekiel 39:10 relates. But, beyond this point begins speculation, and I do not write science fiction.

As to the Second Coming of Christ and the end of human history, St. Paul wrote,

> "Listen, I will tell you a mystery! We will not all die, but we will all be changed, in a moment, in a twinkling of an eye, at the last trumpet. For the trumpet will sound, and the dead will be raised imperishable, and we will be changed." [1 Cor. 15:51-52]

> "For the Lord himself, with a cry of command, with the archangel's call and with the sound of God's trumpet, will descend from heaven, and the dead in Christ will rise first. Then we who are alive, who are left, will be caught up in the clouds together with them to meet the Lord in the air; and so we will be with the Lord forever. Therefore encourage one another with these words." [1 Thes. 4:16-18]

So, the history of mankind will be ended "in the twinkling of an eye." Pay no heed to what some gray brains say about the matter. The world has many birds. All statements to the effect that human history will end with Armageddon are erroneous; to the contrary, the best wine is being saved for last.

In verses 11-15, John succinctly described the Last Judgment. Verse 1 stated,

> "…the earth and the heaven fled from his presence, and no place was found for them."

This means that the world and the Church, i.e., secular and religious affairs, ceased: mankind was simply removed from the planet. Of this was Christ thinking when he said,

> "Heaven and earth shall pass away, but my words shall never pass away" [Mt. 24:35]

In verse 12, John wrote,

> "…the dead were judged according to their works, as recorded in the books."

The reign of Antichrist was the time for the separation of the wheat from the weeds, but the Last Judgment will be the time of separation of the sheep from the goats. All will stand before the Omniscient One, even those from Hades.

Then, John simply stated,

> "Anyone whose name was not found written in the book of life was cast out unto the lake of fire." [20:15]

I do not think I need here explain what that means. Note that Death and Hades in verse 14 were also cast unto the lake of fire, "the second death." This means that, when the history of the world is ended, there logically will be no more first death and Hades; and, so, John means that, ultimately, there are only two everlasting "places": heaven and hell. Each person will end up either in the one or in the other. The Apocalypse is perfectly clear on the point that Hell is forever, and also on the point that human beings who go there will suffer both in soul and in body, as the Beast and the False Prophet shall know "unto the ages of the ages." That, dear reader, is the exactitude of God, even to every "white hair" on Christ's head. Amen.

Chapter 24

—

Apocalypse Chapter 21

In this Chapter, John looped backwards and resumed the narrative of events. Since Chapter 21 describes the Church and its beneficent effect upon mankind during the "millennium," it can be inserted immediately after 20:3, the point where Satan has been bound in the abyss.

Verse 1 states,

> "And I saw a new heaven and a new earth. For the first heaven and the first earth passed away and the sea is no more."

The forepart of this verse is almost identical to that of Isaiah 65:17, which reads,

> "For behold, I am about to create new heavens and a new earth; and the former things shall not be remembered, and they shall not come upon the heart."

By restating so closely the forepart of Isaiah's verse, John indicated that the fulfillment of that prophecy will come in the "millennium" after Antichrist.

The term "new heaven" means the Church ripened and refreshed and restrengthened in all graces and virtues after her heroic conflict against the very powers of hell. Elijah has, indeed, done his part "to restore all things," [Mt. 17:11] and Enoch "to give repentance to the nations [Eccl. 44:16]." Like the survivors in Chapter 7, so here the Church stands: the achievement, the triumph of the Lamb. More than ever before, beautiful of infallibility, catholicity, immutability, and holiness, this is the bride of Jesus Christ. The perpetual wedding feast has begun.

The term "new earth" means the changed state of society; and, to clarify this term, John added: "and the sea is no more." The rebelliousness of the wicked against God is gone; where there was the restless "sea" is now calm, a willingness to obey the Creator, as Dante Alighieri long ago wrote, "In his will is our peace." Society, henceforth, in all its secular institutions, will receive the radiance of the Church's dogmas and moral laws, by a clergy expurgated of all serious flaw and fault, and by a laity who witness in word and deed the mind and heart of their Lord.

The "new heaven" shall include the nation of Israel and the city of Jerusalem, as Isaiah has written [65:18-20],

> 18 For I create Jerusalem to be a joy and its people to be a delight;
> 19 I will rejoice in Jerusalem and exult in my people. No longer shall
> the sound of weeping be heard there, or the sound of crying; 20 no
> longer shall there be in it an infant who lives but a few days, or an old man who does not round out his full lifetime; he dies a mere youth who reaches but a hundred years, and he who fails of a hundred shall be thought accursed.

And, it will include all nations, as Isaiah stated [66:22-23]:

> 22 As the new heavens and the new earth which I will create shall endure before me, says the Lord, so shall your race and your name
> endure. 23 From one new moon to another, and from one Sabbath to another, all mankind shall come to worship before me, says the Lord."

Verse 2 reads,

> "And the city the holy one New Jerusalem I saw coming down out of heaven from God, prepared as a bride adorned for her husband."

The term "Jerusalem" here denotes both the city, in particular, and the Church, in general. Many passages in the prophets tell about Israel's redemption and the exaltation of Jerusalem in messianic times.

In Isaiah 62:1-5, the meaning of this whole Chapter and Chapter 22:1-5 begins to become clear:

> For Zion's sake I will not be silent, for Jerusalem's sake I will not be quiet, until her vindication shines forth like the dawn and her victory like a burning torch. Nations shall behold your vindication, and all kings your glory; you shall be called a new name pronounced by the mouth of the Lord. You shall be a glorious crown in the hand of the Lord, a royal diadem held by your God. No more shall men call you "Forsaken," or your land "Desolate," but you shall be called "My Delight," and your land "Espoused." For the Lord delights in you, and makes your land his spouse. As a young man marries a virgin, your Builder will marry you; and as a bridegroom rejoices in his bride, so shall your God rejoice in you.

To discern the meaning of this passage and scores of others [see Is. 60, 61, for example], recall the crown on the head of "the woman clothed with the sun" in Chapter 12: Another meaning of the noun "στέφανος" [stephanos] is the wall that encircles a city. The new Jerusalem shall be, within its "wall," a garden of the Lord's delights, as prefigured in the Song of Songs, in which the bride, responding to her brother's plans, declares her virgin chastity,

> "I am a wall, and my breasts are like towers. So now in his eyes I have become one to be welcomed." [Sng. 8:10]

How appropriate that spring is the time to renew the face of the earth, the season in which the song is sung, the season when the fig tree begins to bear fruit:

> For see, the winter is past, the rains are over and gone. The flowers appear on the earth, the time of pruning the vines has come, and the song of the dove is heard in our land. The fig tree puts forth its figs,

> and the vines, in bloom, give forth fragrance. Arise, my beloved, my beautiful one, and come! [Sng. 2:11-13]

However, John reminds the reader in Apocalypse 21:3, that this is the temporary dwelling of God on earth,

> "...Behold the tent of God is with men, and he will dwell with them, and they will be his peoples, and God himself will be with them..."

The "σκηνὴ" [skënë], or "tent," here alludes to the same in 15:5 and the "meeting tent" in Exodus 40:35 [mentioned in the second part of the commentary on the Apocalypse]. The "tent" signifies that a time will come when "heaven and earth" will "pass away"; and, so, the pilgrim church must never forget her ultimate destination [as Gog and Magog will forget].

Speaking about Jerusalem as a city, in particular, Isaiah, in 66:12, wrote,

> "Behold, I will spread prosperity over her like a river, and the wealth of the nations like an overflowing torrent."

It is this wealth that will attract the greed of Gog and Magog in "the end of years," as Ezekiel 38 and 39 relate. The Church needs an earthly center; and Jerusalem, the "navel of the earth," as the prophets called it, shall become that center. It is reasonable to assume that a great basilica will be built on Mt. Zion, "the recesses of the north." Note the use of the definite article in "THE tent," and the plural "peoples."

In verse 4, John stated,

> "...He will wipe away every tear from their eyes, and Death will be no more, and mourning and crying and pain will be no more, for the first things passed away."

The last clause of this sentence modifies the parts previous: John does not mean the state of the blessed in everlasting heaven but the state of the world under the Messiah. If one cross-refers the language used here with that in 7:16-17, the point becomes clear: the survivors believe in Christ who has conquered

Death, and, therefore, the first death means nothing to them, i.e., in their hearts and minds, "Death will be no more." Disbelief has passed away, and, so, sorrow over physical death has passed away.

There will still be problems in the "millennium": God will always give man the choice between good and evil. But, most people will follow the teachings of the Church; and this will make life's typical problems much easier to bear or, in some cases, will remove them altogether. Evil men will be very few in number, and society will know what to do with them and will not hesitate: people will not have any doubt about the consequences of permitting anti-theistic individuals [including agnostics] to infect the minds and hearts of many. So, the new "heaven" and new earth will be a blessed state; but, if one falls down and scrapes a knee, one will still feel the pain.

John is talking from a spiritual point of view in these verses, because, ultimately, it is the one that counts. Verses 5-8 corroborate this explanation; for, in them, Jesus promises the "water of life" as a gift [recall his words to the Samaritan woman at the well in Jn. 4:4-42 to those who conquer, i.e., to those who enter the city "by the narrow gate" that is Christ. Verse 8 gives a general list of those who shall not enter:

> "...the faithless, the impure, the fornicators, idolaters [which includes the greedy], and all liars."

Jesus pronounces the eternal certainty of the fulfillment of the visions with the words, "it is done!" [v. 6]

In verses 9-27, John described,

> "the holy city Jerusalem coming down out of heaven from God."

As the prophet was carried into the wilderness to see the evil city of Babylon the Great [Chapter 17], so, here an angel [probably, the same one as in 17] carries him to a great, high mountain to show him the New Jerusalem. Obviously, the physical description is symbolical, but always keep in mind that a symbol stands for something real.

Note that John repeated the idea that the city comes "out of heaven from God." Please, do not think, at this point, that a redundancy has been committed. The words simply emphasize that it is Jesus Christ who makes [creates] "all things new." The new "heaven" and new earth belong to those who are "the new creation," i.e., the Christians. Implied here is the prophecy of Ezekiel 34:23-31, in which is prefigured ONE SHEPHERD, ONE FLOCK.

> 23 AND I WILL SET UP ONE SHEPHERD OVER THEM, and he shall feed them, even my servant David: he shall feed them, and he shall be their shepherd. 24 And I the Lord will be their God: and my servant David the prince in the midst of them: I the Lord have spoken it. 25 And I will make a covenant of peace with them, and will cause the evil beasts to cease out of the land: and they that dwell in the wilderness shall sleep secure in the forests. 26 And I will make them a blessing round about my hill: and I will send down the rain in its season, there shall be showers of blessing. 27 And the tree of the field shall yield its fruit, and the earth shall yield her increase, and they shall be in their land without fear: and they shall know that I am the Lord, when I shall have broken the bonds of their yoke, and shall have delivered them out of the hand of those that rule over them. 28 And they shall be no more for a spoil to the nations, neither shall the beasts of the earth devour them: but they shall dwell securely without any terror. 29 And I will raise up for them a bud of renown: and they shall be no more consumed with famine in the land, neither shall they bear any more the reproach of the Gentiles. 30 And they shall know that I the Lord their God am with them, and that they are my people the house of Israel: saith the Lord God. 31 And you my flocks, the flocks of my pasture are men: and I am the Lord your God, saith the Lord God.

To remove all doubts about this point, including any doubt about the conversion of the Jews to Christ, verses 12-14 about the city read thus,

> It has a great, high wall with twelve gates, and at the gates twelve angels, and on the gates are inscribed the names of the twelve tribes of sons of Israel: on the east three gates and on the north three gates and on the south three gates and on the west three gates. And the wall

> of the city has twelve foundations, and on them are the twelve names of the twelve apostles of the Little Lamb.

John indicates that the city to be described is the kingdom of heaven on earth, the Church, by the phrase, "a great, high wall," which corresponds and alludes to "a great, high mountain" in verse 10. The symbolical number "twelve," in regard to the "wall," absolutely confirms that this vision presents the Church on earth in Messianic times, and that the Jews will be of the Church in those days: one Christ, one faith, one flock.

This is a dire and solemn warning to the more than 2,500 pseudo-Christian denominations in our own day. There is only one Christ; there can be only one true Church. The world, at present, is an enormous abnormality, collective offense and blasphemy against the One Living unto the ages of ages, against Him who is master of exactitude. Human imagination is too weak to comprehend how terrible the consequences that shall be incurred during the reign of Antichrist.

Before the invention of gunpowder, a city was a defensive structure: it was built with a high wall encircling it, and with towers along the wall, and placed atop a hill or mountain, if possible. Many writers have compared an ancient city on a mountain to a "crown." The "crown of TWELVE stars" on the head of the "woman" in Chapter 12 symbolizes apostolic authority to teach the Truth; the "wall" around the city also symbolizes the Truth: for the Truth is the Church's defense against all attacks of evil or falsehood. The very size of the city signifies that it is a mighty fortress, indestructible; and the children of the Most High will dwell in full security.

Remember, this description is symbolic. Ezekiel made special mention of the fact that the cities of Israel will not have walls around them when Gog and Magog come to despoil Jerusalem. This means that never again will the Israelites trust in anyone or anything except the Truth, Jesus Christ. He alone will be their defense.

The city's measurements are 12,000 stadia [12 x 1,000] in length, in width, and in height: a perfect cube about 1,379.5 miles per side. The number 12,000 is obtained by multiplying 1,000 times 12, and this corroborates the interpretation of the number "1,000," for the years of Christ's reign, as symbolical.

The idea suggested by these two instances is spiritual maturity. Many saints pondered the statement, in Isaiah 65:20, about the length of life men will have during the "Millennium," and some concluded that people would live many hundreds of years. This alludes to the Old Testament, wherein it is told that the farther the world got away from the time of Eden, the shorter did the average age of man become, until, in John's day, a life span of 40 years was considered "old." St. Justin attributes this to the fact that men could no longer eat of the "tree of life," and the effect of that "tree" upon posterity gradually weakened.

Such interpretations arise because the reader, a human being, errs in discerning between literal and symbolical. In the case of the number "1,000" are found many errors, but those are quickly corrected if truth and literalness are not set into the same concept. The Bible tells the truth, but it tells the truth in various ways; for God inspired various men to write it. It should not surprise that metaphor and symbol are used to express fact and truth in the Bible.

Therefore, the decrease in the average life span recorded in the Old Testament, and the restoration of the "longevity" enjoyed by such as Methuselah, as indicated in Isaiah 65:20, relate to spiritual maturity and the mentality that accompanies it. The older a man is, the wiser he should be. Youth is the high day of the blood, impetuous and impatient; and senectitude, the much calmer, contemplative of things.

St. John was probably in his seventies when he wrote the Apocalypse, and that is why artists have always presented him as an old man with long, white hair. Christ himself is described as having white hair in Chapter 1; and it is Christ, as St. Paul said, who is the second Adam. It logically follows that the Apocalypse, which relates the development of the Church according to the mysterious wisdom of God, should culminate in the spiritual maturity of Christ.

The Church will no longer be a child after the days of Antichrist, but "the bride, the wife of the Lamb" [21:9]. St. Paul's words apply here:

> "For we know only in part, and we prophesy only in part; but the perfection comes, the "in part" will be ended. When I was a child, I spoke like a child, I thought like a child, I reasoned like a child; when I became an adult, I put an end to childish ways. For now we see by a mirror with a riddle [ἐν αἰνίγματι = en ainigmati], but at that time

> [τότε = tote] face to face: Now I know only in part, but then will I know at once and fully. And now faith, hope, and love abide, these three: and greatest of these is love." [1 Cor. 13:9-13]

Love "rejoices in the truth," St. Paul said [1 Cor.13:6], and, so, for this reason did Isaiah write of the time that would eventually be,

> "As a young man marries a virgin, your <u>Builder</u> will marry you; and as a bridegroom rejoices in his <u>bride</u>, so shall your God rejoice in you." [Is. 62:5]

Obviously, the maturity of the soul is not absolutely dependent on the maturity of the body, as shown by the fact that some saints at a very early age were spiritually very mature. As always, common sense should be exercised in reading scripture. The important point to remember here is that the number "1000" in Chapters 20 and 21 is symbolical, and it signifies nearly total perfection, in the spiritual sense, for the earth is not heaven everlasting above.

The Church is the bride and wife, i.e., the "second Eve" who will be the "mother" of all the living, i.e., the ones who keep their lives in Christ. She stands in contrast to the "Great Harlot" of Chapter 17, whose illegitimate children inherited neither the "new heaven" nor the "new earth." The marriage of the Little Lamb and the Church will be solemnized when those people not yet converted [baptized] will "enter the city" soon after the "μαρτύριον" has been ended.

Remember, in Chapter 15, the sanctuary of the tent of witness did not admit anyone until the separation of the wheat and the weeds was ended. To baptize the peoples who are not Roman Catholic will not take long, because not many shall have survived the "μαρτύριον." From the start of the second woe to the end of the third, I <u>suspect</u> that as much as 75%–85% of the human race will die. This range of percentage may be unrealistically optimistic. Much depends on the success of the missions in Asia, which for 450 years has been little.

Today is November 17, 1998, and the sky is very dark. Perhaps, on such a day did John "eat" the very small scroll. God is most exact.

In love's season, the hope of life will tell
That faith forced its march where the many fell.
Reader, remember, and remember well:
It sometimes comes that only God can tell
The course of heaven from the curse of hell.

An angel guards at each of the twelve "gates" [v.12], and each "gate" is a "pearl" [v.21]. This means that the angels will not allow any corrupt individual in or into the Church; they will keep her pure and free of whatever worldly evils had previously crept into her. No one will be able to enter, unless he enters with the <u>wisdom</u> of Christ, the "pearl of great price." [cf. Mt. 13:46]

The number "twelve" here indicates that the entire priesthood, the Four Living Beings, especially, will be zealous in their duties and obligations.

Note that the names of the twelve tribes are written on the "gates." This suggests a special honor will be bestowed upon the Jews, for they were God's chosen nation, his "gate," through which salvation came to the whole world. The text suggests that the <u>leadership</u> of the Church will be given to them, because they will "sell," i.e., renounce, all that they have, their worldly desires, to "buy" or obtain the "pearl," the wisdom of Christ. Christ was born of the house of David, and He meant exactly what he said, "the first shall be last, and <u>the last shall be first</u>."

> 4 Behold I have given him for a witness to the people, for a leader and a master to the Gentiles. 5 Behold thou shalt call a nation, which thou knewest not: and the nations that knew not thee shall run to thee, because of the Lord thy God, and for the Holy One of Israel, for he hath glorified thee. [Is. 55:4-5].

The foundations of the "wall" are twelve, and each is adorned with a specific kind of "precious stone." The "jewels" are symbolic of spiritual things; three of them I have already explained in part two of this commentary. As for the others, I have not yet been able to find their precise meanings. I will neither opine nor speculate. If I find their meanings, I will inform you. Isaiah 54:11-12 contains a description, in part, similar to the one John gave.

Verses 22-27 allude to passages in the Old Testament, such as, Isaiah 60:3, which reads,

> "Nations shall walk by your light, and kings by your shining radiance";

or 60:11, which reads,

> "Your gates shall stand open constantly; day and night they shall not be closed, but shall admit to you the wealth of nations, and their kings, in the vanguard." [John does not mention "night" because the "millennium" will be unending "days," spiritually speaking]

There are too many to quote, and it is better for the reader to "browse among the lilies," so that he or she may judge how closely John has restated many of the prophecies in the Old Testament.

One fact is made perfectly clear: Israel shall be exalted and glorified in the "millennium," and Jerusalem, especially. It was impossible <u>for me</u> not to receive the impression that Jerusalem will be the <u>center</u> of the Church in the world during that time. The reader must keep before the mind that Chapter 21 describes Jerusalem, in particular, and the Church, in general, the former being understood as within the latter. Since Jerusalem will be the "crown" upon the "mountain," like the "crown" upon the "woman" in Chapter 12, I have concluded what I have concluded about Jerusalem and the Jewish people.

As for verses 22 and 23, their meanings must be deduced according to the context. St. John made it absolutely clear that there will be NO TEMPLE, i.e., the TEMPLE of Solomon, as in the Old Testament. <u>That</u> temple will never be rebuilt, and the reason for this is simple to understand: in the New Jerusalem, the presence of God will no longer be hidden under a Shekhinah or shadowy form in a temple; rather, <u>God and the Little Lamb will be the temple</u>: God's "σκηνὴ" or "tent" will be "his peoples." God will be in them and they in Him.

Thus, verse 23 is the perfect complement to verse 22,

> "And the city does not have a need of the sun or the moon, for the glory of God is its light, and its lamp is the Little Lamb."

God will be PRESENT in each human being, and his literal presence will be the illumination in the will and intellect of each person's soul. This implies a heightened mentality. When a person is conscious of himself, he has entered the mode of spirit; and, when that person is conscious of himself, consistently, on a daily basis, as one in whom God is literally present, then progress toward spiritual maturity and "adult" mentality is possible. Such a person extends this heightened perception to all others. Imagine a world in which individuals will be consistently conscious of themselves and others, as everywhere and always, literally, IN THE PRESENCE of GOD…and act accordingly. Each will be the living fulfillment of the two great commandments; full love of God and love of neighbors as oneself, here symbolized as "sun" and "moon."

What John implies in verse 23 is that people will not need external commands; rather, their internal motivation will be love, the greatest light of all. "God is love," said John, "and whoever does not love does not know God" [1 Jn. 4:8]. So, where love is, there also God is. Since all nations shall walk in his "light," shall progress toward spiritual maturity, it cannot be that the Temple of Solomon shall be rebuilt; for "new wine is not poured into old wineskins."

Chapter 25

—

Apocalypse Chapter 22

Verses 1-5 are the conclusion of what was begun and developed in Chapter 21. The same angel who showed John the outside of the city now shows him the inside. The interior has "the river of the water of life" and the "tree of life"; it is a garden, the second Eden, so to speak.

In Genesis, it is written that Eve desired the fruit of the forbidden tree, the "tree of the knowledge of good and evil," in order to gain wisdom [Gen. 3:6]. God banished Adam and Eve from Eden, then "stationed a cherubim with a flaming sword, to guard the way to the tree of life" [Gen. 3:24]. In the New Jerusalem, the "angels" at the "gates" do not guard with flaming swords to bar access to the "tree of life."

The "river of the water of life" flows along through the middle of the street of the city, and the "tree of life" grows on either side of it [which suggests two rows]. The "tree of life" bears 12 kinds of fruit throughout the 12 months of the year, and the leaves of the "tree" are for the healing of the nations [v.2]. Thus, God provides his people with "food" and "drink," the two physical necessities for life, symbolizing spiritual sustenance.

The "tree of life" obviously stands in contrast to the "tree of knowledge of good and evil." Since, for man, the latter "tree" symbolized <u>having dominion over being</u>, the former symbolizes <u>obedience in activity</u>: to eat the fruit of the latter incurred spiritual death, but to eat the fruit of the former brings spiritual life. The act of eating the fruit from the "tree of knowledge" was rebellion, a departure from the natural order, a finite being's attempt to equal God who alone is infinite and has authority and power over finite being. The act of eating the fruit of the "tree of life" is obedience, a conforming to the natural order, a finite being's proper activity of worshipping the Supreme Being.

When Adam and Eve ate the forbidden fruit, they did not gain wisdom, but spiritual ignorance, i.e., they lost knowledge of God—they lost Him who is love. Violation of the first great commandment plunges the soul into utter darkness: the "sun" no longer shines, and, so, the "moon" no longer gives its light. But, Jesus as the Son of Man, the new Adam,

> "…did not regard equality with God as something to be grasped at, but emptied himself, taking the form of a servant." [Phil. 2:6-7]

Adam and Eve became spiritually naked, and that kind of nakedness is what St. Paul had in mind when he wrote,

> "Above all, clothe yourselves with love." [Col. 3:14]

The language of the Bible may sound quaint, and its stories may appear, at times, odd, but Truth, by whatever sound or appearance He comes, love easily cognizes or recognizes, because knower and known become one. It is accurate regarding men, in general, to assert that those who absolutely cannot understand the Bible, which includes those who continually misunderstand it, do not love God. Sin to the soul is like a wound to the body; serious sin is a mortal wound. The leaves of the "tree of life" will heal the nations, because love can heal all wounds to the soul. Love is wisdom.

In Chapter 7, John mentioned "springs of the water of life" [v.17], but, in Chapter 22, those "springs" have become a river flowing from the throne of God. This means that God's graces, through the sacraments, will easily quench the survivor's thirst for Truth, and where the faithful may wash their robes of love clean. Hence, Jesus says in 22:17,

> "And let everyone who is thirsty come."

In verse 3-4, John wrote,

> "...The throne of God and of the Little Lamb will be in it [the city], and his servants will be worshipping him and they will see the face of him, and the name of him [will be] upon the foreheads of them."

Note that John did not say that people would see the Little Lamb, but the "face" [mask] of the Little Lamb [the mention of the throne here is the same as that in Chapter 4-5]. What John means is the Eucharistic Lamb, Jesus Christ under the appearance of bread and wine. Again, Christ's name upon the worshipers' foreheads is symbolical of their having the mind of Christ, like the 144,000 virgins in 14:1.

This passage also implies that people will not turn their "faces" away from him, and he will not turn his "face" away from them. As Isaiah 30:20-21 states,

> The Lord will give you the bread you need and the water for which you thirst. No longer will your Teacher hide himself, but with your own eyes you shall see your Teacher, while from behind, a voice shall sound in your ears: "This is the way; walk in it," when you would turn to the right or to the left.

Adam and Eve fled from the presence of God because they were afraid; but, in the new Eden, love of God will be such that it will drive out all fear of God. Men will not try to "hide their plans too deep for the Lord" [Is. 29:15]. They will "see his face," in the sense that the thought of his presence will be ever before their minds, and men will see the "face" of every other member of the Church, as the "face" or "mask" of Christ. Even if someone thinks of "turning his eyes away" from the Teacher of wisdom, the "voice" of the Holy Spirit will "sound in their "ears" that "this is the way; walk in it."

The faithful will seek to do God's will first and foremost; and so it will be, even as Christ, in Mt. 5:8, said,

> "Blessed are the pure of heart, for they shall see God."

Psalms 23:3-4 likewise says,

> "Who shall ascend unto the mountain of the Lord, or who shall stand in his holy place? The innocent of hand and clean of heart."

In Apocalypse 20:3-4, John did not write about the Beatific Vision, but a more enlightened faith and keener love of God. As the heart loves, so the mind sees. The magnanimity of Christ will magnify the minds of men, so they may fittingly know their friendship with God: for friendship is love, love bears immortal eyes. "Behold, I make all things new," says the Little Lamb from the throne [21:5]; and this will be realized when men see all things from the viewpoint of Eternity.

St. Paul, many years before St. John wrote the Apocalypse, epitomized the principal theme of Chapter 21 and the forepart of 22 in 2 Corinthians 5:17, which states,

> "So if anyone is in Christ, there is a new creation: everything old has passed away; see, everything has become new!"

I do not see how anyone can believe in Christ and not believe in the "millennium," and, yet, many opine that the "mystery of God" among men will end at Armageddon. That is far short of the Truth.

In verse 7, the phrase, "the words of the prophecy of this scroll," pertains to the entire Apocalypse, for prophecy concerns "things that are, and things that must soon take place." The admonitions in the first three Chapters were written for the whole Church throughout its history, even unto the "end of years," and, therefore, they are important, because those who will not "hear" them will be less motivated to practice "patient endurance" and to overcome.

Three more times, in verses 7, 12, and 20, the reader is reminded that Christ will come soon, an admonition that applies not only to large collectives, such as a nation or empire or global civilization, but also to each individual who knows not the day or hour of his own death. Life is very short, and Christ always comes very soon for the individual.

Verse 10 is quite clear: men shall be permitted to exercise free will either to weal or to woe; verse 12 is quite clear: Christ will repay according to each person's work.

Verse 15 tells how Christ regards those who do serious evil: no more than dogs. The wise man will heed "the words of the prophecy" and direct his life, accordingly. Proverbs 49:21 speaks tersely,

> "Man, for all his splendor, if he have not prudence, resembles the beasts that perish."

In verse 16, Christ himself witnesses to the contents of the Apocalypse; and, in verse 17, the Holy Spirit and the bride [those spiritually mature] declare the time right and fitting for the coming of the Judge; and, thus, the Apocalypse returns to the readiness indicated by the "voice like a trumpet" in 1:10, the verse where the visions began.

Verses 18-19 deliver the final warning. It is presented here in full:

> I warn everyone who hears the words of the prophecy of this scroll: if anyone adds to them, God will add to him the plagues described in this scroll. And if anyone takes away from the words of the scroll of this prophecy, God will take away his share from the tree of life and out of the holy city described in this scroll.

This warning pertains to any willful alteration or subversion of the teachings in the Apocalypse, not to any unintentional error in copying or interpretation. Repeated inadvertence, resulting in errors and other ilks of incompetence, from exegetes, commentators, translators, and instructors cannot be excused: if one cannot do the task right, then, one ought not to pretend.

Since opinion is here defined as "a belief, or judgment, that rests on grounds <u>insufficient</u> to produce certainty," it, too, cannot be excused. Opinion, in this case, is self-assertion, the imposition of an individual's own meaning upon God's, a la Adam and Eve. Hence, fudging, also, cannot be excused. Either a substantial argument can be presented or it cannot be presented; and, if it cannot be presented, then, suspicion or probability must be declared, even ad nauseam, if necessary.

Translation should adhere to literalness and should practice consistency as much as possible; that this advice is sound and sane has been demonstrated, most especially, in regard to verb forms and the definitions of vocabulary. Translation that does not get the point cannot make the point. In brief, beware of false prophets: this admonition must be so expanded as to include oneself.

John has declared simply and plainly that the Apocalypse is PROPHECY, and this means it is a "μαρτυρία" divinely inspired: every word PROCEEDED FROM THE MOUTH OF GOD. Therefore, beware; do most beware, of putting words in God's mouth, for to do so is to commit spiritual suicide. This prophecy shall enlighten and encourage the Church in her darkest hour; and, therefore, anyone who alters its meaning, without valid excuse, must fall under one word: ANATHEMA.

Note how John transposed the verbal order from verse 18 to verse 19: the former emphasizes "the words of the PROPHECY," and the latter emphasizes "the words of the SCROLL." This means that one must not take anything out of its context. Each verse belongs where it is in the Apocalypse; and each word belongs where it is in the Apocalypse.

Verse 18 refers to the "plagues" and, with them, threatens those who would change the meaning of any term in the revelation, especially, those who would read into the words a meaning that is not there.

Verse 19 refers to the rewards of the "holy city" and the "tree of life," and menaces with the loss of them those who would conveniently "lose" a word, or would ignore a part of what the Spirit has said to the Church.

Whoever reads the Apocalypse [or any text of Scripture] through his own personal prejudice or opinion shall, in the instant of doing so, forfeit his citizenship and inheritance in the "holy city." When a person reads the Bible, that person reads unto life—or death: for The Bible is the word of God, there is no other.

In verse 20, the last words from Jesus are "Yes, I am coming soon." And John replies very simply, "Amen, come Lord Jesus!" The "Amen" is the solemn close to the revelation; it is also the Seer's acknowledgment of the perfection of the revelation. And, regarding the words, "Come, Lord Jesus!," John had in mind the whole evolvement of the divine plan, as shown to him from the first vision to the last, and desired with all his heart the final triumph of the King of kings and the Lord of lords, of the Redeemer and Sanctifier who justifies the ways of men to God, of the Living One, the Little Lamb.

The grace of the Lord Jesus be with all. Amen.

AFTERWORD

Dear Reader,

It has been five years since Steve passed away. Attempting to preserve and pass on this work, I have studied the Bible, read books by Church fathers, studied other books and writings on the Apocalypse, and prayed a lot as to what to do with this. My decision to publish came about as I reflected on the magnitude of the effort that Steve put forward as well as my own observation that the time depicted can't be too far away.

Current events since the time of Steve's passing include; laws recently passed in our own country and abroad that force physicians and religious-based hospitals and pharmacies to violate their religious beliefs. We have begun to see pastors and protestors arrested for preaching the Gospel in public. And we are seeing the removal of all references to God and religion from public places. Meanwhile, Christian Churches are burning to the ground in Indonesia, Kosovo, Bosnia, Sudan and Congo. Humans are being conceived and discarded for "scientific research" and for their parts. The seriously injured are ordered to starve to death and euthanasia is being legalized. Many clergy won't even mention the evil of artificial birth control from the pulpit, only one generation after it was condemned as a grave evil and as a path to abortion, divorce, and homosexual marriage.

The European Union refused the Pope's request to include any reference of Europe's Christian heritage in their now rejected constitution. The formerly Roman Catholic Country of France cut illegal deals with a brutal dictator to enrich herself with Oil and then not long after, her own Islamic population set Paris afire. A precursor to Babylon the Great?

In Spain, less than 10% of an overwhelmingly Roman Catholic population attends Church, following a trend found across Europe. Doctors are being required to perform abortions there against their conscience and Roman Catholic belief. The great cathedrals of France are largely vacant tourist attractions.

Catholic Colleges are seemingly run as autonomous secular institutions with studies showing that they actually deaden the faith of their students instead of nurturing it.

Steve often said that the Apocalypse was not a book of consolations but if one can take hope from it, it is that every activity we witness is the evolvement of God's plan for mankind. The spiritual battle must be joined because He wills it. What side you take will be determinate as to your fate. And the reward is disproportionate to the sacrifice involved. To see God face to face surpasses infinitum any persecution or scandal suffered here at this time.

I am reminded of two signs from the World Trade Center collapse. In the shadows of all the broken and destroyed skyscrapers, man's temples to money, stood the little chapel of Sts. Peter and Paul with nary a cracked stained glass window. The church is a vessel, the ship we ride to eternity. And the other sign was a cross on top of the pile of ruins from the towers. It was the result of two broken girders that were the last to remain standing. The rescuers saw it and knelt before it. In fact, they brought it to Rome and presented it to the Pope. The cross is the sign of our destination, our redemption and salvation. The cross calls to all of us. Most of all, the two signs said, God is in charge here, not the terrorists, not the government, not wealth or power.

I find myself in the uncomfortable position of being the one who will need to answer to objections about this work. And I am not nearly as qualified as my brother-in-law. Two points that have come up seem easily answered though. Perhaps the issue he spent the most time lecturing about was the Great Sign, The Woman Clothed with the Sun. Most people assign her to the Virgin Mary. Steve refutes that quite well in the book. I noticed a footnote in an older copy of the Douay-Rheims, Challoner version of the Bible that states that the "woman" is The Church. It also occurred to me that the Virgin Mary, since she was conceived without sin, would not suffer from the curse that original sin brought upon women, travail in childbirth. Nowhere in the Gospels does it mention Mary to be in labor. But the Woman Clothed with the Sun is "in great travail."

Another objection was raised by a Catholic apologetic who informed me that most Catholics are amellinialists and not premillenialists, that is my brother-in-law says the millennium is yet to come while most say we are in it. Pondering this, I considered the prayer of St. Michael:

> St. Michael the Archangel, defend us in the day of battle;
> Be our protection from the wickedness and snares of the devil;
> May God rebuke him we humbly pray,
> And do thou, O Prince of the heavenly host
> <u>Cast into Hell Satan</u> and all the evil spirits prowling the world
> Seeking the ruin of souls. Amen.

So, if this has supposedly already happened, why do so many Catholics recite this prayer?

"Oh, and by the way, the title Apocalypse—Letter by Letter, is of course a play on words concerning the detail to which Steve used the grammar and form of words to prove the meaning of the Apocalypse as well as his mode of transmission—letters. Most of the New Testament was composed of encyclical letters. The final irony is that Steve worked for the US Postal Office—as a letter carrier of course.

Yours,

A Friend of the Lord

APPENDIX A
—
GREEK ALPHABET

Α α	Alpha	1
Β β	Beta	2
Γ γ	Gamma	3
Δ δ	Delta	4
Ε ε	Epsilon	5
ς	Digamma	6
Ζ ζ	Zeta	7
Η η	Eta	8
Θ θ	Theta	9
Ι ι	Iota	10
Κ κ	Kappa	20
Λ λ	Lambda	30
Μ μ	Mu	40
Ν ν	Nu	50
Ξ ξ	Xi	60
Ο ο	Omicron	70
Π π	Pi	80
Θ (1) (Ϙ ϙ)	Qoppa	90
Ρ ρ	Rho	100
Σ σ	Sigma	200

Τ τ	Tau	300
Υ υ	Upsilon	400
Φ φ	Phi	500
Χ χ	Chi	600
Ψ ψ	Psi	700
Ω ω	Omega	800
Ϡ ϡ (1)	Sampi	900

Glossary

accusative

- adjective, *Grammar:* (in certain inflected languages, as Latin, Greek, or Russian) noting a case whose distinctive function is to indicate the direct object of a verb or the object of certain prepositions. Similar to such a case form in function or meaning.

active

- adjective, *Grammar:* noting or pertaining to a voice of verbal inflection in which typically the subject of the sentence is represented as performing the action expressed by the verb (opposed to *passive*): *Writes* in *He writes a letter every day* is an active verb form.

alliteration

- noun, the commencement of two or more stressed syllables of a word group either with the same consonant sound or sound group (**consonantal alliteration**), as in *from stem to stern,* or with a vowel sound that may differ from syllable to syllable (**vocalic alliteration**), as in *each to all.*

aorist

- adjective, pertaining to the verb form used to convey the idea that "an action or act is single or simple rather than repeated or prolonged."

assonance

- noun, rhyme in which the same vowel sounds are used with different consonants in the stressed syllables of the rhyming words, as in *penitent* and *reticence.*

apposition

- noun, *Grammar:* a syntactic relation between expressions, usually consecutive, that have the same function and the same relation to other elements in the sentence, the second expression identifying or supplementing the first. In *Washington, our first president,* the phrase *our first president* is in apposition with *Washington.*

case

- noun, *Grammar:* a category in the inflection of nouns, pronouns, and adjectives, noting the syntactic relation of these words to other words in the sentence, indicated by the form or the position of the words. A set of such categories in a particular language. The meaning of or the meaning typical of such a category. Such categories or their meanings, collectively.

clause

- noun, *Grammar:* a syntactic construction containing a subject and predicate and forming part of a sentence or constituting a whole simple sentence.

complement

- noun, *Grammar:* a word or group of words that completes a grammatical construction in the predicate and that describes or is identified with the subject or object, as *small* in *The house is small* or *president* in *They elected her president.*

finite verb

- noun, *Grammar:* a verb form that distinguishes person, number, and tense, and also mood or aspect, as *opens* in *She opens the door.*

genitive

- adjective, *Grammar*: (in certain inflected languages) noting a case of nouns, pronouns, or adjectives, used primarily to express possession, measure, or origin: as *John's* hat, *week's* vacation, *duty's* call.

imperative

- adjective, *Grammar:* noting or pertaining to the mood of the verb used in commands, requests, etc., as in *Listen! Go!*

indicative

- adjective, *Grammar:* noting or pertaining to the mood of the verb used for ordinary objective statements, questions, etc., as the verb *plays* in *John plays football.*

intransitive verb

- noun, *Grammar:* a verb that indicates a complete action without being accompanied by a direct object, as *sit or lie,* and, in English, that does not form a passive.

mood

- noun, *Grammar:* a set of categories for which the verb is inflected in many languages, and that is typically used to indicate the syntactic relation of the clause in which the verb occurs to other clauses in the sentence, or the attitude of the speaker toward what he or she is saying, as certainty or uncertainty, wish or command, emphasis or hesitancy. A set of syntactic devices in some languages that is similar to this set in function or meaning, involving the use of auxiliary words, as *can, may, might.* Any of the categories of these sets: *the Latin indicative, imperative, and subjunctive moods.*

nominative

- adjective, *Grammar:* (in certain inflected languages, as Sanskrit, Latin, and Russian) noting a case having as its function the indication of the subject of a finite verb, as in Latin *Nauta bonus est* "The sailor is good," with *nauta* "sailor" in the nominative case. Similar to such a case in function or meaning.

passive

- adjective, *Grammar:*(a) noting a voice in the inflection of the verb in some languages which is used to indicate that the subject undergoes the action of the verb. Latin *portātur,* "he, she, or it is carried," is in the passive voice. (b) Noting or pertaining to a construction similar to this in meaning, as English *He is carried* (opposed to *active*).

participle

- noun, *Grammar:* an adjective or complement to certain auxiliaries that is regularly derived from the verb in many languages and refers to participation in the action or state of the verb; a verbal form used as an adjective. It does not specify person or number in English, but may have a subject or object, show tense, etc., as *burning,* in *a burning candle,* or *devoted* in *his devoted friend.*

perfect

- adjective, *Grammar:* noting an action or state brought to a close prior to some temporal point of reference, in contrast to imperfect or incomplete action. Designating a tense or other verb formation or construction with such meaning.

phrase

- noun, *Grammar:* a sequence of two or more words arranged in a grammatical construction and acting as a unit in a sentence. (in English) a sequence of two or more words that does not contain a finite verb and its subject or that does not consist of clause elements such as subject, verb, object, or complement, as a preposition and a noun or pronoun, an adjective and noun, or an adverb and verb.

preposition

- noun, *Grammar:* any member of a class of words found in many languages that are used before nouns, pronouns, or other substantives to form phrases functioning as modifiers of verbs, nouns, or adjectives, and that typically express a spatial, temporal, or other relationship, as *in, on, by, to, since.*

subjunctive

- adjective, *Grammar:* (in English and certain other languages) noting or pertaining to a mood or mode of the verb that may be used for subjective, doubtful, hypothetical, or grammatically subordinate statements or questions, as the mood of *be* in *if this be treason.*

synthetic language

- a language characterized by a relatively widespread use of affixes, rather than separate words, to express syntactic relationships: *Greek is a synthetic language, while English is analytic.*

tense

- noun, a category of verbal inflection that serves chiefly to specify the time of the action or state expressed by the verb.

transitive verb

- noun, *Grammar:* a verb accompanied by a direct object and from which a passive can be formed, as *deny, rectify, elect.*

voice

- noun, *Grammar:* a set of categories for which the verb is inflected in some languages, as Latin, and which is typically used to indicate the relation of the verbal action to the subject as performer, undergoer, or beneficiary of its action. A set of syntactic devices in some languages, as English, that is similar to this set in function. Any of the categories of these sets: *the English passive voice; the Greek middle voice.*

978-0-595-67591-3
0-595-67591-3

Printed in the United States
76624LV00008BA/13